RELATIVE
DISTANCE

RELATIVE DISTANCE

A Memoir

DAVID PRUITT

Published by SparkPress, a BookSparks imprint,
A division of SparkPoint Studio, LLC
Phoenix, Arizona, USA, 85007
www.gosparkpress.com

Published 2022
Printed in the United States of America
Print ISBN: 978-1-68463-169-8
E-ISBN: 978-1-68463-170-4
Library of Congress Control Number: 2022907468

Formatting by Kiran Spees

Disclaimer
This is a work of creative nonfiction. When appropriate to add context, perspective, and narrative, "best recollection" detail and dialogue have been added and, in some cases, events have been sequenced and additional details have been included to augment story flow. In telling my brother's stories, I prioritized key life events (based on our discussions) and tried to put the reader in those critical moments as best as their memories and my imagination would allow. In some cases, throughout the book, names and identifying details have been changed to protect the privacy of the people involved.

To Paula, a good wife, who made me a better man,
and my children, Zachary and Matthew,
two good sons of a wayward son.

Author's Note

The story of my brother Danny's life was gathered over several contacts between March 2018 and March 2019. I visited him at his home in Wichita Falls, Texas, for two long days in 2018. We also spent time, over the course of phone calls, ironing out details as best as time and memory would allow. He also reviewed a draft manuscript in February 2019. My brother Billy's input was gathered at a lengthy meeting in October of 2018 and he reviewed a draft manuscript in February 2019.

"The turning point in the process of growing up is when you discover the core of strength within you that survives all hurt."

—Max Lerner

"Where I was born and where and how I have lived is unimportant. It is what I have done with where I have been that should be of interest."

—Georgia O'Keeffe

Contents

Part I
At Eighteen

One
The Park

WHY A SEEMINGLY MERCILESS God decided it was *his* fate to be born into a damaged home is a fair question to ask, though not one with an easy answer.

He could've been born into the historic mansions of Old Irving Park, with their rolling hills and emerald putting greens, or the fresh-moneyed estates of New Irving Park, with their impeccable red-bricked homes backed by placid, clear waters and fronted by wrought iron gates. These are the places of privilege in Greensboro, North Carolina, in 1979.

It could've happened that way—but it didn't. That the fates have been unkind to him is beyond dispute. That he's been hurt by people he loved and trusted is fact. That he, without early expectation or intent, has lied, stolen, and disappointed those who loved him is an unfortunate truth.

And now he's here in this pivotal moment, these most uncertain of times, on a warm Sunday evening, alone, in a large local park with a small name: Country Park.

He hikes the lengthy trails in tepid silence and, despite his troubles, can't help but notice the beauty of his surroundings. The white oak and sugar maple leaves that dance beneath the clouds. The dogwoods in bloom, stray berries resting above shallow roots. Twin lakes nestled amid verdant woods casting a long shadow that cools the paired-off lovers as they lie in repose, gazing at one another, on their rumpled blankets along the grassy shorelines.

With tired feet and a weary glance, he finds an empty park bench overlooking a lake. Taking a seat, he drops his backpack on the thin pine straw at his feet, looks out, and spots a young boy fishing—his willowy line hanging from a thin bamboo pole with a half-red, half-white sinker floating aimlessly atop the tranquil pond.

He stares at its slow, hypnotic drift and remembers a time not so long ago when he eagerly cast his line in these waters. There were fish he caught—and some that got away.

Brown-haired, sunburnt, and long-limbed, at twenty years of age he stands taller than most and is lean and sinewy in a manner that prompts notice from the occasional passerby. His hands are strong and capable, lending him to excel at challenging, physical work. He may not design the building, but he can align the studs and straight-cut the two-by-fours. And despite his occasional struggle with the truth, at his core, he's a decent soul and possesses a discrete but present charisma. There's real good in him and some can see it. But somehow, in the recesses of his anxious mind, any faith about what he can accomplish in this life has long been stripped away.

In the lonely quiet, he ponders the last few difficult months while the darkness continues its rapid descent.

He was ordered to leave his home and not come back—and not without reason. He made mistakes and did things that were just plain wrong. It's also true that he was raised by a man who survived hard things as a youth and zealously passed them on—as if he was supposed to, as if it was all he knew, as if it was the right thing, as if it was the only way. Maybe it was. And maybe his leaving was for the best.

He spots a bathroom some fifty yards to his right near the dense woodline. With his backpack and its frayed straps resting heavily on his tired shoulders, he walks over and steps through its open door. It's quite dark inside. Finding no light switch, he carefully relieves himself in the low-set urinal and throws cold water in his face before stepping back outside.

The park is now empty. He checks his watch. It's 9:58 p.m., and other than a few streetlights on the main park road, it's dark out—time to bed down. He takes a seat at the picnic table under the attached shelter to take inventory of his few possessions. He has a small blanket, a pair of jeans, a UNC baseball cap, a gray hoodie, assorted underwear and socks, three T-shirts, a toothbrush and toothpaste, a comb, and a Milky Way bar.

He removes the blanket and the hoodie from the backpack, zips it closed in a half-circle across the top and quickly decides he'll sleep behind the bathroom: it backs up to the woods and is hidden from the main road. He walks around behind the building, spreads his blanket, drops down on his backside, and places the backpack under his head. He pulls the hoodie up tight around his shoulders—it's getting cooler—and lies quiet and motionless on his left side, but the hard ground, lightly carpeted in apple-green centipede grass, is unforgiving. His eyes stretch wide open as he listens to the echoed sound of chirping crickets and the hoot of a nearby owl perched high in a skinny-boughed pine. He tries to manage his nerves, but the uncertainty of his surroundings causes sleep to elude him until exhaustion finally takes over.

A bit after 3:00 a.m., a patrol car stops, and two officers, flashlights in hand, exit the vehicle. They slowly walk the grounds by the lake; after a brief reconnaissance, they take a look behind the bathroom and, sure enough, find the young man fast asleep. With flashlights beaming on his motionless back and after a vain attempt to rouse him with a perfunctory call, one of the officers walks over and places his boot on the young man's hip to jostle him awake.

"Hey, you," he decrees. "Get up. You're not allowed to sleep here, this is city property."

No response. He's out cold, dead to the world.

"Hey, come on, get up!" the officer implores, more forcefully this time.

The young man suddenly feels the boot on his hip and, alarmed, scrambles to his feet. He backs against the rear wall of the building in confusion and tries to get his bearings, his mind slowly coming to life. One of the officers shines a bright beam directly in his eyes.

"Hey buddy, you can't . . ." He turns quiet for a moment, and then: "Danny, is that you?"

Danny tries to look closer, but for a moment can't make him out through the light. Then it hits him. The cop's name is Mark Carroll—they went to high school together.

"Oh, uh, hey man, how ya doing?"

"Well, I'm okay, but what're you doing out here?"

"I've had a few problems at home. Um, I'm just trying to get some rest." He pauses. "But I'm not botherin' anybody."

"Yeah, I can see that. Look, I'm sorry man, but you can't stay here. This is public property."

"Oh? Okay. I'm just trying to get some sleep. But . . . but, I hear you. Uh, let me get my stuff together."

He pulls on the hoodie, zips up, and bends down, fumbling with the blanket and backpack.

Mark watches the sorry scene and mercifully reconsiders his request.

"Look, Danny, this is not usually allowed. Just leave the blanket, you can stay tonight, but just for the night. If you come back here in the future, I'm going to have to take you in for loitering, okay?"

"Yeah, uh, thanks, Mark. I—I really appreciate it, man."

The two officers start to head back to the car, but then Mark stops in his tracks and turns back around.

"Hey Danny, do you need anything? Can I drop you anywhere?"

Danny looks up from re-spreading the blanket on the ground and locks eyes with his old friend. He has a sudden, desperate urge to unburden himself and, for the first time feeling the full weight of his vulnerability, nearly breaks down in tears. But instead, he stubbornly gathers himself.

"No thanks, man. I'll make this work for now."

Two
The Woods

Across the city, farther east, Billy exits the woods and brushes himself off as he steps into the backyard of an empty house. The elderly couple that owns the place left earlier this morning. He knows—he watched discreetly from behind the trunk of an aging red maple as they drove away.

Initially, he felt a little strange walking around the yard while they're gone, but not anymore. With time, his guilt and constant fear of detection have passed. He walks toward the spigot and rationalizes to himself that at least he's not a total stranger here. He sorta knows the homeowners. They're a friend's parents.

His friend, a former coworker, told him about this place, this stretch of woods—thick the first twenty-five yards in, but then more accessible. And one morning, after running out of any other option, he trekked in deep, past the thicket, set his bag down, and made himself at home. He's been hiding out here now for over three months, and he tells himself it's not all bad. The undergrowth has a small creek running through its center whose persistent flow provides a soothing burble. His ears welcome the calming sound—though unfortunately his bladder doesn't. On more than one night, he's had to venture out in the darkness to relieve himself and gotten nicked up in the process. But it can't be helped; he can't use his flashlight for fear of alerting his none-the-wiser landlords.

Amazingly, he's survived this long in these wooded environs silent and alone—except for the infectious mosquitoes and ticks, the stinging fire ants, a few jittery but industrious squirrels, and the occasional foraging raccoon. It's not easy, that's for sure. But he gets by. He always has. In his brief life, he's learned to expect and require little. And his current circumstances are made somewhat easier by the fact that he is, plain and simple, a loner, a man content in his own company who has no hint of pretension or curiosity about a perspective that's not his own.

At twenty-two, he has prematurely thinning hair and a wide girth. But he's not fat—just thick and sturdy. His back is broad and also a bit too hairy, an unfortunate genetic trait passed to him by his paternal grandfather. Book smart but not street smart, he has no allegiance to society's expectations or norms. He is simply a young man in search of an elusive understanding. His life, after a difficult beginning, seemed to be on track for a while but has since gone completely, irreparably wrong. And he doesn't know why. He only knows he can't move forward until he figures it out. So, alone in these woods, he searches for answers.

He stops a moment to further dust himself off and take in his surroundings. The old couple has a nice place: a single-story brick ranch sitting on three acres near the local shopping mall and US Route 29, a major highway that carries travelers north to Danville, Virginia, or south to South Carolina, near Blacksburg. Sometimes he can hear the speeding cars roll past, most vividly in the wee, dark hours of a lonely, sleepless night.

He gets himself moving again—there are things to do and time is limited.

He has little money or food. He gives plasma when he's desperate for cash, and his pockets are currently empty except for some loose change he'll use to pay the bus driver. He'll catch a ride at the mall and head downtown to the local plasma center, where he'll bleed, collect his cash, pick up some supplies, hop back on the bus, and return to these woods—all before 5:00 p.m.

But first things first: he stinks—badly. In his right hand, he carries a bar of Dial soap and a washcloth. In his left, he has a small, thin duffel bag containing a clean pair of underwear, his last pair of khaki shorts, and a green Chicago band T-shirt. There's no house to the right or left of him, so he kicks off his sneakers, drops his pants, sheds his shirt and turns on the water spigot.

He dreads the cold but mission firmly in mind, yanks the garden hose off its reel cart. He takes a deep breath and braces as he squeezes the nozzle and fires the frigid water, first at his upper torso and then over the balance of his soiled body. Streams of dirt and water follow gravity to the grass beneath his feet. His beard is long and grungy, filled with dried-in dirt and broken pine needles, so he soaps up the rag and begins to scrub—first along his face, then all over his head, neck, and shoulders. He washes under his arms, between his legs, and down around his butt, rubbing hard against the baked-in grime. He then cleans his feet, legs, and genitals before again washing his thin but still coal-black hair. In a final rinse, he shoots the nozzle full throttle in continuous rotation at the mass and various crevices of his bulky physique.

In fifteen minutes, he's clean and done. He peeks around the corner of the house. The coast remains clear, so he pats himself down with the damp rag, walks over, and sits naked in an aluminum patio chair next to the sliding glass door that enters the back den. He rests quietly for a few minutes and dries off, eyes closed, enjoying the warm rays of the mid-morning sun. He then puts on his clothes, ties his shoes, and carries the duffel bag, now filled with dirty clothes, back to the edge of the woods. He hides it under dry leaves behind a rotting hickory stump then turns toward the waiting streets below.

On workdays they're usually home by five-thirty so he has to hurry, and he does. Ten minutes later he's on the city bus—but sitting quietly, a sudden, ominous thought enters his mind: *In a few months, it's gonna be the dead of winter. What the hell am I gonna do then?*

Three
The Fight

I'M EIGHTEEN, STILL HERE in Greensboro—and still in this damn house. It wasn't my choice to be born here, in this time and place, or to this family.

None of us get to choose where or how our lives begin. The circumstances we're born into—skin color, gender, nationality, level of affluence, physical appearance, and, of course, the character, integrity, and mental acuity of those who raise us—are assigned to us by fate.

And fate can be gloriously beneficent, passively indifferent, or savagely cruel.

For the blessed at birth, the inherited advantages are real, the benefits undeniable. Though no outcome in life is guaranteed, the journey is somewhat iterative; after all, a story with a strong beginning tends to end well. And later in life wistful reflection is generally optional, not required, because, while no life is perfect, for those raised and loved with care the few cuts sustained produce minimal scars that require less care in the healing.

Those of us born less fortunate are silently, permanently aware of our past difficult circumstances—the dark times in our adolescence when fate was unkind. Sadly, some never get past the arbitrary unfairness of it all. But for many, our early mistreatments and short-comings are willfully and deliberately cast aside, ignored; while we do not forget them, we learn to, in some functional manner, compensate for our losses. But it's not so simple. There is no puzzled-out, clean exit from the labyrinthine escape room occupied by those of us damaged in youth. The cracks in the mirror of our lives, compared to that of others, are sometimes reflected back at us. And when that happens a somber realization sets in and leaves us with nagging feelings of resignation, inadequacy, anger—as if we were somehow short-changed, even cheated.

But today—today I don't feel cheated.

Today I feel churning anxiety and the ignorant worry of a grown-man wannabe.

My mind is restless, my thoughts are shaky, and I'm fearful about what lies ahead. High school—an experience that left me feeling unaccomplished, marginalized, failed as a scholar, a near social outcast, and led me to the clear-eyed realization that doors open to others are closed to me—is behind me. My indolent behavior and indifferent attitude have put me here, on the outside looking in, feeling like a kid with empty pockets standing on his front stoop watching the ice cream truck pull away while the other kids lick the melted cream off their fingers before leaning in for the next delicious bite. They greedily inhale the crispy waffle cone, while I can only imagine its sugary taste.

I've been busy in my young life so far, chasing acceptance and normality but distracted by ever-present fear. The storms have come often but I learned early to be on watch, and when the signs pointed to a higher alert—a warning—I learned to take shelter. Even so my father, the great force of nature that he is, blew my walls down until I was left cowering on all fours in the bathtub, the safehouse crumbling around me. Sometimes I stubbornly—foolishly—poked my head over the rim of that tub and opened my mouth, only to encounter the bitterest and strongest winds.

And now I'm here alone with him and my stepmother, Helen. The three of us cling to an uneasy truce and I to a tenuous occupancy. But today . . . today I have a plan, an idea, and—is it possible—perhaps even hope?

I hear the two of them talking in the small kitchen of our modest ranch home as I tentatively make my way up the hallway from my back bedroom. One last time, I mentally rehearse my carefully selected words—but I lose focus when I hear the roaring engine of a passing car and the loud, insistent honk of its impatient driver. Busy Cone Boulevard, a major east–west thoroughfare in Greensboro, lies about a hundred feet from our front door.

I enter the kitchen. "Pop, can I talk to you about something?" I ask uncertainly.

My father is seated at the kitchen table, paying our monthly bills. I watch him record dollars and cents on the check register as he dutifully satisfies his creditors. Ten years ago, when my mother was sick, when debt almost overwhelmed him, he lashed out at us, at the world, at the seeming injustice of it all. He was determined to break free, and he did. He found Helen, and together they've gotten to a better place. Now I need to find out if there's a better place in the world for me.

He glances up at me as he stuffs the check in the envelope. "Yeah?"

"You wanted me to work and I'm doing it. I've been running projectors at the movie theater for almost two years now."

"Yeah, okay?" He peers back at Helen, who is behind him washing dishes in the sink. "He must want something."

"Well, I do," I admit. "I want to go to college at UNC-Greensboro in the fall, and I was thinking I could continue to work at the theater and between the money I make there and your help, I could afford the tuition."

There, I've gotten it out.

Pop shakes his head. "That's going to be expensive. You could go right over to Guilford Technical Community College, sign up, and in two years you'll be done. You can learn you a trade, and when you get out, you can get a job. It'll be less money. I might be willing to help you with that," he offers as he writes out the check to Duke Power for last month's power bill.

"Pop, you know I've never been good working around the house," I rebut. "I'm not going to make a living working with my hands, I know that much already."

"Boy, there's nothing wrong working with your hands," says the strong man before me who makes his living with his.

"No, I know that. It's just not for me. I want to get a four-year degree. I'll find a major I'm interested in and go after it. I'll work all this year and into the summer of next year. I hope to eventually save enough money to move on campus my second year and have the full college experience," I say, proudly but naively.

"Yeah right, you'll get the 'full' experience. You'll flunk out in a year, guaranteed!" he says sarcastically.

There it is; my overly sensitive emotional antenna captures his clear signal. I ask for his help and instead I get his prevalent view of my limited capabilities. A feverish heat rises in my body, flushing my face red and leaving the back of my neck uncomfortably hot.

"You're good at telling me what I can't do," I say. "I figured you'd say that."

"Well, I don't think you exactly tore it up in high school, and I know what you've been doing at night with your friends. You couldn't even get out of bed on New Year's morning a few months back. You didn't come out of your room until five o'clock in the afternoon!"

"You don't know what my grades were in high school," I shoot back. "You never asked. And I go out with my friends to get out of this house."

Pop's face begins to flush as well. "I don't think I'm wrong on the grades. Besides, you going and living on campus is a waste of money when you have a place to live right here."

"Pop, it's just time for me to get out of the house," I plead. "I want to be out on my own. I took the SAT; that's the test colleges use to determine your potential as a student. I did better than I thought I would, and it gives me hope that I can do the work at a college level if I apply myself. It's true, I haven't worked hard in the past, but I swear I'm going to now."

"David, your daddy and me don't have money to throw away on you going off to party just because you don't want to work for a living," Helen chimes in.

"What do you mean? I'm working now, at the theater!"

Pop's eyes narrow. "That's not real money, and you couldn't even keep a job washing damn dishes," he snaps, bringing up a sore spot from my past failed employment at the local pizzeria.

"Look, I haven't been perfect, but nobody is," I say, knowing but somehow no longer caring where this is going to lead. "You-all haven't been either."

"Here we go—it's always somebody else's fault," Pop says as he drops his pen and slides his chair back from the kitchen table.

"No," I say, "I've made my mistakes. But I didn't have a lot of help along the way, that's for sure."

"What do you mean you didn't have help? I kept a roof over your head and food in your stomach. If it had been up to your real mama, you wouldn't have had a pot to piss in!" he retorts.

Dammit, he always brings up Mama! I look in hard-eyed frustration at my father. I can feel the rage bubbling, pulsing inside me and my breath quickens. Adrenaline and resentment coalesce as I grit my teeth and straighten my back. Too much shit has happened over the years in this house. I'm not sure if I'm trying to hold it in or bracing to scream it out.

"Yeah, you fed me, and you're right, Mama didn't help us—but she had mental problems, at least she had some kind of an excuse," I fire back. "And yes, you clothed us and kept us out of an orphanage. I'm thankful for that. But no matter what Mama was capable of doing or not, you were still our father. We were your responsibility. We didn't ask to be brought into this world. You can't beat up on us or tell us how bad we are one minute, then pet us up the next minute and make it all better. Because it wasn't, and it's still not!"

"David Pruitt, don't you talk to your daddy like that!" Helen yells and steps toward me.

"And yeah, I had food in my belly," I press on. "But God help me if I spilled a crumb of that food on the floor. 'Cause we know what would happen then: you'd beat the shit out of me."

Pop rises angrily from his chair. "I was just trying to keep the house clean and you were a damn messer!" he shouts.

"No, I was just a clumsy kid who was scared to death to make a mistake because I knew what would happen if I did!"

I pause for a moment and try to dial things down, but my hurt won't let me.

"Look, you're right. You kept me when Mama left us. I appreciate that. But I knew you couldn't have what you wanted out of life because I was in the way; you always made that clear. And I know I didn't come first in your eyes. You told me that too. Hell, I had to wear winter clothes in the springtime just to cover up the damn stripes and bruises running up and down my legs! A dog shouldn't have had to live like that!"

"I raised you the best way I knew how!" he yells back, his voice breaking in the effort.

"Yeah, you did your best all right. You told me all my life I wasn't worth a shit for nothing! But you were fucking wrong. I am worth something!"

"Well if you can do so much better without me, then you go right ahead. The door's right there. Nobody's stopping you!" My father is now speaking in the derisive voice that alarmed me as a child but only angers me as a grown-man wannabe.

I determinedly step toward him—edging closer to the storm.

"David, you need to calm down. Stop it!" Helen places her hands on my arms as she, once again, steps in between me and Pop. In previous years, she sought to protect me from Pop, but now her goal is to protect both of us from each other.

Pop isn't backing down. He never has. His indignation is registered clearly in his raging, contorted features.

He edges closer to me.

But I'm no longer afraid. I weigh two hundred pounds, and after playing football and lifting weights for the last two years I can bench press over three hundred pounds. I'm as strong as I've ever been. I'm not gonna hit anybody, but nobody's gonna hit me either—not this time.

"Your mama wouldn't work, and I did the best I could," my father proclaims. "I didn't see anybody else signing up for the job." He fully believes the broader tenets of the father–son contract have been faithfully executed, but he's forgetting the fine print that's been violently breached.

Still, my anger breaks for a moment; other, torturous, pent-up emotion rises; and I make a final attempt to find my father's heart.

"Was it the best you could do? Really? Don't you get that I'll be living with what you did to me for the rest of my life?" I croak. And then, wastefully, tears fall—unacknowledged, unheeded.

My chest heaves, and I try again. One more time.

"Did you ever have any dreams for me? Did you want something better for me than what you had?"

"I didn't have time for dreaming," Pop snarls. "I had to work for a living. Nobody gave *me* anything."

"Don't you understand?" I plead. "You made me lose faith in myself." But I mumble these words, hanging my head in exhaustion. I have finally made a definitive statement of my pain and loss. I wait hopefully for some tacit acknowledgment of mistakes made, regrets contemplated, some recognition of the fact that things could have been done differently—that maybe, just maybe, Pop is sorry for things that happened, things he did. In these last, brutal days of my adolescence, I need him to extend a hand—I need a regretful, repentant bridge to help me stumble across the breach between us.

"All I can tell ya is, don't let the door hit ya in the ass on your way out," he says coldly.

My spine stiffens. My defiance returns. My tears dry.

"You ain't gonna do to me what I watched you do to them. If I ever have kids one day, I'll never treat them the way you treated me!" I say, eyes narrowing, and angrily step even closer so our faces are inches apart.

"You want to hit me? Well, go ahead!" he baits me.

I never thought I would but right now, for a moment, I consider it. Then Helen, who remains tightly sandwiched between us, aggressively shoves me, looking to create separation, and when I refuse to move she bounces off of me and falls to the kitchen floor.

"Boy, don't you touch her," my father screams. "She's treated you better than your own Mama!"

"I never touched her," I protest. "She fell on her own."

I reach to help her up, but Pop pushes me away. He helps her to her feet and then turns to me in disgust.

"I think you better get your stuff and get out."

"Helen, I'm sorry you fell," I tell her. "I didn't mean for that to happen."

But somehow I'm not quite finished; before I walk away, I drive the last nail in the weathered coffin of a father–son relationship that died some years ago, when one beating too many turned love and respect into resentment and apathy.

"You can turn this around on me all you want," I say, "but you'll have to live with the things you've done. You know, maybe I ain't worth a shit for nothing, just like you say. But you raised me. Well, if I'm shit, where does that leave you?"

"David, I think you better go now!" Helen shouts.

I turn on my heels and head back to the bedroom to grab some clothes. There's nothing left for me to say. I started this conversation with the hope of getting support for college, and now I've ended it not knowing where I'll sleep tonight. I should've held my hurt back a little longer. But I just couldn't do it.

I grab my few things, throw them in a bag, head out the back door, start my used Chevy, sigh deeply, and curse under my breath, "Jesus Christ! Why was I born into this shit?"

But then, as I back into the busy street, it suddenly hits me: *My God, Billy and Danny are out here too! How can my brothers and me all be homeless at the same time?*

I drive up the hill and, about a mile up, reach a stoplight. I apply the brake and watch cars pull up beside and behind me. I look up and take note of a darkening sky.

Cold reality sets in. And fear.

What in the world have I done?

Part II
Boys to Men

Four
Oak Grove

Our small, off-white, weathered wood home sits quietly on Oak Grove Avenue in the eastern end of Greensboro. While the western side of the city is thriving with new restaurants, commercial office buildings, and expansive retailers springing up in hot pursuit of the wallet share of a rising professional, mostly white constituency, the east end is mired in a slow but steady decline. There is a creeping rot to the aesthetic here that is visible in the light of day. Not as visible in the cover of night are widening pockets of violence and desperation in the form of drug and alcohol abuse, domestic disputes, and even the occasional shooting.

But it isn't the outside world that threatens when I'm inside the walls of our tired bungalow.

Pop is not a large man, but he is clear-eyed, ham-fisted, and hot-tempered—and he dominates my life in my early childhood. I can't imagine, at my age, anything or anyone he can't handle. But we don't call him "Pop" quite yet. Our parents to us, at this age, are "Mama and Diddy." Not Daddy, Diddy. The "I" speaks to where and how we live—the blue-collar South, not so far from where, a few years back, lunch was belatedly served to four resolute young Black men at the local Woolworth's.

Naptime is almost over and I'm lying awake in the too-small spring-green crib to the right of the doorway in the small bedroom I share with my brothers. At the appointed time, I kick my blanket off, climb over the narrow top beam, and hop down onto the hickory-colored hardwood floor. My brother Danny's small twin-size bed rests to the left of me as I scramble upright, rising quickly from skinned-up knees to bare, dirt-stained feet. My oldest brother Billy's bed is against the wall directly across from me, and there is a window to my right. Sometimes that window is open on late summer nights and I enjoy a slight, but precious, cool wisp of a breeze. I often feel comforted by my brothers' presence, as we lie in the inky black darkness of this small, shaded room.

Exiting the bedroom, I step into the small den that leads to the front of the house. It's lightly furnished with an older dark brown couch, a pressed wood end table, and a rarely used lamp with a plastic, slightly torn cover on the white shade (the torn part is strategically rotated away from view, nestled close and tight against the wall). We do most of our living, as a family, in the kitchen in the rear of the home and the large, poorly maintained yard surrounding it. My parents sleep in the nondescript bedroom to the back left of the kitchen.

I continue now out the front door to the low-sitting concrete front porch, jump the two steps down, and land in the front yard, where my brothers are playing with neighborhood kids. While the front yard is large and green, with a feckless combination of grass and weeds, the right side of the lot is simply brown dirt with a large oak tree that shades the ground and protects that side of our home from the late-day summer sun. Water and neglect have left the outside of the house looking like my sunburned shoulders days after running a game of "red light, green light," shirtless in the thin grass.

My brothers mount their two-wheelers and ride down the street with the others. I wander beneath the old oak and begin playing in the dirt. In my underwear and a T-shirt, I sit and poke at the ground, digging for ants and worms with a small, sharp stick.

As darkness descends, I am toppled over drowsily, lying closer and flatter to the ground, when, suddenly, Danny whips around the corner, pedaling hard, and runs over my right leg, snickering as he passes. I let out a yelp, climb to my feet, and stomp toward the front porch to tell my father.

Overcome with concern, Danny tries to head me off—"David, don't tell Diddy. You'll get us both in trouble"—but I ignore him.

"Diddy, Danny ran over me with his bike!" I cry, angry tears rolling down my cheeks.

My father looks over from where he's sitting on the front porch steps near the lightnin' bugs my siblings caught in a 10-2-4 Dr. Pepper soda bottle. "What?"

"He ran over my leg!" I show him the dirt-stained streak on the side of my leg just below the knee.

"Did you run over him, boy?" he asks Danny.

"It was dark. I was circling the house. I came around the corner and he was there. I didn't see him!" Danny splutters.

"He laughed!" I vengefully report.

"Boy, did you laugh?" Diddy asks in a tone and glare that says my brother had best not lie.

"No!" he shouts.

"Yes, you did!" I cry out between sniffles.

It's silent for a moment as Diddy says nothing, but a hard gaze at Danny says he knows the truth. He rises from the low-slung porch and strides toward my now cowering sibling.

My brother's words come quickly: "Diddy I was just playing. He's not even hurt—"

"You know better than to lie to me, young'un. Take that damn bike, put it up, and get inside that house—now!"

Danny skitters away, relieved, but out of the corner of his eye he cuts me a look that acknowledges my betrayal.

"David, get over here," Diddy calls to me. "Let me see that leg."

I walk over and can see he is unimpressed by the damage. He leans over and looks down at me and then slowly sniffs the air—and is displeased by the result. My underwear is dirty from the ground but also other things, things Diddy has been trying to break me of— harder in the last week or two.

"Boy, did you piss in your pants again?"

I put my head down. At almost five years old, I still haven't quite figured out how to control my bladder.

"You get your ass inside that house and put on some clean under-wear," he orders—but as I walk away, he grabs me by the arm. "Bring that dirty underwear back here when you get done. You get right back out here, ya heah me?"

Inside, I drop my soiled pants, grab a clean pair out of the chest of drawers, and pull them up quickly around my waist. Then I return, dirty underwear in hand, as ordered.

"Get over here young'un. Get right here." Diddy points to a spot directly at his feet.

I uncertainly comply.

"You put that underwear on your head, and you get ya ass runnin' around this house then get right back here to me!" he commands and points toward the old oak.

I stare up at him, bottom lip poked out, eyes watering. "No Diddy, don't make me," I beg.

"I've told you to run to the bathroom if ya gotta go, but I see you're still pissin' yourself. I'm going to put a stop to it. Put it on your head—NOW!"

"Please, Diddy. Don't make me. I promise I won't do it again," I plead once more, still refusing to move.

Sensing my resistance, his hand draws back. I flinch and back up a step. I take a long look. I can see the harshness, the insistence. He's not gonna stop until I run. Resigned, I turn and walk slowly, uncertainly, dirty underwear clutched in my right hand, still hanging loosely at my side.

"On your head and run—NOW!" he roars.

Tears roll down my face. I've gotta run. I hesitantly place the wet yellow underpants on my head and take off. I angle toward the oak and turn left at the far-right corner of the house. I circle the rear of our rented abode. I feel the underwear bouncing, moving on my head, and I smell—in full—the piss stains as I run. I adjust my grip and feel a dampness on my fingers. I come back up the other side, still crying but now also angry, resentful. I stop roughly three feet from where I started, directly in front of him.

I take the underwear off my head.

"You gonna piss in those pants anymore?" he asks and steps forward.

"No, sir!" I respond as I shudder with rage and embarrassment.

I wipe my eyes clean, then glare at him.

He reads my defiance like a surly headmaster disciplining an obstinate plebe.

My head snaps hard to the right as the back of my father's hand and his taut knuckles connect with my temple. The blow puts me on the ground, splay-legged like a fawn. Through blurry eyes, I look up in shock at the ruddy face towering over me. I'm silent for a moment; then I bellow out a high-pitched wail and wet, salty tears cascade down my cheeks.

My father hesitates, then sums up his position.

"Boy—hard heads make for sore sitting-down places," he says.

I continue to cry.

"Stop that hollerin'!" he demands.

I try to swallow down my anger and slow my tears. But it's no use. I can't stop myself. I bawl unabashedly.

"You shut that damn racket up—NOW!" he screams in full-throated fury.

Fear overtakes rage. Silence displaces noise. My body shudders at the effort.

He surveys the pitiful scene. "Stop pissin' your pants, and you can stop wearin' piss on your head," he says. He looks me over one more time, then steps up on the porch and strides into the house.

After a while, I get up. I stand for a moment, feeling a painful shame that will soon enough become repetitive and familiar. I slowly climb the two steps to the front porch, walk inside, and drop the briefs in the clothes basket outside the bathroom, which I use before climbing into bed. Mama remains an elusive visage, nowhere to be found.

I lay quietly in that spring-green crib.

Danny says, "See, I told you not to say nothin'," but follows with, "Are you okay?"

Billy chimes in: "You all right, David?"

"No, I'm not!" I respond, still whimpering in self-pity.

"Shhh, I hear Diddy coming!" Danny whispers.

All noise stops.

And the door opens. It's Diddy, and he comes over to the crib, reaches a callused hand down, and rubs the top of my head softly— "You know you're Diddy's baby boy. Diddy loves his baby boy."

I lie very still.

Five
The Biting Words

I SAY GOODNIGHT, GIVE MY wife, Paula, a peck on the cheek, and lightly pat Cody, our spirited black poodle, on his scruffy head. It's late Sunday evening, and while my body is fatigued my mind is racing. My thoughts are scattered and apprehensive and it's all I can do to suppress my sense of heightened anxiety. I desperately need to get some sleep, but sadly it's obligation, not exhaustion, that sends me upstairs to bed.

I enter our bedroom, leaving the door cracked open behind me, then head into our master bathroom with its vaulted ceiling and sky-blue walls to brush my teeth. After brushing, I climb into our queen-size Sleep Number bed and, lying on my right side, take my Kindle firmly in hand and speed-read Walter Isaacson's *Einstein*, impatiently chasing his Theory of Relativity in hopes that it will calm my nerves and occupy my brain.

After a lengthy but fruitless effort I put the Kindle aside, reposition onto my left side, and pull the thin blanket tight to my shoulders. I take several deep breaths, then close my eyes and begin my nightly conversation with God.

Dear God,

Tomorrow is one of the biggest days of my life. Lord, please don't let things go south on me. I have pride in my accomplishments and if this thing fails on my watch the shame, the embarrassment—well, dealing with it is almost unimaginable. While I trust I've worked hard and done a lot of the right things, so far, it's not been enough.

Lord, I'm not praying for me tonight. You've given me so much, for me to complain or ask for more, it's not something I'm gonna do. But there are other people, people who have families, people who need their jobs. And I need time. Lord, I'm asking that You give me that time. Let me rest tonight and find the right words in the morning. If it's your will, I know it will be done. I pray it is your will. And I pray that I live in your will.

Thank you again for the many blessings you've given my family over the years. You've helped me so much in life and I'm just so grateful for it. But I'm asking that you put your hand on tomorrow too. It's important—I know you know that. I love you and believe in you.

In Jesus's name, I pray.

Amen.

Praying calms and focuses me. Talking with God makes me feel like I'm not alone in my struggles, although until I met Paula, I willfully trusted no one and soldiered through life's challenges alone.

And the struggle continues now. My active mind allows only a small window for me to fall asleep. Either I'll go quickly or not at all. I'm physically exhausted, having worked long days and nights for months on end, so my body relaxes but my mind continues its dogged pursuit of the insightful answer, the miracle solution, that will alter the course of seemingly inevitable events.

My head burrows deeper into the thick pillow as my fingers feel the binding seam on the outer lip of the mattress. It's quiet. It's dark. I'm almost there.

But the window passes, and a weary body concedes defeat to an indefatigable mind.

What will they say tomorrow and how do I best respond? If they're on the fence, how do I get them on my side?

The pillow, like my thoughts, has grown hot, so I flip it over. My worried head now rests on the cool side, temporarily refreshed.

If I can make it past these guys, it could change everything. But if it somehow goes sideways, how do I tell our associates? Shit, how do I tell my kids?

I roll over again to my right side. The room begins to lighten as my eyes flicker open and shut, adjusting to the dark. The floor fan in the closet next to my side of the bed hums on medium, my primary weapon against the noise outside the door and the voices inside my head. But tonight, the familiar white noise is not working.

My thoughts move in other directions.

I hope Pop's new nurse works out. I need to move some money out of his annuity into his checking account—he's burning through cash and she's not cheap.

I pause for a moment.

And it looks like he could be right about me after all—he always told me I wasn't worth a shit for nothin'.

More than forty years later, I still hear those venomous words in my head.

The biting words—the judgmental verdicts issued by our parents when we're young—abide for a lifetime in the dark and hidden places of our private souls. They lie dormant and fallow through the passage of unexceptional days only to surface and echo in our greatest moments of trial and doubt. They challenge our certitude, our sense of self-worth, our aspirations for the future. They can do irreparable harm and break our spirits for a lifetime, or they can fuel a white-hot fire that becomes despicable but effective fodder to drive us forward. The biting words that cut us so deeply as children can control the very course and trajectory of our adult lives—but only if we let them.

I check the time. It's just past midnight. I inhale, then exhale, deeply and slowly begin to drift. I feel movement in the bed next to me but I don't speak. At last, spent and exhausted, I pass out.

At roughly 3:00 a.m., I'm awake again. Sleep, it seems, is over for tonight.

At 4:25 a.m., I turn off the alarm with five minutes to spare and save Paula the dreariness of a rainy Monday morning. I grab a quick shower and head downstairs to get dressed.

It's early 2016. I'm the CEO of the largest specialty retail bicycle business in the United States, Performance Bike, and have been for over five years. We have over one hundred stores nationwide, as well as an established online presence. I've been with the company for more than twenty-five years, and in that time we've grown in revenue from approximately 30 million to over 250 million dollars. By any measure, I've had a successful career, more successful than I could ever have imagined so many challenging years ago. But none of that matters right now.

I grab my vintage leather bag and carefully slide my presentation materials into it, then step outside, climb in my blue Beemer, put the car in reverse, and back out into the cul-de-sac of well-kept houses filled with doctors and various hard-charging, high-powered executives. I pull forward, moving uphill now in the heavy rain, and begin the eighteen-mile drive from our home in Chapel Hill to the Raleigh-Durham airport. I arrive at the gate well before the 6:30 a.m. boarding time.

Today, I'm flying into LaGuardia Airport en route to a meeting that could impact a lot of lives—and not necessarily for the better. The thought weighs heavy as I board and plop down in a narrow aisle seat near the front of the plane. I stow my bag under the seat in front of me, close my eyes, and tilt my head back, arching my neck as I desperately seek sleep and additional leg space.

I find neither.

After landing, I catch a ride into the city and meet one of our subordinate lenders, Greg, at a crowded Starbucks at 9:30 a.m. sharp. We briefly strategize about the meeting to come, then walk down a few congested blocks and enter the pristine foyer of an intimidating high-rise. After clearing security, we board a gleaming, elegantly silent elevator, ride up several floors, then step out to find a receptionist working busily at an L-shaped front desk in a large waiting area bathed in warm light and framed by opaque glass and modern upholstered furnishings. We announce the purpose of our visit and, nodding in recognition, she walks us around the corner, down the hallway, and into a large formal conference room with a substantial, boat-shaped table in its center. There are at least twenty black midback chairs to choose from and Greg and I take ours next to each other. I pull the presentation materials from my bag.

In the next moment, the door bursts open and ten bankers spill into the room. Each of them heads to the other side of the table, pulling the rolling chairs over to "their side," leaving Greg and me to sit alone, facing them like hopeful inmates at a parole board hearing.

They're intimidating in number and countenance and I'm acutely aware this might go in a bad direction quickly.

But I have a chance here.

GE Capital has been our senior lender for years, and I have served in both the CEO and CFO roles for our company during that lengthy relationship. I'm confident, despite current circumstances, that they respect me. I've had some success and they've taken note. In particular, when I took over as CEO, my team and I raised profit dramatically and paid down a significant amount of debt. I've also been a straight shooter—even when it hasn't been easy. When I've said the company's going to do something, we've done it. If for whatever reason we've been unable to follow through, I've told them early on, explained why, and then communicated our plan to make it right. And I've made sure we've done just that. I'm pretty sure a few of those faces across the table, despite their current stony demeanors, trust me.

But in the last couple of years, we've put that trust to the test. With the rapid growth of Amazon, the change in consumer buying behavior (moving online), and the fact that millennials aren't riding bikes as their boomer predecessors do, we, like many other brick-and-mortar retailers across the country, have been struggling to get an acceptable amount of traffic in our stores. This reduction in traffic has negatively impacted both sales and profit.

To make matters worse, we're owned by a private equity firm that paid very little cash at the time of the sale. Instead, they borrowed the money to finance their purchase and put that large amount of debt on our books (it's called a leveraged buy-out), reducing our free cash flow and constraining our ability to reinvest in the business. But none of that matters to GE. They simply want to know how we're going to pay back the money we owe.

That's what Greg and I are here to explain. If we can't raise GE's confidence that they'll eventually be repaid, they may call the loan immediately, which could bankrupt the company. Potentially, two thousand people could lose their jobs, and we could join the many other brick-and-mortar retailers who've shuttered their doors in the last few years. But I'm determined. It's not going to happen. I've got to win them over, and, by God, I'm going to find a way.

Greg gets the ball rolling.

"We appreciate each of you taking your time with us this morning," he begins. "We know you're busy, so we'll get right to it. David and I want to talk with you about our plans going forward to get the business back on track, and some things we intend to do relative to the capital structure of the company long-term. Then, of course, we'll field any questions. Sound good?"

Crickets. Silence.

Finally, Tim, the leader from GE, gives him the nod to proceed. Greg is a finance guy talking to a room full of finance guys. He's also done other deals with GE and, I suspect, knows many of the players in the room. He rightly leads the discussion from our side.

"We've spoken with the current owners and the parties have mutually agreed that we will take over majority control of Performance Bike, and in exchange for that control will forgive some of the money we're owed by the company. This will reduce a large amount of debt on Performance's balance sheet."

Greg and I discussed doing this a while back and it was a huge win for Performance when he agreed. But for the GE folks, it's only a nice thing to hear. They're our senior lenders and will get paid first anyway. Tim nods his head in acknowledgment but seems nonplussed.

Greg continues.

"We've worked with David for years now and he and his team have consistently outperformed a difficult bicycle industry. We know some of you have worked with him as well. We believe, with some changes he's going to make to the business and one other initiative we'll discuss in a moment, we can get things back on track and, of course, get you all comfortable with where we're at. And with that, I'm going to let David step in."

More crickets. More silence.

I pass out the materials and methodically, but quickly, layout the various positive actions we're taking to improve our situation—then also detail the extremely difficult action I took recently to reduce staff.

"We're partners, and while we'll provide a generous severance to those affected, it's the right thing to do given the sluggishness in the industry," I hear myself say. "I'm here today to strongly reassure each of you: we'll do what has to be done to protect our larger base of associates—and the critical interests of GE."

Heads nod approvingly. Bankers, and boards in general, love overhead reduction. And I need to protect our remaining employees and buy time to turn this around. The body language of the GE group tells me I might have made a bit of headway here.

Greg jumps back in.

"One last thing we think you'll be pleased to hear: We've signed with an investment bank to help us find a buyer for the business. David also has a few leads he's working with inside the industry. Some vendors might want to invest in the business. Our goal is to add additional capital to our balance sheet and strengthen our business model with a new investor."

I add a few reassuring comments and then—a stubborn silence fills the suddenly motionless room.

I hold my breath. I feel every one of our employees and their families on my shoulders in this critical moment. The thing I fear the most, the question that kept me up last night and so many nights before, is about to be answered.

Tim takes his time before he finally speaks.

"Okay," he says slowly. "We'll continue to work with you on this . . . for now. But David—we'll expect written business updates from you monthly, including your progress on finding a buyer. My credit team will hold a weekly call with your staff to monitor payment distributions and incoming sales receipts per the plan you've provided. We'll also expect you to be available to us when needed."

"Absolutely," I respond.

I take a long, deep but discreet breath. *This thing is not over yet! Dammit, we can still save it!*

There is little small talk as the meeting breaks up quickly. The bankers' faces remain stoic—not a single smile—as they exit the room, pinstriped soldiers marching in stolid formation back to their cubicle trenches.

I gather my things, say my goodbyes to Greg, and make my way back to LaGuardia. I have several hours before the flight, and although I'm exhausted, there is more work to be done.

At the boarding gate, I take a seat and pull out my phone and laptop to get started. But focus escapes me. It's been a tough day already and I've got a long way to go before landing in Raleigh and eventually climbing into bed for another attempt at a good night's sleep.

I'm an even longer way from my father's house all those years ago.

Six
Mariachi Sounds

POP—NO LONGER DIDDY—decides to move us from Oak Grove Avenue to a slightly larger place on Huffine Mill Road, still in the eastern part of the city. And this time we're not renting! He's bought us an older, ranch-style home with partial brick frontage, white trim, and a small, unattached garage in the back. Entering the house from the backyard, I climb three concrete steps (not two), open a screen door, and enter a combination kitchen/den. To the left, three bedrooms are located down a long hallway and a small living room anchors the front. It's about 1,200 square feet, a little small for a family of five. But it's nicer than I'm used to, and I like it.

I watch him closely as he carries our meager belongings in. Though not a tall man, he's rock-solid: one hundred eighty pounds, with Popeye-like wrists and forearms. His face is smooth, and his black hair is parted on the left and combed over to the side, then swept around into a "ball" with a slight curl peaking high on his forehead. I pass him in the bathroom on some mornings just as he splashes on a bit of Vitalis and fingers that final sweep. It's sort of a Bill Haley look, a product of an earlier time.

My father is a handsome man. And a working man. He believes that a man should "rightly" work for a living—he tells us that all the time. And he does. He's a mechanic at Lorillard, a cigarette manufacturer whose main plant is convenient to our new place. He's also a smoker, and smoke quickly fills the house in a vaporous fog as we bring our things in. Within a few weeks, we've settled into our new routine.

In a normal week, Pop's an eight-to-five, Monday-through-Friday worker while Mama works varying hours at a local department store. In her frequent absence, Pop cooks and cares for us. He's not one to sit around—he's a doer, a mover. He possesses a relentless restlessness that's constantly in play in our everyday life. If a day passes and something's not been accomplished—whether it's his job, washing the car, mowing the lawn, doing laundry, or cooking a meal—it's a wasted one.

His energetic approach also applies to the weekend, and Saturday is our day to make sure the house is just so. He cleans inside in the afternoon after working in the yard all morning, doing everything from scrubbing toilets to dusting furniture. We also complete our assigned chores, knowing full well what's at stake. Pop's expectations are high and his patience level is low—he'll give us a second chance, but not a third one, to get the job done right.

While working, he sorts through his vinyl collection of country, bluegrass, and early rock and roll. Today he makes his choice, places *Ring of Fire* on the turntable, drops the needle, and the music blares, sound filling the entire house, including the living room—which, other than the stereo system, remains unfurnished. Sometimes, when I'm working, I laugh to myself while he sings along because for the most part he can't carry a tune in a bucket.

We have a chain-link fence surrounding our backyard, and this Saturday it's a sunny afternoon and our chores are done, so

Danny and Billy are outside playing football. The ball flies back and forth. Danny is on the left side of the yard, closer to our neighbor Mr. Bowers, who diligently hangs wet clothes on the line to dry. He mumbles impatiently to himself as he fumbles with the clothespins. He seems bothered.

The kitchen window is open, and despite Johnny Cash's echoed crooning, Pop can hear everything.

"Hot out today, huh boys?" Mr. Bowers begins, casually initiating a conversation with my brothers.

They both nod and Danny politely responds, "Yes sir, it sure is."

"Been like this for a few weeks now and, geez, my air conditioner—I'm running it all the time. Just got my electric bill for the month—it's off the charts!" he remarks offhandedly.

"Yes, sir. Well, Pop don't run ours too much. I don't think our bill was that bad." Danny tosses the ball back to Billy.

"Really? Oh well, at this rate, maybe I'm gonna have to cut back on mine too," says Mr. Bowers as he pins another snow-white T-shirt on the thin line.

After he finishes pinning the remaining items, he picks up his clothes basket and heads back inside. The sun punches down through a cloudless blue sky and the clothes will dry quickly in the shimmering heat.

The football continues to spiral while I'm inside, playing with my Hot Wheels cars on the den floor. I lie on my right side, my left hand pressed firmly atop the roof of my green Ford Mustang as I roll it back and forth under our black leather couch. "Vroom, vroom," I say, gunning the engine as I roll.

"Danny Wayne Pruitt, get in this house!" Pop suddenly shouts, startling me, as he interrupts the mariachi trumpet sounds on "Ring of Fire

My antenna goes up immediately. I sit upright, my butt now directly on the tile floor. I look on as Danny steps through the back door.

"What the hell are you doing out there?" Pop sputters.

"Billy and I are just throwing the football around," Danny answers, unaware of any issue.

"I heard you talking to him!" Pop says accusingly.

"I was just throwing the football with Billy!" He pauses for a moment, and then it hits him. "Oh, you mean Mr. Bowers?"

Da, da, da, da, da . . . the trumpets blare. *Da, da, da* . . .

"What do you know about how much our electric bill is?" Pop asks, his voice rising.

Danny looks at my father quizzically.

"Boy, it's none of his damn business what our bills are, and you don't know nothin' about it anyway!"

"Pop, we were just talking. I didn't tell him anything," Danny says, vainly trying to calm my father.

"You keep your mouth shut about our bills or about anything else that goes on in this house. Is that clear? You keep it shut or I'll shut it for you."

"Pop, he was makin' conversation with me. What was I supposed to do?"

Pop steps forward. Now right in my brother's face, he reaches out and grabs him by the T-shirt and pulls him close.

"Just keep your damn mouth shut, ya heah me!"

"But I was just answerin' him, Pop!" my brother repetitively and foolishly responds.

My father does nothing for a moment, then releases his grip. He steps back and starts to unbuckle his black belt.

Danny, temporarily stunned, stares at my father's waist, then looks up at his roiling, seething eyes and suddenly he knows what's about to happen. He starts to beg.

"No, Pop. Don't. I'm sorry! I won't say anything from now on, I promise! Please!"

Da, da, da, da, da . . . da, da, da . . .

His voice and body quiver as the familiar fear takes hold. He backs away, vainly seeking safer ground.

Pop decides against the belt; instead, he reaches out and slaps Danny viciously on the side of the face with his open right palm. He strikes firmly, sending him immediately to the floor. He continues to swing as Danny kneels, ducks, and covers. I hear the smack of Pop's large hand as it connects with my brother's head, shoulders, and upper back. Danny rises, then falls to the floor once again. But Pop is unsatisfied.

Unable, in his mind, to inflict an acceptable level of damage, he snatches my brother up off the floor and shoves him hard against the wall where the kitchen trash can sits. Unbelievably, Danny caroms forward, staggers, and falls back over into the open trash can. His backside sinks in deep and he's caught like a turtle on its carapace, trying to flip itself back over. Neck extended, his hands grasp anxiously at the rim of the can, seeking escape.

I stand up now, mouth open, and slowly back away.

"Get your ass outta there, get outta that trashcan NOW!" Pop screams.

Danny's eyes bulge in utter panic. Desperate to escape, he rocks back and forth, tips over the can, falls to the floor, wiggles free and scrambles to his feet. Unfortunately, trash spills on the floor in the process. A second cardinal sin has now been committed. He tries to run but Pop grabs him by the back of the shirt, swings him away from the back door, and unceremoniously deposits him down like a soppy wet rag, flat on his back, in the middle of the kitchen floor.

He straddles him, leans down, puts his index finger in his face, looks him eyeball to eyeball, and screams, "I told you—you keep your damn mouth shut about my business! Ya heah me?"

"Yes Pop," Danny whimpers.

"Now get up from there!" Pop backs off enough so Danny can stand. "Pick up that trash, get your ass out that door, and you better keep that damn mouth shut!" he says in a manner that holds the promise of worse things to come if his edict is not followed.

As ordered, Danny staggers to his feet, cleans up the mess, then sprints outside. The screen door slams behind him.

Pop turns away, walks over to the kitchen counter, and grabs his open can of Schlitz beer. He takes a deep swig and then turns around to see me standing there—open-mouthed, unmoving, gawking back at him. Our eyes meet and I, needing no encouragement, drop the green Mustang on the black leather couch and run out the screen door behind my brother.

Once outside, I look to my left and see Mr. Bower's clothes fluttering in the wind. Danny sits off to the left side on the porch steps, head down between his legs, crying softly. Billy stands to the right in the grass, silently tossing the football up and down, back and forth, shifting it from hand to hand.

"Danny, you'll be okay," he says.

I say nothing. I step around Danny and run away from the porch steps, looking for the safety of greener grass. Billy nods at me, then throws the football. I make the catch and, seeking normalcy, toss it back. But Danny doesn't rise to join us.

After sitting for a while, his tears dry. He gets to his feet, unlatches the gate, and, without saying a word, deliberately moves down our driveway to the open road and takes a left.

From the backyard, Billy cradles the ball as the two of us, standing side by side, cling to the rusty chain-link fence and watch him walk away, slow-footed and glassy-eyed, down the empty street.

Seven
Phoenix Rising

Restless, DANNY HEADS WEST once again. His feet, his wits, and his right thumb take him in a northwestern direction, away from southern Arkansas. He crosses efficiently through several states along the way.

In his wanderings, he carries along a small Bible. He prefers the gospels in the New Testament when he can settle his mind and read, but he also can't help but be struck by the imagery in the Old Testament of Moses taking his people, the Israelites, from Egypt, where they wound up wandering in the desert for forty years before defeating the Canaanites and finally reaching their promised land east of the Jordan River.

Weary from the constant travel, he considers the fact that he's been on the road for almost twenty years himself. Where's his promised land? Screw that, when can he stop running, settle down, and just be satisfied? He's had people in his life, women that loved him, and he tried to love them back, but after a while he stopped kidding himself—he couldn't do it. So he runs instead—it just feels better. But why? What does God want of him? What does he want for himself?

He pushes these troubling questions to the back of his mind.

He stops in Phoenix, Arizona. He's always wanted to see Phoenix.

He's a Carolina boy—and while he's spent some time on the road in the cold, he much prefers the warmer weather. But this is pushing it—it's hot as blazes here, nearly 100 degrees in the shade! Still, he rolls into town on this late afternoon with the vague hope he usually feels when landing in a new place. He also has a nearly empty wallet.

Down to his last five dollars, he heads for the downtown area, working his way toward Central Arizona Shelter Services on South 12th Avenue. Slow-walking the city streets, he takes apprehensive note of the beggars and the damaged, who stand in abundance to the simultaneous disgust and neglect of the urban sprawl that passes by undeterred.

Various sheet-covered encampments dot the area on 9th Avenue close to the shelter. This tells him the shelter itself will be packed and unruly. Phoenix, he surmises, is a popular home for the homeless.

But still, he has no idea the level of squalor and depravity he's about to confront.

He finally reaches South 12th and enters the front door of the shelter to find a three-level dormitory with approximately 400 beds and eight available toilets. Seven of them sit unflushed and full of shit. He bites the bullet, relieves himself quickly, and for a moment considers the growing possibility that he'll be sleeping outside for the night.

But this time, he gets lucky.

Not all the beds are full of the mentally ill, the substance abusers, the down on their luck, or the just-released prisoners discreetly dropped there by the local authorities. He's somehow caught a break: there's an open bed, which means he's avoided the hard floors of the nearby St. Vincent De Paul facility or, worse yet, sleeping outside under the sweaty stars near tents with God knows who lurking inside them.

After checking in, he showers, eats a decent meal and sleeps well.

He is up the next day at 4:00 a.m. It's an hour's walk to the local labor pool, and they start handing out jobs as early as five. And he needs to work.

He steps outside onto 12th Avenue under the bulbous white lights and mostly silent streets of early-morning downtown Phoenix. A fellow transient outside the door says to him, "You better watch your ass out here."

He plans on it. He's wearing black tennis shoes, gym socks with a double red stripe, cut-off jeans, and a gray T-shirt. His backpack is pulled tight to his shoulders and his Walmart work boots are resting on his chest with the tied strings looping around the back of his neck. A man on a mission, he starts north towards 13th Avenue.

Five minutes into his journey, he hears the quiet exchange of unintelligible words emanating from across the street and behind him. He tentatively looks back over his right shoulder to see two men under a streetlight, huddled together, returning his glance. Their teeth are scant and rotten.

Oh man, he thinks. *Meth and they're probably bat-shit crazy.* He averts his eyes forward, showing no sign of panic but moving more quickly now, hopeful of leaving any potential trouble behind.

But then he hears it—the rapid footfalls. The meth-heads are walking faster. They cross the street and move in directly behind him. Just out of his sight-line, he can feel them coming on, their footsteps getting closer and closer. In an instant, acceptable distance is breached, pretense is dead, and, in these wee hours of the morning, that time when the veil between life and death hangs at its thinnest, he knows what they want and what they'll do to get it.

They're within thirty yards of him when he turns to face them.

"We want the damn backpack," the thin but well-muscled tall one demands, waving the knife he holds menacingly in his right hand. He has scraggly dark hair and a wiry, scruffy beard that comes to an innocuous point, while the other one is thicker and shorter, with a purple Phoenix Suns cap pulled low and tight on his head. It almost looks too tight, vise-gripping a melon head that is, fortunately in this case, too fat—he looks unfit.

He takes a quick inventory. *They're both younger than me, but I can probably kick the skinny guy's ass and outrun the stumpy one*, he thinks. Individually no problem, but together—both crazed on meth and carrying knives—engaging with them could be fatal.

When a homeless person dies on a city street in the United States of America, nobody gives two shits—and he knows it. And these men mean to do him serious harm. He now realizes this will be a run for his life. With a quick mental "fuck it," he abruptly takes off, determinedly toting the intended prize on his back.

Ironically, the backpack has nothing in it that would make a difference to his pursuers. He carries a sleeping bag, some clothes, toiletries, a few tools, water, five dollars, and other miscellaneous nothings. Is he going to die for five bucks? But he's fit and reasonably strong, his body undisturbed by the trespasses of alcohol, drugs, or tobacco. And he can run. Even on the wrong side of forty, he can still run. Also, importantly, he's gotten a good jump on his pursuers with his sudden take-off.

Still, he's struggling to carry the weight of the prize. He can choose now to drop it and end this. But all he owns in the world is in this red canvas bag. It keeps him clean. It gives him a place to sleep. So, he's not gonna give it up—they're gonna have to take it. Accordingly, he wills himself to turn it up a Gump-like notch.

His increase in speed lengthens his distance from the fat one—but the thin one begins to come on.

He can hear the threatening shouts behind him.

"That backpack is mine old man," the thinner one slurs.

"You better drop them damn boots!" the fat one bellows, his strides hampered somewhat by the thickness of his inner thighs.

Danny turns right onto West Jefferson Street, moving back and forth between darkness and light as he passes under streetlights in the concealed blackness of the early morning. He glances at a lush, tree-filled area on the left, a hundred yards up. He can't make it out clearly, but it looks like some sort of gentrified park. He thinks about turning but instead decides to keep going—and anyway, didn't he recall a police station up ahead somewhere? Screw it, if he has to stand and confront these meth-crazed bastards, he'll do it on the main drag, and if they kill him—because they're gonna have to before they get his backpack—let the whole damn city get a good look at it. He maintains his course and continues his determined pace, but the thin one continues to close in.

Taking a stand isn't an option until it becomes his only option, so, hamstrings now fully warm and loose, he picks his feet up and moves even faster, shifting to his final gear. His heightened adrenaline jack-pumps his legs, but his fear also speeds his breathing and now his lungs begin to push back. He ignores it. He sees a left thirty yards up; he races to it quickly and makes a sharp turn. He flies up 7th Avenue.

His backpack bounces slightly on his shoulders as his boots pound hard, their beat echoing that of his pulsing chest. It's completely quiet now except for three sets of feet smacking against the soon-to-be-overheated pavement. Then, suddenly, it's only two sets of feet—the fat one is walking! But the thin one . . . is he tiring at all? *Can I wear him out too?*

Danny steals a backward glance.

"I'm gonna cut you, asshole! You better drop it!"

No, he can't. *The son of a bitch is going to kill me!* he thinks. There's a right; he takes it and sees a large, well-lit building up ahead. His panic rising, he now realizes he can't outrun the younger man. He has to find help here, or he'll have to stand and fight. He runs on another fifty yards, toward the light, bypassing small trees in rectangular planters with brick façades stationed in broken rows to his left. It looks like some sort of courtyard. This is it. If there is no help ahead, no open door to run into, he's in real trouble.

Then he sees it! There's a row of police cars parked just outside the lit-up building. He was right! It's the Phoenix Police Department! It's right in front of him, forty yards ahead! *My God*, he thinks, *I'm almost there. Lord, don't let me fuckin' die now!*

And suddenly, all is silent in the world. He hears no sound and has no sense of proximity to his pursuer. He can only see the dark and silent sirens atop the empty black-and-whites parked just ahead of him. His legs relentlessly pump like fast-wearing pistons and the concrete punishes his cramping quads with every insistent stride. Then—like a spent miler who extends to his fullest and breaks the tape ahead of an unrelenting clock and his diligent competitors—he arrives safely at his destination.

He dodges in between two of the cars and, lungs burning, climbs the flight of stairs in front of the entry door to the department. He turns, hands clutching the top railing, looks out into the darkness, and sees nothing.

He doubles over weakly, his heart pounding, lungs gasping, straining for breath. His pursuer must have discreetly dropped from his heels. He drops the backpack to the ground but keeps a firm grip on one of the straps, never losing hold. He's never been so frightened in his life. Even Pop never scared him like this. He thought he might have to fight them—he thought he might even die. As he straightens his back and continues to search for any threatening movement in the darkness, a final thought enters his mind: *I gotta get some money in my pocket—cause I'm gettin' the hell out of Phoenix.*

Part III
Scenes of Survival

Eight
Pictures

THE LARGE BOOK SITS heavy in my lap. The cover's light brown, its bold red-lettered title centered. It's unwieldy and the pages are thick as cardboard between my fingers. I try to focus, read the stories, follow the endless stream of words, but the pictures—my imagination is captured by the pictures.

I turn the pages slowly.

I see a serpent and a man and woman holding a prized apple. Animals, two by two, climb a precipitous height to a towering ark resting on dry ground. I see a chariot of fire leaving a gray field ascending to the heavens: a great prophet has been called home— Elijah. I see a coat of many colors and an enslaved boy who will grow to lead a nation—and restore a family.

I see the pictures.

I see a ladder that climbs to the stars, where angels tread upon it. A father stands over a son that lies prostrate on a sacrificial altar while a sparing light shines down from above. A whale leaps mightily from a rolling sea while a straying sinner rests fitfully in his belly. A bush burns red flame but isn't consumed by the fire, and bare feet step lightly on ground that seems too perfect to touch. Fierce lions lie meek and mild at the foot of a man of faith.

Two armies face off against each other across desert sands but their weapons lie unused on the ground. A mighty man-giant dares the enemy horde to send forward a champion but is instead met by a young boy with a sling and a stone. The stone flies and an army is conquered. I see a woman with a jar on her head, gathering water. She is beautiful and the boy who flung the stone is now a king—and a man.

There is another wise king on a throne. Two women stand before him with one child—and a soldier draws his sword. I see a blind man chained between two pillars. His hair is long, his strength revived, and a throng of Philistines fall to the earth. A towering wall crumbles at the sound of warriors shouting—and a ram's horn.

I see shepherds and canes, a great star, rolling fields of wheat and animals transfixed on the face of a child. Atop a fiery mountain, a God and a devil converse. I see a temple and rage—a table tumbles and evil men run. A simple speck of fish and bread feeds a worshipful multitude and holy hands touch eyes that now open where they were once closed.

I see the pictures.

A small boat sits perilously on roaring seas, carrying the fears of faithless men. But holy feet walk on water, the storm calms, and the doubtful witness the power of God. I see a woman wash the heels of holiness with the locks of her hair. A teacher and his disciples gather at a banquet table to share bread and wine—a ritual that will span centuries. There is a lush garden in the evening twilight, and the temple guard arrests a great healer.

A crown of thorns draws rivulets of blood. I see a cross carried through a crowd of vipers. I see nails in wrists and three crosses in a field. A godly head slumps forward and a dark sky opens in angry torrents of rain. Angels roll back a stone and a holy one leaves the earth, rising to the highest heavens, surrounded by the brightest light.

I chase the words in the heavy book—but my eyes catch and hold the captivating pictures.

When I'm not doing anything, when I say I'm bored, Pop says, "Boy, get that Bible out I bought ya and read it."

And I do.

When Pop reads us his Bible, I don't always understand all the words but I remember the pictures I've seen in mine.

His Bible is the King James Version—the best one, he says. It's smaller than ours and the cover is made of black leather, the pages are as thin as toilet tissue. They land lightly as he thumbs his way to a chosen passage.

On a Saturday night, we gather in the kitchen at a purple dinette table with flecks of white and a bowl-shaped light fixture hanging above its center. The window is open over the kitchen sink and the crickets chirp riotously in the dark. Pop sits at the table head with Billy to his right and Danny to his left. I sit next to Billy, and tonight Grandpa's with us too. He sits across from me while his only living son thumbs through the good book, searching for the right message to share.

Grandpa's been with us for a week so far, and I love him—but he scares me. Pop told us that when he was a boy, Grandpa used to put his head between his knees and whip him with a razor strap.

I see the picture.

With our spiritual growth in mind, Pop reads a simple story about a man that Jesus brought back from the dead. His name is Lazarus. He was buried in a cave when Jesus called him to come out:

"And he that was dead came forth bound head and foot with graveclothes . . . and Jesus saith unto them, loose him and let him go."

I don't know what "grave clothes" are, but in my head I see the picture of Lazarus leaving the cave and death behind.

Pop ends by saying, "Jesus came back from the dead and he brought Lazarus back too. He's our savior and he watches over us, he protects us. You boys remember that. Now, time for bed. I'll come in and check on ya in a few minutes."

He and Grandpa lean forward to talk as we head down the hall. That's good, I think. I don't see them talk that often. While I sense they share a tolerant mutual respect, the love is unspoken—or perhaps it passed because of the razor strap.

Later, when I'm lying with my covers pulled tight to my shoulders, Pop walks in, leans over, and pats me on the head.

"Did you say your prayers?" he asks.

"Yes sir."

"Night. Diddy loves you."

He finishes checking Danny and announces, "Now I don't wanna hear no racket in here. Ya heah me? Y'all go on to sleep."

He closes the door. I lie motionless in the dark silence and think about a line from the prayer Pop taught us to say each night before we close our eyes: "If I should die before I wake, I pray the Lord my soul to take."

That line confuses me, even scares me a little—but I don't think I'm gonna die tonight. Jesus is watching over me.

Nine
Wynken, Blynken, and Nod
—and Herman

POP SNAPS THE REYNOLDS Wrap off the cardboard roll. I hear the tear before he puts the box in a small drawer to the left of the black-eyed stove and places the shiny foil across the top of the pan. With cobalt-blue crayon in hand, I color Spider-man's legs, trying hard to stay between the lines, as I half-watch Pop pull hot dogs from the refrigerator and Ore-Ida fries from the freezer drawer. It's gonna be an easy supper today—I won't have to choke down any beans.

The whistling starts and I set my crayons and coloring book aside. It's my favorite time of the day during the school week—5:00 p.m. The narrator says it's *The Andy Griffith Show* but people in the town of Mayberry call him Andy Taylor. It's a little confusing—but to me, he's just Andy. And I see him now—walking through the woods toward the lake, fishing pole resting on his shoulder. I take happy note of his arm around his boy Opie's shoulder.

And I like the way he calls Opie "son."

"Mornin' son."

"Howdy son."

"Bye son."

"Nite son."

In an earlier episode, Opie was being picked on by a bully who, each day, demanded the nickel he used to buy milk at school. Andy discovered this and, after a father–son day at the lake, told Opie about his nemesis when he was a young boy—mean ole Hodie Snitch. Hodie tried to steal the spot the two of them had just fished so successfully. Andy confessed that he was scared but eventually chose to stand and fight.

"What happened?" Opie asked breathlessly.

"Well, you and me just fished that spot, didn't we?" Andy responded as he ties Opie's shoe.

"Yeah? Yeah . . ." Opie acknowledged as his eyes widened in sudden realization.

His courage bolstered, Opie took on the bully. He received a black eye—but gave better than he got. When he returned, he had the nickel he owed Andy.

"And here's your nickel back, Paw."

"Why, thank ya, son!"

I could sense his pride in Opie when he said the word "son"—and that was my favorite way he's ever said it.

Today, Opie's in trouble again. He's hit a mama songbird with his new slingshot. She falls lifelessly, lost in the grass. He picks her up, tosses her to the skies, beckons her to fly, but it's no use. She's dead—he killed her. Andy told him to be careful with his new weapon but he recklessly shot a stone high in the trees. In tears, he runs inside the house, slamming the screen door behind him.

I don't like to see Opie cry.

When Andy arrives home a few hours later, he finds the dead bird and soon figures out that Opie's the culprit. He heads upstairs to confront his son's careless disobedience. I see the anger on his face. Is he gonna hit him? I hope not. I don't want Andy to hit him.

"You gonna give me a whippin' Paw?" Opie asks.

"No, I'm not gonna give you a whippin'," Andy responds.

Instead, he walks to the bedroom window, opens the sash, and commotion floods the room. The baby songbirds chirp hungrily in their motherless nest.

"You hear that?" he says. "That's the sound of those young birds chirpin' for their mama who's never coming back. Now, you just listen to that awhile."

Opie sits in silence, the weight of his transgression delivered in piercing, anguished twitters.

Watching intently, I think, *How are those birds gonna make it without their mama?*

My heart aches at the sound of the birds chirping—and it's an ache from a place that's still tender and sore.

As the Old Gold cigarette commercial plays on the Philco, my mind goes back to a few weeks ago, when Pop took Herman away.

Herman was our soft, brown, short-legged weenie dog. His belly skidded the ground and his tiny feet skittered on the linoleum when he chased us around the kitchen. I loved to rub the short hairs on his back and watch him look up at me with his deep brown eyes, enjoying my affection.

But Herman had a problem: he peed on the floor a few times. And Mama didn't like him in the house anyway. Then one Friday afternoon, when Pop got home from work, there was poop on the floor.

"That's it," Pop informed the three of us—Herman had to go.

But go where? Pop said he'd drop him on a country road out by some woods. He said Herman was a dog and dogs can hunt and take care of themselves. But I didn't believe it. Herman's snout was barely above his fuzzy-green tennis ball when he leaned down to snatch it off the floor!

We stayed up late that night and did our best to talk Pop out of it. We told him we'd take Herman outside more often and teach him to go in the grass. But he wouldn't budge and quickly got tired of our whimpering.

"Don't ask me again," he finally said coldly.

The next morning, we got up early, filled Herman's dish with food, and gave him some clean water. We rolled the fuzzy tennis ball until Pop said it was time to go. Herman's legs churned and clicked the linoleum until his momentum finally propelled him forward in hot pursuit.

He's not so fast, I thought. *How's he gonna hunt anything?*

We begged Pop to let us ride with him. We wanted to be with Herman as long as we could. He warned me, the youngest, not to come, but I kept on until he relented. I thought that maybe, somehow, we could get him to change his mind.

Danny and I climbed in the back of the Marlin Silver AMC Rambler and Billy sat passively up front. Pop took the wheel. We passed Herman back and forth on the ride to nowhere.

"Let me have him—no, let me have him!"

I squeezed Herman and rubbed my face on his as he instinctively twisted away.

Finally, Pop stopped the car at a quiet but steamy place. There were pines, oaks, maples, and poison oak. There was an isolated country road, cracked and soft from the heat of so many hot summer days.

He warned me about trying to stop him, but I no longer cared, and neither did Billy or Danny.

"Please Pop, don't do it. We'll clean it up. You won't have to do it anymore. We promise!" we begged.

Pop was unaffected and angry at us for disobeying him, for our continued begging.

"Hand me that dog and don't let me see you getting out of this car!" he warned, his steely eyes dismissing our panicked faces.

He brusquely snatched Herman from Danny's arms, walked several paces down the road, and dropped him in the grass to the right of the hot pavement. He patted him on the head, ran back to the car, cranked the engine and shifted into drive. We took off and skidded hard left as the tires squealed. Danny and I looked out the back window. Herman ran after the car, ears flying—and our tears came down in droves, hot and fast. Billy told us it would be all right.

He chased us for a while, then stopped and stared as we continued to speed away. His deep browns turned to the dense woods as we climbed up over the rise. Barreling downhill, we quickly lost sight of him. My heart pounded and my chest heaved. I felt nauseous as I tumbled back down in the seat.

"I told you not to come," Pop reminded me.

I wished I hadn't.

The baby songbirds are in trouble—but Opie has a plan. With Andy looking on, he pulls worms from the ground, climbs a tall ladder, and feeds the starving babies. When Mrs. Snyder's cat returns next door, he retrieves them from the nest, puts them in a cage, and continues his diligent care. And soon enough, they begin to grow. They still chirp loudly but it's no longer a cry for their mama—they're fat and singing!

Andy, the proud father looks on.

"And Paw, there's three of 'em," Opie says one morning. "I call 'em Wynken, Blynken, and Nod."

"Them's fine bird names," says Andy.

A second commercial plays and I think back to Herman running after our car and I can see it now—I handled it all wrong! I was so busy petting him that I didn't pay attention to how we got to that country road. And now I'll never be able to go back and get him. Opie's saving Wynken, Blynken, and Nod—but I let Herman down.

One morning, before school, Andy takes Opie aside and tells him what he already knows: it's time for the songbirds to be set free.

"What if I didn't do all the right things? What if they can't fly?" Opie asks.

"You did all the right things," Andy assures him. "I expect they'll be able to fly."

Father and son continue to talk. But mostly the father listens, quietly and intently, and the son does the talking. Slowly, the child turns the idea over in his mind, sharing his logic with his father—an easy progression that happens because the child has been taught, and loved. He gets to the right place. He loves these birds but he must let them go. And so he does, one by one. They soar majestically into the trees—but they take a little boy's heart with them.

The familiar ache.

A good father is there to help.

"The cage sure looks awful empty don't it Paw?" Opie asks regretfully.

"Yes son, it sure does," Andy agrees as his eyes drift slowly up the old oak to the highest branches. The songbirds jitter and shake happily from limb to limb, tailfeathers wiggling in the damp leaves. They sing lustily.

"But don't the trees sound nice and full," Andy says, and puts his arm around Opie's shoulder again.

I like Andy and think about him a lot, even when he's not on TV.

I pick up my coloring book and grab a magenta red.

I miss Herman and hope this heartache will ease in time. But I'm gonna remember the way Andy helped Opie's birds fly—and how Pop made my dog run.

Ten
Coffee and the Sixth Floor

THERE IS AN INTELLIGENCE in her words that I don't hear in the rest of our family. She is statuesque and, at 5'9", stands a bit taller than Pop. She's quite pretty: light brown hair, straight white teeth, light-blue eyes, and a lithe, lean figure.

We arrive at the department store some nights to pick her up at the end of her work shift and I see men walk away quickly, cutting their eyes at my father as they pass. She has both beauty and brains but her behavior can, at times, be undisciplined. She succumbs to the advances of other men and is also a spendthrift. To my father's great consternation, she seems unable to maintain steady employment.

She aggressively asserts her authority over us at home in Pop's absence but laughs off his abrasiveness and cowers in the volcanic wake of his overbearing return. She is, for the most part, an unfeeling woman. She can, on occasion, show affection and concern, but it seems forced, obligatory, like a conversation where one can't handle dead space and fills it with words that hold no relevance, no real intent. She is kind but noncommittal, friendly but distant. The right words are said because they've been learned, not because they're felt. But of all the things she is and is not, what confuses and scares me most about Mama is this: she sees people and hears voices that I can't.

She hears them in the house constantly and often thinks it's us, talking about her. She angrily pulls my brothers and me in from playing outside on summer mornings and has the three of us stand in the corner for hours on end in complete silence.

In a solitude of her choosing, she fights the persistent prodding of her damaged mind—but the battle is beginning to take a toll. I see, of late, a distracted silence that has taken hold. She's slow to respond, her eyes are vacant and empty, and she's vanishing quickly from the day-to-day of our lives. Pop takes the lead in everything and keeps the family moving forward—but just barely.

He pulls us out of bed each morning. After getting dressed and brushing our teeth, we head for the kitchen, where hot oatmeal is placed in the center of the table. I take my seat facing the kitchen sink, and we all recite repetitive prayers: "God is great, God is good, let us thank Him for our food. Amen."

The kitchen is small: the white-bodied, black-eyed, silver-edged stove sits to the right of me, off the back wall of the house, while the refrigerator sits prominently to my left. The purple dinette set, with its faux leather seats, is the epicenter of family discussions, meals, and occasional Bible readings.

But it's relatively quiet so far this morning. Pop wolfs down a bowl of oatmeal and, lunch bag in hand, leaves quickly for work. Billy reaches across the table to pour milk into my bowl. I dip my spoon directly into the milk, mix it with the hulled oat grains, and hungrily scoop a spoonful into my mouth. On this day, Mama sits at the table and joins us. She's here, but she's mostly not.

She sits quietly, her eyes looking off into some impenetrable distance. The radio on the counter, to the left of the kitchen sink and behind the table, is tuned to the local country music AM station. Radio, not TV, is part of our typical morning, and AM, as opposed to FM, rules the radio dial. Eddy Arnold has just finished singing his latest, and the announcer is talking about the expected weather forecast for the day and the coming weekend. Billy, Danny, and I are talking about playing ball.

Suddenly, Mama is talking to the radio:

"I'll drink my coffee if I want to!" she shouts, wide-eyed, staring right at the radio.

I look at Billy, who looks at Danny, who, in turn, looks at me.

Visibly agitated, she reiterates, "You heard me! I can drink my coffee if I want to! Isn't that right Billy?" She turns to my big brother.

"Mama, that man didn't say anything about you drinking coffee. He's talking about the weather."

She laughs, but not in a "just kidding" kind of way. It's less of a laugh and more of a cackle; she seems unaware that her conversation is one-sided.

"I've been drinking my coffee since I was fifteen, and you or anyone else can't do anything about it," she says, eyes still glued tight on the radio.

Danny pokes me in the ribs and points at me, laughing at Mama's imagined snit with the radio announcer. I ignore his joking elbow. My eight-year-old mind can grasp that Mama has always been a bit different. She's done strange things from, well, ever since I can remember. But things have begun to get even stranger now. There is a dawning awareness in all of us that something is terribly wrong with her.

"Hee, hee, hee" she sniggers with a wildness in her eyes that is no longer funny to me or my brothers. She continues drinking her coffee, lifting the cup with an air of defiance and nodding assertively at the voice in the box.

I am struck by the strange smile on her face. I watched a scary movie recently about a young motel clerk who killed his Mama. Her smile makes me think of that young man's face. He talked to the voices in his head too.

"Mama, I got to get to school, you keep drinking and don't worry about it. David, get the sugar for Mama," Billy instructs as he rises from the table, picks up the bag at his feet, and heads out the door.

I see my way out: I jump up, grab the sugar jar off the counter, plop it on the table, and say, "Here Mama, I gotta catch the bus. Bye!"

I eye Danny, who reflects a raised eyebrow look that says, "Are you leaving me here alone with her—like this?" Confirming his suspicion, I snap my books up off the counter and run outside, slamming the thin screen door behind me.

Around this time, Pop and his fellow union workers at Lorillard go on strike. He takes his daily shifts carrying signs on the picket line and gets a small weekly stipend that, unfortunately, does not come close to replacing his normal paycheck. Mama doesn't bring home a big salary either, and things become tighter than normal.

We eat milk gravy and biscuits, corned beef hash, eggs, spam, pork and beans, and mayonnaise sandwiches. The strike goes on for a little over six weeks, and our rotating food lineup remains repetitive and thin. Worse still, I can see Pop and Mama's relationship deteriorating rapidly under the financial strain, like a willowy Kleenex tissue tossed into a roaring fire.

He asks if she can get more hours at work, but it doesn't happen. We hear, though I don't fully understand, as they yell at each other behind closed doors (mostly Pop) that she is unresponsive to his advances in the bedroom.

It all comes to a head one night when we ride over to pick Mama up from work. Pop has been carrying a picket sign all day and is in a foul mood. Mama climbs into the Rambler, sits down, closes the door, and promptly announces she's just lost her job. In the backseat, my brothers and I eye each other warily, not making a sound.

"Dammit, you know we're on strike and we've got to have that money!" Pop swears.

"Mr. Emeritt yelled at me. I told him I didn't have to stand for it, so I quit."

"Did you think about them boys back there when you made that decision?"

"You know we'll be all right." She laughs as if it's only a temporary setback.

Maybe it is to her, but not to Pop. He punches the steering wheel in frustration, curses, turns the car around, and floors it, sending us all tumbling in the backseat.

When we finally pull up at the house, he stomps around the front of the car, unlocks the back door, opens the passenger car door, grabs Mama by the arm, and drags her inside. I hear her say, "No, stop!" as he pulls her up the steps through the back door, down the hallway, and into their bedroom.

We hop out of the car and run in behind them. Following Billy's lead, we stop in the kitchen, tentatively peeking our heads around the corner down the hall. We watch Pop slam the bedroom door and hear what sounds like him throwing her down on the bed. The sound of his screamed words comes flooding back toward the kitchen. My eyes tear up.

"I told you you were going to have to work to help me. I told you to finish that nursing school, but you wouldn't listen to me. 'Oh, I'll work, I'll get a job,'" he imitates her voice in a high-pitched derisive squeal. "Now look at where we are! We don't have a pot to piss in!"

"I'll get another job!" Mama promises.

"You can't keep a damn job, and you ain't a wife to me either. I ain't putting up with this shit anymore!" Here, his voice breaks in a way that I've not heard before. It's not just anger; it's violent desperation.

"Well, don't forget YOU have those boys in there to take care of."

In a world where the two of them might split apart, Mama always makes it clear that we are Pop's responsibility—not hers. I've heard this before.

Billy slowly advances down the hall toward the bedroom door. We follow in tow. We plead with Pop to calm down, speaking our impotent words to the closed bedroom door—"It's okay, Pop, it'll be all right."

"We can't pay for the house, the refrigerator is empty, and I know about that shit going on at work," Pop growls.

"What do you expect, the way you treat me?" Mama screams.

Carefully, Billy opens the door. I tiptoe behind him and tentatively peek around his haunches. Mama gets up off the bed, but Pop's balled fist comes crashing down across the right side of her face, causing her to fall back down. She again bounces back up to his waiting, rigid, fingers, the veins popping blue and hard in the tops of his hands, which are now locked tight in a vise grip on her slender shoulders. He shakes her, and her head rolls to and fro like a dinghy rocking in a stormy sea. A weak mind and a short fuse make for a combustible, but not yet final, encounter.

"Pop, stop—don't do it. Don't hit her!" Billy pleads as he cautiously edges farther into the room.

"Yeah, stop Pop—don't hit Mama," Danny and I add in a high-pitched, fearful chorus.

Pop looks up. "Get out and close the damn door!" he roars.

"Pop, don't hit her—it ain't right," Billy says again.

Danny and I stand behind him, wide-eyed and crying.

"Get out!!" Pop screams, his hands still clutching Mama's shoulders. Her face is contorted and washed with rolling tears.

We do, but perhaps the sight of us, scared and begging, strikes a nerve, because although there is more yelling, crying, and violent cursing deep into the night, I do not hear bone on bone anymore.

I lie there, quietly listening—waiting for it all to end. Finally, the commotion dies down, and the house becomes quiet.

The next morning, carrying brutal memories of the night before, we're packed up and sent to a lost and seemingly unimportant day at school.

There is no sign of Mama when I get back home later that afternoon—the bedroom door remains closed—and she is even less present in our family in the weeks and months that follow. But she is still hung up on the damn radio station. She now calls and cusses them out weekly for talking about her drinking her coffee. I sit and listen quietly as she rants at them over the phone.

One afternoon, the station manager calls Pop at home to complain. I hear her tell him Mama needs to see a doctor. Pop says he'll take care of it.

He sits down with her in their bedroom—the door closed. As we listen outside, he says he'll stay with her and help, but only if she tries to help herself by going to the doctor.

Begrudgingly she agrees.

The doctor says Mama is mentally ill and places her on the sixth floor of Moses Cone Hospital, where shock treatments are to be administered. Mama may have agreed to go to the doctor, but she never agreed to have her brain shocked; she wants no part of it. She fights with Pop and asks us not to let him do it. Billy, and to a lesser extent

Danny, have hardened toward Mama by now because of her notable absence from our lives, so I feel singled out when she appeals to the three of us that she wants to come home. It is frightening and confusing. I feel guilty that I don't stand up for her. But this is happening no matter what. The treatments are to be given.

Pop takes us to visit her on the sixth floor of Cone for the first time one night after supper. We step off the elevator, get past an initial foyer entryway, turn a corner, push a button to the right of the locked grey metal doors, and enter hallways with slanted, broken, human shells slowly but determinedly wandering the halls on sliding feet in umber socks. Eyes, vacant but feral, cast about feverishly before landing dead on me. They seem to dare me to look back. Disheveled hair, stained clothing, hunched-over shoulders, gnarled hands loosely gripping IV poles carrying mounted drip bags, all mix inaudibly with quiet mumbling, loud shrieking, or cackling laughter. Billy tells me this is where the "crazies" hang out.

My fearful anxiety grows as we continue to navigate the eerie hallways, which smell of a dichotomous mixture of Pine-Sol and poop. I carefully remain close to Pop's impatient stride until we enter Mama's room—one shared with a roommate who matches the description of her cohorts traveling the hallways.

Mama eyes Pop warily. "You shouldn't have brought me here. Get me out now—please."

"We talked about this. And you know what the doctor said. These treatments might help. Don't you want to be a mother to these boys? Don't you want to come home?" Pop asks, his firm hand resting on my shoulder.

"I am their mother, and I don't want to be here. Boys, don't you want your mama to come home now?" she asks us all.

But it feels like her eyes are only looking at me.

"Mama," Billy interrupts, "the doctors know what's best for you. It'll make you better."

"*I* know what's best for me; these people are crazy," says the woman who has been talking with unseen visages for months. She pauses, then begins to cry soft tears. "Now listen, I'm all right. You boys know I love you. I want to come home."

"We love you too, Mama," I say. I feel the tears well up and my throat tightens.

She leans forward as if intending to peel back the clean white sheets and escape from the rumpled, thin bed. Before she can, Pop waves us out the door. I hesitate but follow Billy, happy to escape her accusing tone and tearful stare but nervous about facing the floating apparitions in the halls without Pop. As we step out, I hear noises inside. Mama's still edging out of the bed, but Pop quickly stems the tide of her movement.

We go back in a bit later. I sense the noticeable tension in the room between my parents; it's as thick as the bowl of tomato soup mixed with saltine crackers I had for supper.

We return several times over the next few weeks and see Mama in fluctuating states of lucidity. She's getting more confused, and at times acts like she doesn't even know us.

After a few more troubling visits, she is, supposedly, well enough for us to take her home. But when we do, she just sleeps a lot.

In time, she gets back on her feet. But she remains unemployed and emotionally unavailable, and the relationship between my parents does not improve. I still love my mother, but she's not around, so my brothers and I are left to deal with Pop on our own.

Very soon, just like my older brothers, I no longer rely on Mama—no longer need her.

Eleven
A Father's Name

I WALK HOME SLOWLY, KNOWING the fight that just ended was far less violent than the confrontation ahead. My dread is palpable; each step is taken hesitantly, and time is not my friend. If I stall, meander, or procrastinate to steal more time, my sentence is delayed but its severity is compounded. If I run quickly and forfeit time, perhaps my sentence will be commuted. But no, that's foolish thinking. The rules are clear, and the tear in the knee of my jeans will not escape my father's observant eye.

I'm late and he'll already know something is up. I could sneak in and change my clothes, but he'll find them, and the weight of my transgression will be multiplied—and so will my punishment. Still, it's my fault. He told me the rule: money is tight, so take care of your clothes. We've each got two pairs of jeans for the new school year, period. "You tear them up, you're getting your asses torn up"—those were his exact words. I'm in trouble, real trouble.

I decide to compromise: I don't stall but I also don't run—I keep a steady pace. Home is now three houses ahead on my left. In my head, I search feebly for acceptable excuses.

Think! What can I possibly say to save myself? I didn't want to fight. Two boys were arguing with Danny at the bus stop and I walked over to make sure he was okay. He's my brother! The next thing I knew, I was rolling around on the ground.

Oh God, I'm almost there. I regretfully eye the tear in my jeans one last time. My feet are, somehow, still moving forward. Is his car home yet? Another house up, and I can see it. It is—the Rambler is parked front and center in the driveway.

I turn left. I begin walking up to our driveway to the latched fence. I prepare to beg.

But it wasn't always like this.

On a warm Saturday morning, the sun is shining bright in a sky colored in scattered whites and azure blue. I'm excited because Diddy is taking us to the playground at the local elementary school. The three of us stand eagerly by the car as Diddy loads a baseball bat and three softballs into the car trunk, along with a football, a basketball, and three new gloves he recently bought from K-Mart. We ride, and Danny and I buzz happily in the backseat as Diddy talks about some of his favorite baseball players.

"Willie Mays was great but if Mickey Mantle hadn't got hurt, he'd have all the records. And nobody could touch Bob Gibson pitchin'—nobody," he declares to Billy.

We arrive at the playground. Diddy tells us to grab our gloves from the open trunk and head to the backstop. He drops the football and basketball in the grass by the car and follows. Billy walks along with him but Danny and I take off running, testing our speed against one another. We prance like newborn colts who've just discovered their legs and are experiencing the warmth of a summer breeze and the softness of tall grass for the first time.

Wow, Danny's fast, I can't keep up with him, I think. *But he's older than me*, I remind myself.

Diddy, now at the backstop, tells Billy to grab a bat and step up to the plate. He sends me to the right and Danny to the left and directs us to move just beyond the dirt on the fringe of the infield to the green grass. He walks out to the pitchers' mound and lobs one in high and slow. Billy takes a cut, and the ball comes my way on the bounce. I miss it but run full speed to retrieve the ball. I toss it back to Diddy on the bounce.

"Come on now, young'un, get that ball up here," he tells me.

Billy's got the hang of it. He sends one after another beyond the dirt into the grass as we race to see who can get to the ball first. Danny even catches one.

The sun is getting hotter now but we're spared by a cool wind that moves with gentle purpose. I feel like I could run all day.

Next, Danny's up. Although he doesn't hit it as hard as Billy, he makes solid contact. Diddy is satisfied he's got it.

Now he waves me in. It's my turn.

He takes a few steps closer to the plate and tosses it in. I swing and miss and then swing and miss again.

Diddy sets his glove down and walks up behind me. After telling me to get in my stance, he grabs my right elbow and lifts it high.

"Keep that elbow up," he counsels.

He steps back in front of me.

"Keep your eye on *this* ball," he says, holding it up. "When you start your swing, don't look where you think the ball's gonna go, keep your eyes right on the ball and swing the bat where your eyes tell you to swing it, okay?"

"Okay, Diddy."

He takes a few steps back and gently tosses it in—and I make contact! Then, I do it again. It's not going very far, but at least I'm hitting it now.

Diddy picks up the bat, calls Billy in, hands him the ball, and tells me to get my glove and head back in the grass to the right.

I run happily. Diddy's gonna hit now.

Billy throws it up to the plate and—SMACK!—the ball jumps off Diddy's bat and sails low and fast on a line. It reminds me of when I snap my wrist hard and my yo-yo unfurls quickly from my middle finger to hover just above the ground. The ball lands deep in the green grass and insistently keeps rolling, almost to the school. Danny has a long way to go running it down.

"You boys back up!" Diddy calls out.

"Diddy can really hit it!" Danny says with a smile.

Diddy sends us scurrying, one ball after another flying fast and far until he's had enough, and so have me and Danny. The young colts are spent.

He calls us in.

"I've got work to do at home," he says. "Y'all stay out here and play awhile. There's a water hose there behind the backstop. See it?"

We nod.

"If you get thirsty, get ya some water. I'll be back in a few hours. Billy, you're in charge."

Billy nods and Diddy hustles to the silver rambler, climbs in, and takes off.

We guzzle water from the hose. The sun beats down and sweat gathers on my brow, but we're not tired; we've got our second wind.

We grab the football. One of us plays quarterback, one plays receiver, and the other plays defense. We score touchdowns, make hard tackles, and roll all over one another in the itchiness of the green grass. It's not wrestling, our favorite thing to do in the backyard at home, but it's pretty close.

After a while, we tire again and head back for the garden hose.

Billy tells us to line up and he holds it while Danny and I take a drink. He tells me to lean over and fires the water onto my head, face, and neck. I shake my head and shoulders like a frisky collie rinsed clean after a soapy bath, then run up the hill to grab the basketball before my brothers finish.

I flip it over in both hands as I head toward the court, liking the feel of it. I'm younger and smaller than my brothers but I have a knack for putting the ball in the hole. We have a backboard and rim at home, nailed to a sturdy pine in the far-right corner of our backyard just in front of the dark woods, and I practice on it all the time—this is my best sport.

The school playground basket has an orange metal rim and a net, which means we can get a good swish. Danny and I team up against Billy until a kid my age shows up. Now it's me and Danny against Billy and the new kid. I'm learning to move my feet, to make space to get my shot off. I run around Danny's pick, he hands me the ball, I bend my knees, push off, and—swish!

After a time, the little boy has to leave, and when he does we sprint down the hill to the backstop and water hose one final time. Despite my best efforts, I come in a distant third.

Afterward, Billy and Danny sit on the concrete and lean against the fence surrounding the court while I continue to shoot and dribble. We talk about the basketball game, Diddy hittin' the softball, the latest Captain America comic book, and Herman the dog while I continue to shoot on the orange-rimmed goal.

Finally, Diddy pulls up and waves us back to the car. We gather the balls and bats and hustle. We got chores to do.

"Did y'all have fun?" he asks.

We happily concur.

"Thanks for takin' us Diddy," Billy says.

＊ ＊

Once we get back, we put the balls and bat in the garage and Diddy ushers us inside. We have a seat at the kitchen table and Diddy passes out glasses of grape Kool-Aid. He clinks the cubes in the clear glass and the deep cold on the back of my throat makes me pause before I continue guzzling.

Diddy then herds us into the living room and we stretch out, worn and exhausted, on the carpeted floor. We have our window unit, the only air conditioning in the entire house, here.

"I'm gonna turn the air on," Diddy says. "You boys lie there and cool down a few minutes."

I lie on the thin carpet and close my eyes while the air conditioner turns the moisture on my face from damp sweat to dry salt.

A half-hour later, Diddy returns and turns off the AC.

"All right," he says, "time's a-wastin'. Get them chores done."

We hop to it.

Diddy is a man who works hard, who accepts responsibility, who pays his bills, who teaches his children about Jesus and loves them when his thin patience will allow, who apologizes profusely when he ignores his better angels and gives in to his obsessive need to diminish and control by using spiteful words or a battering hand.

"Diddy's sorry," he says to us over and over again.

But the father who tosses the softball, who reads us the Bible, who pours the grape Kool-Aid and turns on the window air conditioning has a different response in mind today.

I step through the back door and he is waiting, eyeing his watch. It doesn't take him long to spot the tear in my jeans and determine I've broken one of his rules. He uncinches his belt, tells me to drop my pants, and yells, "Get over here!"

Frozen, immobile with fear, I try to tell him what happened, but he ignores my weak explanation. He reaches over, grabs me by the wrist, yanks me into striking range, and proceeds to whip my ass, lower back, and upper legs as I run in a circle to avoid, as much as possible, the bite of the belt.

His tongue hangs out the corner of his mouth as he leans in hard. Typically, real pain is inflicted but the end comes soon enough. This time, however, he will not stop. As I wail and run, newly raised, bloody stripes connect my mid-torso to the backs of my legs down to the bend of my knees.

At some point, my mind seems to numb and my running and his swinging seem to unfold at a slower speed—and suddenly, I'm flying back into the kitchen stove. Its protruding silver metal handle cuts hard into my upper back and I immediately fall into a doubled-over heap on the kitchen floor, splattered like a not-so-deft fly hit by a stealthy swatter.

I make it to my knees and crawl, desperately praying no more strokes will come. And the swinging stops. Sensing he's completed his work, I ease down on my stomach and lie still, the left side of my face pressed flat against the cool linoleum tile of the kitchen floor. I watch my detached father re-thread the leather belt through the loops on his work pants. I hear the tick of the clock above the stove and try to calm myself, my nerves. It's over. I reach down and gently touch the tender spots on my upper legs, then eye the watery layer of blood on my fingertips as he works at making supper in the kitchen.

Danny arrives home a few minutes later, clothes dirty and torn, and he receives similarly rough treatment. After several belt strokes, Diddy releases his death grip on his wrist and a second frightened child stumbles back against an unforgiving kitchen wall and that damned stove with all its sharp edges, perched quietly but pointedly waiting on its next victim.

Slaps to the face come quickly now—right hand, right hand—and then it happens: the side of Danny's head bounces off the sharp corner of that old stove and blood flies. He's cut badly on the side of his temple. As it streams down the side of his face, I see the fear in Diddy's eyes: his kryptonite shows itself.

Diddy does not like blood, and on rare occasions, it can make him faint. His eyes widen at the sight of Danny's head wound, and the brutality stops. Maybe it's the blood, maybe it's the realization he's gone too far, but the recriminations quickly start and the "look what you made me do" words are delivered—resentfully, but from a thankfully calmer disposition. A warm washrag is applied to the cut, and when the bleeding stops, rubbing alcohol is applied. After getting past the stinging burn of the unwelcome antiseptic, my brother's sobs begin to slow, strongly encouraged by my father's demand, "Boy, shut that damn racket up!"

That evening at the dinner table, as Danny wears an oversize Band-Aid and a gauze pad on the side of his head, I stare at the damage done and think, *What kind of father does this?* Danny was late and tore his clothes. He deserved to be punished. But did he deserve this?

I look briefly at Diddy, resentfully convicting him with my eyes. He coldly looks back at me. He asks if I have a problem. I say, "No Sir," and quickly turn my eyes back to my supper. But I think he knows that I know he's gone too far this time.

This revelation leaves him unaffected. Not another word is spoken between us, and Mama, as usual, sits quietly at the table, silent on the subject.

It's at this moment, at the supper table, that I question for the very first time what kind of man my father is and the unfortunate circumstances of my young life. It's also at this time that we grow beyond calling him "Diddy" forever. I'm the youngest son, but I take the lead in calling my father "Pop" because I can't call him "Paw," like Opie calls Andy, or "Dad."

I can't ever imagine calling him "Dad."

He's not like some of the wise and caring fathers I see on TV whose kids call them by those respected names. No, he is something different.

We will call him Pop instead.

Twelve
Ya Ain't Worth a Shit for Nothin'

IT'S A SPRING SATURDAY morning and I'm out mowing the lawn. Pop likes to keep a few small tomato plants growing in our backyard—he was raised on a farm by my sharecropping grandpa. He places wire fencing in a circle around each plant, then ties them off with string to keep them growing upright towards the warm sun.

Without care, I run the mower up close to one of the circular fences and lift the front end to get the high grass around it. The thin wire gets sucked into the bottom of the mower, clogging the rotating blade and bringing the mower to a screeching halt. I flip it over on its side and immediately know I'm in trouble. After unsuccessfully fiddling with the tangled mess around the blades, I walk, head down, up the back porch steps and through the screen door to tell him.

"Pop, I messed up."

He's washing dishes in the kitchen sink and also has the washer going, preparing to eventually hang laundry on the clothesline outside. We have no dryer. Like Mr. Bowers, we have clothespins and sunshine to dry our clothes.

"What's the matter?"

"I think I screwed up the lawnmower. I'm sorry Pop. I'll help fix it."

He looks at me quizzically, opens the screen door, lightly steps down from the porch to the ground, and heads to the right corner of the backyard. He takes one look at the mower resting on its side, next to the plants, and says, "What in the shit?"

Like the tomatoes on the vine, his face reddens quickly.

"I was trying to get the grass around the tomato plants, and I accidentally hit the fence and got it tangled up."

"Boy, you pull that grass up by hand; you don't mow that close to the fence."

"I won't do it again. I'm sorry."

"Dammit, just get out of my way." He shoves me to the side and walks to the garage, where he grabs his pliers and work gloves.

"Boy, you're gonna have a hard row to hoe in life if you don't have any more sense than this," he spits as he makes his way back to the mower. I follow behind him.

Kneeling on one knee, he surveys the damage, then begins to work the wire fencing around and off the blade. I stand in the mid-morning sun and feel the heat rising off the grass. Beads of sweat build on Pop's forehead.

"I can't ask you boys to do a damn thing around here," he mumbles as he continues to work the wire.

I lean over, reach my hand out for the pliers, and say, "Here Pop, I can do it."

He looks back over his right shoulder, twists his upper torso around, and slaps me hard in the face with the back of his hand. His knuckles connect with my cheekbone, and I stumble back a few steps before falling hard to the ground. I'm dazed for a moment. Then I hear the familiar words.

Through gritted teeth, he declares, "Boy, you ain't worth a shit for nothin'!"

I'm embarrassed by my mistake. I deserve to be chastised or punished. But his words, these words, I've heard before. They've been said to me and my brothers over and over, time and again. Usually, I accept the judgment and, if circumstances allow, skitter away. But somehow, it's different this time; I hear a new, dissenting, voice in my head. I don't know where it comes from but it informs and whispers to me that I don't deserve to be dismissed for who I am and what I can be. And for the first time in my young life, I respond to his scornful charge.

"I am worth something, and I'm gonna show you one day. You watch!"

"Boy, you better get your ass out of here and get in that house!"

I pick myself up and lumber, dejectedly, toward the back porch. But I can't stop myself so I turn and yell, "I was just trying to help! Why do you always have to get so mad?"

"Yeah, you helped me all right. Don't make me get up from here. I've told you smart mouths make for sore sitting-down places. Get inside that house NOW!"

I hate it when he hits me in the face. But the belt—I don't want to see the belt. My defiance wanes.

He looks me over in full-on pissed-off mode, and I know I have to go—right now. So, I do.

As I turn away and leave him to fix my mess, I realize he believes what he's just said about me. And the truth is, I spoke back only to spite him. I portray an indignant façade, but in the deepest pit of my heart, I suspect what he says is true.

I don't feel good about who I am. I feel stupid and worthless. Maybe he's right. Maybe I ain't worth a shit for nothin'.

Thirteen
The Orphan

OUR FAMILY UNIT IS not working. Mama's madness melds poorly with Pop's anger and lack of patience. She survived the shock treatments, but Pop's voice is too loud for her, too constant. It interferes with other, beckoning voices calling to her from a damaged mind. My parents have had enough and they both want out of the marriage. I hear them discussing how things will work. Mama wants all she can get; Pop just wants out and is willing to do whatever it takes to make it happen. A year ago, we traded in the old Rambler for a slightly used Chevy Caprice. Not surprisingly, Mama wants the Chevy as part of the settlement. She also wants half of whatever equity there is in the home. This means the house will have to be sold. I hear Pop appeal to her to leave the house alone, so my brothers and I can be raised in it—but she won't budge.

Inevitably, the even more difficult question of who will take care of us has to be decided. Pop is willing to take all three of us, and Billy and Danny immediately opt to stay with him. Knowing the brutality we'll continue to absorb, my brothers' quick commitment to Pop is a clear condemnation of Mama. Once she hears Billy and Danny have chosen Pop, she backs away from them and focuses her attention on me.

One day, she takes me aside and asks me to live with her. It's not an easy choice. I deeply resent Pop's abuse and erratic behavior. Even more frightening, my anger and resentment are showing more clearly now when he comes barreling at me with his tongue, his knuckles, or that damn black belt. I know he'll never back off and I wonder, at ten years of age, if I'm too stupid to back down, to get the resentful glare off my face, or to choke down the defiant words. *Maybe it's best for me to get out before I get myself killed*, I think. I drag out my decision as they negotiate back and forth over the next month.

Ultimately, it comes down to Billy and Danny. We have jointly survived the domestic battlefield of our adolescence and there is a bond between us that is real, if unspoken. We are three wayward sons—the bruised fallen fruit of a damaged family tree—but we are also brothers, and I love them.

That means I will be staying with Pop.

I tell Mama I love her, but I'm staying with my siblings. She is disappointed but understands. She soon moves out of the house and our day-to-day lives. The house gets sold and we move into an apartment on Cone Boulevard, a little farther west in the city, where a large backyard is replaced by a concrete sidewalk leading to a black-top parking lot. And more changes are coming.

Mama is being replaced too.

Mary Helen Rumley grew up on a farm and, by her account, had a happy early childhood. Much like Pop, but with a nod toward her gender, she did light work on the farm, and she often talks of helping her daddy cure tobacco in the small barn behind their shotgun shack home.

Tragically, her birth mother died young. Helen was only twelve at the time. Her father, a genial but poor and uneducated man, soon remarried. His new wife, after an initial—and, from her perspective, unsuccessful—trial did not want the burden of taking care of Helen, so Helen's daddy, in an amazing betrayal, shipped Helen off to the local orphanage. She lived there from age twelve to sixteen, during which time she got rudimentary schooling and an occasional ice cream cone; after those four years, she was required to leave. Her father, still unable or unwilling to take her back, pawned her off to Greensboro to live with his younger brother. She became close to his wife, who gave her love and care she'd not received in years. After several years she decided to get married; when the marriage failed, she moved into a small, run-down trailer. Like Pop, she works at Lorillard; that's where she and Pop met.

When Pop brings Helen to our apartment for the first time, the only thing she has to her name is a 1970 Ford Cortina and the little money in her pocket that came from her most recent paycheck. However, she smiles at me and my brothers, greets us shyly but enthusiastically in an almost indecipherable southern drawl, and then hands us each a dollar bill! Maybe it's a bribe, but I see it as a sign that she wants to make it work with us. And in fact, she does.

She and Pop marry. It's 1972. Helen becomes our new stepmother, moves into our small apartment with thick shag carpet on Cone Boulevard, and enters our lives with no experience or idea of how to raise kids. Some adjustments have to be made, and she's making most of them. I wonder sometimes what she thinks about all of it: three irascible boys and a moody, volatile husband. But she's here, trying to make it all work. And she's a strong woman. With what she's lived through, she's a damn strong woman.

The two of them come in from work one afternoon and Pop whips up a quick dinner of salmon cakes, cream corn from the can, and pinto beans. I'm not feeling well today and Pop isn't in a good mood, railing about some infraction, real or perceived, that happened at work. All five of us are at the table eating. I finish early, walk into the kitchen, and begin the process of scraping my half-eaten dinner into the wastebasket. As I do, I lose my grip on the plate and drop it. It breaks and suddenly spilled food is all over the kitchen floor and a bit of the adjacent carpet.

I'm in real trouble.

Pop springs up from his chair.

"Pop, I'm sorry. It was an accident. I'm cleaning it up. See?" I say quickly as I take the lid off the trash can and kneel to pick up the pieces of the broken plate.

"Dammit, that's not going to come out of that carpet. We got a deposit on this place! You're a damn messer!" He moves quickly toward me. "Clean it up, NOW!"

I shrink away from his quick advance to no avail. With momentum, he slaps me, his open palm connecting firmly with my left cheek. I tumble back against the kitchen cabinet, and though I'm dazed, I can see him coming forward. I've got to move. I've got to quell his anger, show him I'm going to fix this.

I stumble to my knees and crawl past him to get more of the bean/corn mix off the floor. I'm on my knees, cleaning, and he's standing menacingly above me, hand raised, when I feel someone brush by my shoulder and come to a sudden stop.

"Bill, don't hit him again, he didn't mean to do it. It was an accident." Helen steps in, plants her feet, and gets between the two of us.

I rise and stand back quickly—and look on in shock.

"You get out of the way, now," Pop warns. "This is between me and him. Look at that damn mess on the floor!" He lunges for me again.

Helen presses her hands patiently but firmly against my father's chest. "We'll clean it up; it's not the end of the world," she says, calmly but defiantly.

"If you don't get out of my way, I'm gonna have to move ya," he says, and he has that wild-eyed look in his eye that tells me he'll do it in a hurry.

"I'm not moving. I know he made a mess, but you goin' crazy is not going to get it off the floor. Let the boy clean it up." Her feet are still planted on the yellowing linoleum tile.

Pop draws back, and I can see the back of his hand and the small golden ring on his finger.

She doesn't flinch—not a bit. "You go ahead and hit me. I've been hit before. But you better hit me good, 'cause I'm still gonna be standin' here when you're done. And I can hit back too."

"Sweetie, you get out my way now—you ain't gonna hit nobody," Pop says, but as he says it, he starts to laugh.

Is he amused at her audacity, or is he a bully trying to downplay someone finally standing up to him?

"I mean it," she says, her hands now on his upper arms. "Just stop and let him clean it up. He can't do it with you standing over him and yelling like that. Just back up, and let him do it."

I don't think of it now, but in the future I'll feel sure that Helen had to fight throughout her life, whether it was with an abusive stepmother, a drunken husband, or all the potential confrontations a teenage girl might have faced running loose in an orphanage. And I'll also know this: She has no intention of moving. He will have to fight her to get to me. And while the outcome is certain if he decides to take that tack, there is more to it than a beatdown and verbal lambasting of me at stake. While I have seen him hit Mama in the past, he and Helen are newly married. How is it going to work out if within weeks of her moving in he's slapping her around and then makes her look on while he finishes beating the shit out of me? I shudder to think of what that life might be like.

"All right, boy, you heard her. Clean it up. NOW!" He steps away from her and walks back to the bathroom down the hall. I grab some paper towels, get down on my knees, and begin to more aggressively clean and pick up the spillage.

"David, hurry and get that up," Helen says. "We'll get out the carpet cleaner and scrub it when you finish." She goes over and returns to her seat at the table.

There are still tears in my eyes as I look down at the floor and continue to clean. Between my sniffles, I do not look up at her. I don't know why. "Thank you," I mumble between my tears. It seems like so much more needs to be said, but for me, for what she just did, there are no words.

She, Billy, and Danny go back to their meals. I clean quickly, and then Helen helps me clean the carpet, just as she promised.

Later that night, I sit in bed listening to an Atlanta Braves baseball game on the blue transistor radio that sits on my three-legged pressed-wood nightstand and marvel at how bravely Helen stood her ground in my defense. She's been nothing but strong, kind, and supportive since she entered my life. I know Mama has her issues, but she never stood up for us like that—and I hardly even see her these days. Still, she's my mother and Helen's not—or is she?

When the traditional family home is broken, who is our family and where is home?

When we're a child in a broken home we tend to be stubbornly loyal to blood over behavior. We long for our mothers and fathers to be who we want them to be without being fully cognizant or accepting of who they are. Even though they let us down, treat us badly, and even leave us behind, we stubbornly seek their love and approval, because it provides us with a sense of self-worth. We need our parents to love us when we're young, to reassure us that we're okay—because if they don't, then something must be wrong with *us*. This is the false reality that a needy, naive child accepts as painful truth.

When we reach adulthood, we become more pragmatic and tilt toward behavior over blood. Who loved us, fed us, and nurtured us when we were young? Who taught us right from wrong? Whose actions demonstrated care as opposed to indifference? As better-informed grown men and women, our loyalties swing toward our figurative parents, be it a grandparent, a stepmother or -father, an adoptive parent, or another adult figure, as opposed to an absent or indifferent blood parent—deeds not labels hold our sway. We rightfully love those who have demonstrated their love for us.

But no matter how old we are or how much we love those who loved us, we never completely lose the longing for the unconditional love of a blood parent—even if, over time, some of us surrender the need. It's in our DNA as descendants of generations past who were properly cared for and protected by loving mothers and fathers. It is the reason why a well-loved adopted child seeks to know the whereabouts of the parents who bore them. It's why a battered or neglected child stubbornly clings to the abusive parent for a lifetime or why the successful and grateful adult buys their caregiver grandparent the new home or car—but quietly hides the bitterness in their soul for a blood parent that failed them when they were young. There is a real loss to the child of a failed parent—and there is pain. But that pain recedes over time, then eventually numbs with age and life experience. Why? Because time, love, and accomplishment teach us one critical fact: there was something wrong with *them* in that earlier time—not us.

I hear the crowd roar over the radio as Hank Aaron comes to bat, then Pop opens the door and walks over beside my bed.

"Boy, don't think I can't whup your ass just because she's here. You better behave yourself, or I'll show you I can in a hurry."

I want to say I didn't misbehave before, I just accidentally dropped my plate, but instead I sit there, silent.

Hard-eyed, he takes note of me sprawled out on the bed, and says, "Let me make one thing clear to you, and I'm gonna tell your brothers the same. She comes first in this house—ahead of you, and ahead of them. She's my wife, I married her, and that's it. If it comes down to you and her, it's gonna be her, period. Ya heah me?"

My father has chosen his family.

"Yes, I hear you."

He steps away from the bed, walks out of the room, and closes the door behind him.

I quickly lose track of the baseball game. I don't like what he just said. I can't say I'm surprised, but, although I don't want to be, I am a little hurt. To me, this was just another indirect way for Pop to tell me I'm not worth a shit for nothing.

I turn off the radio and fall asleep.

Fourteen
The First Speech

WE MOVE FARTHER WEST, into a small brick ranch home near Lawndale Drive. It's positioned close to busy Cone Boulevard and also sits next to a sizable creek that runs behind and to the right of the property. When there's a lengthy thunderstorm, I silently stare out my bedroom window as the waters rise and rush through the gouged-out gully like the rolling Mississippi. But it's nice to have more space and our own backyard again.

Danny is in eleventh grade, a year from finishing high school. He's seventeen and a brutally abusive home life is about to catch up with him. He has a new champion in Helen, who has seemed to pick him out as the runt in our damaged litter. She tries to save him from Pop, and himself, with limited results. His struggles at school continue.

In history class, he's required to write a paper and present it, a task most of his peers also dread but somehow survive. He's shy, timid, completely lacking in self-esteem, verbally and physically beaten down—a frightened boy, really. Our life at home has put him on his knees; he has no faith, no belief, no control, no love, only fear, a pervasive fear that lingers and influences his every action and reaction. Yet class protocol requires him to make the attempt, to stand up.

His teacher is sure he can do it, but she's very wrong.

He stands, walks to the front of the classroom, and freezes. He stutters, shakes, starts, stops, and starts again. He loses his place, he stares fitfully at his classmates, and then he hears the creak of an uncomfortable shifting of seats—and then, worse still, he hears the snickers, sees the bemused grins of the obnoxious few.

They're laughing at him! Broken and defeated, eyes watering, he tries one last time, but nothing comes—nothing at all. Finally, he gives up. He makes the long trek back to his seat and sits quietly. He feels the persistent heat of curious eyes watching him, seeing if he'll break further, as he wallows in his shame.

After a few minutes pass, he begins to emerge from the dubious thoughts roiling in his head. He tentatively lifts his eyes, surveys his surroundings, and notes the stealthy glances still coming his way, followed by a quick and uncomfortable turning away. Mercifully, other students are asked to come up, and the sting of his moment of humiliation recedes.

But suddenly, the bell rings, and as soon as class ends the heckling starts full-on:

"Pra, Pra, Pru, Pru, Pruitt, gra, gra, great spa, spa speech . . ." one boy mimics, to the howling amusement of his surrounding henchmen.

Humiliated, Danny gathers his books, exits the classroom, and heads to the isolation of the school parking lot. It's the middle of the school day. He turns the key and fires up the White '69 Chevy Impala he's inherited from Billy. He drives and talks to himself, and he cries. He does not return for his remaining classes that day.

Nor will he return the next day, or the day after that.

Days and weeks pass. Danny leaves the house each morning and vacantly drives the streets, killing the seconds, minutes, and hours, scared for a different reason now; he will be caught sooner or later. But, somehow, he feels free. He considers the consequences, but in the end, he simply cannot will himself to walk back into the hallways of Walter Hines Page High School. The fear now rules him.

He tells no one about this, and we know nothing about it for several weeks. But one day a letter from the school counselor arrives in the mail. The message delivered is that Danny Pruitt has not been to class for weeks and is in danger of dropping out. But can a form letter to a dysfunctional family save a beaten child from a diminished future?

Pop angrily confronts my brother.

"What the hell are you doing? Why aren't you going to school?"

No acceptable response, other than that he has a job now (bagging groceries), high school is not for him, and he will do just fine without it.

"Well, where in the hell have you been going and what have you been doing all this time?" Pop demands.

"Driving around, waiting for my shift to start at Food Town."

"Why didn't you tell me up front?

"I knew you wouldn't like it, but I'm not going back."

He is of sufficient age; there is no forcing him to go back. The argument stops, and there is resignation. Danny has decided his path, and after some consternation, Pop accepts it. He could kick him to the streets but doesn't. But their relationship has now changed. It's now a tenancy game. The new ground rules are: if you're not going to school and want to stay in the house, you have to work and pay a nominal rent. And, of course, the alternative is not good. You'll be kicked to the streets if you fail.

Danny understands and accepts the terms. What choice does he have?

Pop issues his final harsh words on the subject with a narrowed gaze and dismissive candor:

"I'll be so glad when you leave here."

Over the next year or so, jobs come and go. There are good ones and bad ones, layoffs and terminations. A great job is lost when an industrial equipment business downsizes. An okay job is lost when Danny simply quits, saying he can do better. When he's in between work and lying around the house, Pop monitors his lack of progress angrily, impatiently.

"A man is supposed to work for a living," he says.

"Boy, you ain't gonna lay up on me in here doing nothing," he growls.

The tension in the house is palpable; our floors of tiled linoleum and tufted carpet feel more like thin ice and fragile eggshell. Pop gives Danny extra chores to further earn his keep. He's not working a job, so the chores must be done right and on time. In my father's mind, there is no margin for error.

But eventually, an error is made.

One night, while in bed, I hear Pop storm in the house after working a second shift at Lorillard. It's after 11:00 p.m. My bedroom door at the end of the hallway is open. I hear the back door slam as he comes in, yelling at Helen that the trash is still in the back, behind the garage.

Danny, who forgot to take the trash to the road, is asleep, and his bedroom door, up the hall from mine, is closed. I hear footsteps moving quickly, almost stomping down the hallway, then, *WHAM!!* the doorknob to Danny's bedroom slams against the wall of my bedroom, causing my bed to shake and startling me to a full state of alertness. I pray for Danny even as I feel relief at not being the target myself.

"Get up! Get up NOW!!" Pop roars in full-throated rage.

"What? What?" Danny asks groggily.

He looks up too late as Pop grabs him by the ankle and, holding him in a vise-like grip, yanks him out of the bed. His hip hits the floor with a resounding thud and he bounces briefly before landing on his backside.

Pop proceeds to drag him by his ankle out of the bedroom, around the corner, and up the hall. "I told you to take that damn trash to the road!" he screams.

I get up and look up the hallway. I catch sight of Pop—a psychotic, deranged look on his face—yanking Danny across the carpet in fitful pulls and lunges, lividly dragging his body forward, toward the back door and the trash can that sits, damningly, behind the garage outside.

My brother's eyes look as big as a new harvest moon. He was dead asleep when Pop violently awakened him and tossed him on the floor, and now he's sliding down the hall on his back like Quint to the shark, turning on his side, twisting his body, his palms clutching at the carpet, vainly trying to escape the shackle grip on his ankle. For a moment, our eyes meet. And his are filled with abject terror.

"I'm sorry, Pop!" he cries. "I didn't mean to forget it. I'll get it right now!"

"That damn can is still sitting behind the garage! You go out runnin' up damn bills all over town and now you're still here living off me! I give you one simple job to do, and you can't even do that!"

"Pop, let me go! I'll get it! Please!"

There's a dog gate that is now open that blocks the entry to the den. It's there to keep our new dog, Pepe, blocked in. With his left hand, Pop yanks the gate up and tosses it aside, all the while gripping that ankle with his right.

"You boys ain't worth a shit walkin' or ridin', but you're gonna take that trash to the road!" he bellows as he drags Danny along.

"Please, Pop," Danny begs.

They arrive at the end of the hall.

"Get up! Get up off that floor! Get up from there, NOW!" Pop releases his grip on the ankle.

Danny tries to get to his feet as Pop, reaching down, swings wildly and violently at his head. Danny lifts his arms in defense, elbows bent and forearms up, protecting his head, trying to block the blows. He staggers to his feet.

"Get out there and get that trash to the road, and I mean NOW!" Pop screams.

Danny runs out the back door. I look on with my mouth hanging open.

"What are you looking at? Get ya ass back in that bed," he orders. I comply, shaking my head in disgust, but doing so only after I turn the corner.

Danny comes back into the house and Pop directs him to get back in bed.

"Don't you let me find that trash can behind the garage again on trash day—you heah me?"

Danny says "yes sir," goes to his bedroom, and closes the door behind him. The house grows dark and silent. After a few minutes, I walk out and peek into his room. I ask if he is okay.

As concerned brothers, we always lay low during the apex of the storm but caringly survey the damage once it passes. It's been that way ever since I can remember, starting in that spring green crib so many years before.

Danny says yes but to leave him alone. I understand.

* *

Danny lies in bed that night carrying a searing image in his mind that cuts through his body like a freshly opened machete wound. And then the tremors come—and they won't stop. He physically shakes until dawn, unable to calm his nerves or go back to sleep.

His critical mission now is to find a job—and, thank God, he finally does at a local department store. But within months they catch him shoplifting (he stole a gift for Helen). He's arrested and briefly thrown in jail, and though my father bails him out, a few weeks later Pop finally—as promised—kicks him out of the house.

And winter is coming.

Fifteen
Looking for Angels

BILLY IS QUIET AND INTROSPECTIVE. He tends to stay in his bedroom and read—either the Bible or comic books—and when Pop goes off, placidly ignores it. He is by no means spared, but Pop whips Billy less because he lies low and doesn't argue. He walks away. He never gets emotional. He comforts us at times, tries to reason with Pop, and will even call out Pop like he did when he got physical back in the day with Mama. But he remains—visibly, at least, and as much as it is possible with Pop's demanding presence—detached.

Billy's situation is difficult. He is the big brother, and Danny and I look to him as a possible safe port in the Category Five storm of our household. In response, he gives us some support, but only some. His measured distance reminds me of Mama.

My oldest brother walks through pain like the Marvel superheroes in his beloved comics. He tried to pick up an injured squirrel in the backyard of our old house on Oak Grove several years ago and got his right hand bitten and scratched up pretty severely. I watched Pop clean it and then apply rubbing alcohol to sterilize the numerous wounds. Billy didn't move one muscle or say a single word. Pop said he had something in him, something that made him strong, resilient.

"You can take the pain," my father said.

Billy is a seeker of answers to larger, seemingly impossible questions. He turns first to the Bible. He reads the Bible cover to cover several times before he reaches the tenth grade. I see him, seemingly every night, at the kitchen table with his head buried in it while I play with my GI Joe or my Hot Wheels cars. That Bible, in some ways, serves as his shield. Even Pop's volatile temper can be held at bay by the sight of one of his children head down, reading the Good Book. But Billy does not read it to placate Pop, he reads it in an attempt to understand the whys of his life: Why is Mama mad and indifferent? Why is Pop so violent and hateful? Why are we living in constant fear? But he cannot find the answers in the Bible, so he looks for other sources of comfort and understanding.

In eleventh grade Billy has a Bible literature teacher, Mrs. Newman, who, in her younger years, was the secretary to a well-known, self-proclaimed clairvoyant named Edgar Cayce. He was a unique individual. A biographer once nicknamed him "The Sleeping Prophet," as he explored broader issues of healing, reincarnation, wars, the mystery of Atlantis, and also the projection of future events, all while claiming to be in a trance.

He is generally believed to be the true founder and source of the New Age movement, a group of religious/spiritual beliefs and practices that, among many of its teachings, takes on a holistic form of divinity that imbues the universe, including human beings themselves. The movement also informs a belief in the spiritual authority of the self and the existence of semi-divine, non-human entities, such as angels and other masters, that humans can contact through some form of channeling.

Unwittingly, Mrs. Newman spurs Billy's interest in Cayce and the New Age movement, to the detriment of anything else of substance in his life. Once he learns about them, my brother starts looking for an angel to save him from the shit going down at our house.

He stops doing homework or paying attention to his studies. Instead, he locks himself up in his bedroom and reads anything and everything he can get his hands on about Cayce and the New Age. He does his shift at a local grocer and physically shows up at high school, but mostly he reads Edgar Cayce books with a fervor that far exceeds his interest in his Bible studies of previous years. Still, somehow, he manages to graduate. While Danny drops out of high school, Billy finishes—but just barely.

Billy maintains limited hours at work and continues to lock himself up with his books in his bedroom. Pop's patience is wearing thin.

Wisely, Billy sees that and acts. He walks into the house one evening and announces a momentous decision: he has decided to join the Air Force.

Pop, given his previous military experience, is thrilled and praises him for weeks. However, as the time for deployment at Lackland AFB in San Antonio, Texas, hastens, Billy gets cold feet. He thinks seriously about trying to back out. But the die is cast, and he is ultimately off to Texas—supposedly with an exciting new future in front of him, yet I am struck by the look of trepidation and anxiety on his face as we see him off at the Greensboro airport. "Boy, you know if your old Daddy can handle it, you can too," I hear Pop tell him.

But I'm scared for my brother.

Billy completes the six weeks of basic training in San Antonio, and after a week's furlough at home moves on to Sheppard Air Force Base in Wichita Falls, Texas. There he is to receive initial training as a medic. He completes it, and within six months is stationed at Travis

Air Force base in Fairfield, California, about fifty miles northeast of San Francisco.

At Travis, Billy continues his education, but unfortunately, not on the assigned military curriculum, as his interest in Cayce and the New Age dogma continues in full. He has no interest in his medical studies and his grades reflect that. He then meets a fellow soldier named Mike. Mike, like my brother, loves marijuana, and Billy's path to success is further compromised. When they're off duty, they take to the open roads, play Pink Floyd, and get stoned.

Billy's studies continue to suffer, and soon his military career is over.

Mike returns to his parents' place in Washington but Billy, for obvious reasons, isn't sure he wants to come home to Pop. His search to understand his life so far evolves into a search to find a different way to live. While in the San Francisco area, he hears about an intentional community, or commune, formed in 1971 in Summertown, Tennessee. It was founded by Stephen Gaskin, a member of the counterculture of the late 1960s and a creative writing teacher at local San Francisco State University. It's called "The Farm." Billy likes what he hears so he thumbs his way across the country looking for a safe place to live and a new start in life.

The Farm lets Billy in. Over a thousand people reside there and live by Gaskin's edicts—among them, no smoking tobacco, no alcohol, and no sex without commitment. Sunday morning lectures, group marriages (officiated by Gaskin) and various teachings around meditational awareness are part of the required strictures, but the regimented lifestyle doesn't resonate with Billy.

Somehow, he doesn't fit there either.

After a few weeks, he moves on and finds himself, thumb up,

on Tennessee I-840 East, looking to navigate the remaining 500 miles back to Greensboro. He catches a ride with a threatening man who shows him a loaded Colt 45 revolver and a large bag of dope in his glove compartment. Discreetly nervous, Billy nods in passive acknowledgment—but keeps riding.

In all, it takes him thirty-five hours to make it home safely, right back to where he started—under Pop's thumb. In silence, he returns to his old bedroom, books in hand. He keeps the room clean, makes himself scarce, but to Pop he's an expense—he eats food, runs water, and turns on the lights. And his employment efforts remain uneven.

A few weeks later, I note the strained, impatient look on Pop's face as we sit at the dinner table on a Sunday afternoon. He looks like a drill sergeant whose direct orders have been violated by a green recruit. Furrowed brow extended, he glares at my submissive brother and then says coldly, "Boy, you better get up off your dead-ass and find some work. I work for a livin'—and you ain't no better'n me!"

"I know, Pop," Billy mumbles back.

And I know too. It's not good enough. Danny's already gone— my father expects his children to work and take care of themselves. His children do not appear to be entirely capable on this front.

I know where this is going.

And once again, I'm afraid for my brother.

Sixteen
The Break

BAD THINGS ARE NORMALIZED in our home, driven by the unrelenting hand of my father's rule. When it happens, I want to scream out that we're damaged, abnormal, that it's not supposed to be this way. Instead, I brood in silence. I slow-boil in isolated anger. Over time and incidents, subtly, almost imperceptibly, I feel my spirit beginning to break. Resentment and apathy discreetly replace hope and ambition. I don't even understand that it's happening. I just feel like I don't belong in my own family. Somehow, I don't fit.

Yet I fit in with my classmates at school, at least early on. I go to Bessemer Elementary, about a mile down the road from our house on Huffine Mill Road. I love my fourth-grade teacher, Mrs. Ross. She is slightly overweight, with ivory white teeth and clear chocolate skin. She is also diligent but patient and holds each of us accountable to learn. And it comes so easy for me. I make straight As under her persistent tutelage. On the last day of school, she tells me she expects I will do great things one day. But her faith is not enough. Because I'm quickly losing faith in myself.

The early break inside me, driven by tumultuous times at home, weakens my resolve to do well. I'm an immature child at an unrevealed but far-reaching crossroads. Small hits from my fellow students, my teachers, start to come. I can't absorb them, put them down, or set them aside. Naive eyes are opened to larger truths about race, class, and poverty, and my pitiable standing in each order now becomes clear to me.

It's seven fifteen in the morning when the school bus arrives to take me to my new school, Claxton Elementary, on my first day of fifth grade. I climb the three steps up, turn left, and move tentatively down the aisle past students who, like me, have a long ride ahead of them. There are roughly fifty of us onboard and I'm pretty much the only white kid amongst my fellow Black passengers. I search for an empty seat and anonymity. Even though I'm a different color, I have much in common with this group of eastern Greensboro kids riding on the rickety bus.

We all wear the same cheap clothes and the same thin coats that cause us to shiver quietly on the bus rides to school in the dead of winter. We also share a common mission: to bring poverty and diversity to the well-off, well-washed faces that dominate the classrooms at Claxton. Over the summer, I heard Pop talk about "desegregation busing." I guess that's what I'm doing on this long ride across town each morning: I'm being desegregated and bused to my new school.

I exit the bus and enter my classroom well before the bell and sit quietly amidst the busy chatter around me. Head low, my eyes wander around the room and I see feet, wearing the latest Converse sneakers, twitching busily under every desk. But that's not what I wear. One of the kids notices and chides me, informing me that I'm wearing "joe laps." Some of them laugh when, while playing kickball, the sole of my cheap sneaker shoots through the blown-out toe when my foot makes contact with the ball. Both ball and sole fly. The laughter stings me, more than it should. It compounds this break inside me. I didn't know anything about "joe laps" at Bessemer.

My fifth-grade teacher is not like Mrs. Ross. She is young, blond-haired, blue-eyed, and impatient. She has a temper and can be short, almost curt. At times, I see a look of disdain from her that is not unfamiliar. I've seen that "ain't worth a shit" look from Pop. One day I decide I don't like her and I think she knows it, because she snaps at me on occasion.

Suddenly, for me, it's over. I'm done with her and this new school, this new classroom. For the first time, homework goes undone and my grades suffer. My academic slide begins and it continues, full force, right into junior high school.

One morning, another negative factor comes into play.

I get up, go to brush my teeth, look in the mirror, and there is a swollen growth on the right side of my forehead. I do not normally stare at myself that closely, but this lump is obvious—angry and unavoidable. I'm concerned, but not yet cognizant enough to know that I should be self-conscious and embarrassed as well.

When I walk into the kitchen, my concerns are not allayed but magnified. Pop is putting oatmeal on the table. He takes one look and says, "Boy, what the hell is that wap on your forehead?"

"Dang, David, did you hit your head?" Danny chimes in.

And with that, I become self-conscious.

When I get to school, it doesn't get any easier.

"Damn Pruitt, what's wrong with your forehead?"

Girls walk by and seem to take loathsome note of the puffed-up knot. Then there are the conversations with classmates where words are coming out of my mouth but their eyes are focused on my head.

I try to buy time with the first cyst, saying it is a spider bite. But they keep coming back and will not easily go away. The spider bite excuse isn't going to hold.

I don't have pimples on my face, I have cysts. They fill with blood and pus and stick around for weeks at a time. I am disfigured, and while my size keeps me from getting totally bullied, the comments are there and they are continuous. When my face is clear, I'm fine, but when the cysts come—and they often do—it is awful and my embarrassment is complete.

The sideways looks and snide remarks continue throughout the school year. I hate life, both at home and at school, and now there is no place where I feel remotely content. Normality, not popularity, becomes my goal. Girls are completely out of the question, academics are an ignored nuisance, and while Helen makes the home better, Pop remains who he is, so home remains what it is: a place to sleep and eat—and survive.

Pop takes me to the dermatologist, who gives me sun lamp treatments and Clearasil, neither of which help. I have a particularly big cyst on my left cheek around this time and Pop heats a needle with a Bic lighter and sticks it directly in the cyst, which does nothing at all besides leave a permanent hole in my cheek. Cortisone shots and Accutane treatments do not yet exist, so there is no relief, and the stares and comments continue.

My school struggles continue to grow as my self-esteem plummets even further.

I start class each day in Mrs. Boyd's homeroom. She's a nice woman, friendly and petite, and I like her. I sit in the far-left row of desks, four back from the door leading to the hallway outside. One day, a student named Wayne, after looking me over, plops down in the seat in front of me, turns, and says, "Good morning, Pimp!"

I ignore him.

He keeps on: "What's your first class, Pimp?"

I continue to ignore him but it continues—day after day and, soon enough, week after week.

"Hey Pimp, why can't you pop that thing?"

"Is that a balloon on your face, Pimp?"

For weeks I've tried to laugh it off or ignore Wayne. But this Monday morning, after a tough weekend at home with Pop and a newly landed cyst on my left cheek, Wayne walks in and goes after me.

"Damn, Pimp, you grew another cheek, didn't you?"

"When's the last time you had some pussy, boy?"

"When that thing pops, it must cover the mirror right?"

That does it. For the first time in my life, I completely lose it. My father beats the shit out of me, my mother has now vanished, I feel like a freak with this shit on my face, and this asshole is on me every day. I have to have some say in how my life is going to go, some control over how I'm treated. I am viscerally, unequivocally enraged, and I feel a rush of vengeance rise in my soul that is not unfamiliar but has, out of necessity, remained buried, held back, until now.

I stand, my seat flies backward, and with both hands I grab the right side of my desk and toss it aside. As it bounces off the wall to my left, I reach over, grab Wayne by the back of his shirt, and yank him up out of his seat—and as he turns to face me, I give him a shove.

He stumbles backward and nearly goes down as the desks behind him slide aside and the nearby kids scatter, moving safely to the front of the classroom. I charge forward and grab him by the throat with my left hand. He reaches for me, but it's too late: I have a vise grip on him. I easily lift him, turn left, and plant him hard against the wall. His body smacks against the sheetrock.

For once in my life, I'm going to do the hitting. Pop's beatings destroy me, but I've never fought back, not until this moment right now. I cannot help how I look. I cannot help where I come from. I cannot help that my mother is crazy and my father beats the shit out of me. But I can end this. All I know is when I get done, he's never going to call me Pimp again, consequences be damned.

I cock back my right fist, and just then Mrs. Boyd comes rushing up behind me, puts her hand on my arm, and screams, "David, stop! Don't hit him! You'll kill him!"

I look at her, wild-eyed, teeth clenched, in search of her empathy. I feel other eyes on me. I see the mouths hanging open. But I don't give a damn.

"He's been talking shit, making fun of me since the first day in class. I'm gonna shut his damn mouth right NOW!"

He squirms, trying to get his back off the wall. I tighten my grip around his neck, look dead-eyed in his face, and say, "Don't you fuckin' move!"

Red-faced and bug-eyed, he doesn't.

"David, I know," Mrs. Boyd says. "It's not your fault. But you'll get in trouble if you hit him. Don't do it. It's not worth it. I won't turn you in, but you have to let him go now. Please!"

I'm bigger, stronger, and angrier than Wayne, and we both know it. There is no fight in him to be had. He just wants me to put him down. The only question is, will he keep his mouth shut and leave me alone?

As I look at his frightened, submissive face, I'm sure he will not bother me anymore. I step back and release him but continue to eye him firmly, communicating the unspoken boundaries that are not to be crossed.

Mrs. Boyd tells Wayne to step outside the door and wait for her to call him back in. Homeroom is minutes from being over, so she sends the other students out to begin working their way toward their first-period classes. They gossip excitedly about what they've just witnessed.

"What happened, David?" Mrs. Boyd queries, but I think she already knows.

I can't explain it, but I'm overcome with emotion. I begin to tear up. Who I became in that angered instant is not who I am, and her kindness towards me makes me want to reach out and share my shame, pain, and frustration. I am worth a shit for something. I am not a freak. I believe I can do something important with my life. I have value and want to be loved unconditionally, by someone who has a real interest in me, who believes in me, who can guide me through the abuse and the remaining shittiness of my life. I need to talk to someone who cares about me, who has faith in what I can be.

Mrs. Boyd is a good human being, but my troubles are not her problem. It will not be her.

"He was picking on me. I couldn't take it anymore."

I don't have to tell her what it's about. The cyst on my face is there to be seen. It stands out, red and angry. The tears are pulled back.

"David, I understand," she replies.

And I believe she does. She calls Wayne back into the classroom.

"Damn, Pruitt," he says, "I was just kidding with you. You didn't have to go ape shit on me."

"Wayne, in the future you will leave David alone. He's not bothering you, and you will not bother him. Is that clear?" Mrs. Boyd interjects.

"Yeah."

"If you don't leave him alone, you're on your own, as far as I'm concerned. Is that also clear?"

"Yeah, I'm sorry," he says, looking at me.

"Can I leave now?" I say, in no mood for apologies.

"Yes. And David?"

"What?"

"Watch your temper, please."

"Yes, ma'am." I turn and walk away.

Later that night in bed, I think of the encounter at school and the happy fact that Wayne won't bother me anymore. I had my moment, backing the bully down, and maybe my life will get a little better because of it—like Opie's did after he got his milk money back.

But then I reach up with my right index finger and feel the tenderness of the cyst on my left cheek, and I realize that my small victory doesn't change the state of my life. I turn over on my left side and bury my face in the pillow, but I'm not trying to sleep. I'm trying to put pressure on the cyst, to flatten my face out. I close my eyes and squeeze them tight. I feel the moisture beneath my lids and a thin stream of salty tears falls. I angrily wipe it away with my left wrist, and the bitter prayer spills out.

Dear God,

I don't understand why my life has turned out like this. Why does Pop treat us the way he does, beating on us and yelling all the time? Why is Mama crazy? She just left us and didn't give a damn! And after that . . . after all that . . . I have to put up with this shit on my face? Is that it? I'm sorry, Lord. I didn't mean to cuss. That's not right. But I don't understand it. I'm not asking to be handsome and I know you can't change anything here at home. But I just want to be normal, God. Please, just let me be normal. I just wanna be normal . . .

Anguished, I say no amen on this night—but I do finally fall asleep.

Despite my blanket apathy and carefully hidden resentment, at times there are flickering thoughts of a better outcome, a stirring of what I can be, a hunger to achieve, a drive to dig out, a desire to prove my worth. But I don't move on it. I can't. I'm fully broken now. The destruction of any future ambitions, any positive expectations for myself, has been comprehensive and complete. So, I continue to flounder academically as I enter high school. And now additional lessons about class and wealth are revealed.

The implacable caste system, the rigid rungs dictating allowable social interaction between me and my fellow students, becomes brutally clear to me in high school. The cliques are omnipresent and restrictive. There are the jocks, the rich kids, the academics, the preppies, the drug-gies, the middle-of-the-roadies, the disadvantaged poor, the bad-asses, and the unique, stand-alone, quirky kids—the one-offers.

I'm borderline jock, definitely not rich, at first glance not very smart, certainly not handsome, a dabbling pot smoker, and—early on, at least—unemployable. All of that, and the occasional severity of my acne, places me only temporarily in the one-offers. But I don't truly feel like I fit into any specific group. I acknowledge that my attitude and behavior play a role in my meager social standing. Yet it's all I have to offer right now.

A cliquey high school is not a novelty, and many have endured or enjoyed that environment, depending on relative placement. But when you grow up on the wrong side of the tracks, a part of you never leaves, no matter how high you rise or how far away you go. You forever see yourself as being from there and imagine that others see you that way too. And sadly, sometimes they do.

To me, the cliques are just another commentary on the state of my worthiness—not good enough. But at least Pop gives me his damning assessment straight up. The unspoken implication of the social barriers at school breeds in me further resentment and apathy. I don't speak of it or show it to my few friends, but inside I bristle at the additional layer of rejection. And my response to it is not good.

Alcohol, cars, and music become my preferred pastime. I'm convinced it's too damn late to move off this broken path I'm on, so I embrace it. My few friends get their driver's licenses before me, so to get out of our houses they pick me up and we ride. We just ride. We grab a twelve-pack, ride to the outskirts of town, play music, pop a top, drink up, and talk about our lives, girls (in my case the lack thereof), sports, family, and, sometimes, our dreams for the future. I listen a lot. I open up a bit, but I don't talk in-depth about the difficult happenings at home. The alcohol and occasional marijuana make it go away, at least temporarily. When I'm in the car with my friends and we drive out—toward the airport, away from the city, away from the cops—pull over, and watch the planes come in or go out, or when we drive even farther out onto the rolling dirt-brown hills of nearby Summerfield and ride those winding, twisting, turning country roads, feeling the freedom and listening to the music, I'm lifted from a comatose stupor.

The alcohol lets me escape, and it's a feeling I crave. I feel happy and invincible when I drink. I feel the bonds of friendship. I forget my problems, my inadequacies. There are no unattended proms in my future and no groups that cast me aside in my past. There is only the road and this beer in my hand.

Most of my friends are in the same boat. For us, there is alcohol, the occasional joint, and escape. There is also reckless driving, near accidents, and barely avoided arrests. We run off roads, hide beers under car seats, and stagger into late-night, poorly lit back doors. At times I just get flat-out drunk and stagger to my bed quietly to sleep it off. Then I get up the next day, skip class, and do it again. But while I refuse to do any real work academically, I stay in class enough to stay on track to graduate. It feels like Pop is just waiting for me to drop out. But, dammit, I'm staying in, if only to prove him wrong.

In quieter, more sober moments, I also take note of Billy and Danny's struggles. The various trials of my siblings are painful to witness, and they stir within me thoughts, for the very first time, about my uncertain future. My brothers are walking a troubled path and moving in a state of desperation. Options are taken, but only in a world of limited alternatives, and always there is an underlying theme of escape: *get out of the house, do anything, but do it quick and get out of that damn house, NOW!* I understand that need. And share it. The brutality we've seen, the judgment we've endured, the harsh words that have been spoken, and the pain we now feel tell us all to run—run away, run now, run forever, and don't look back. Yet the slowly festering issue is that, despite their best efforts, they keep landing back in the house, under Pop's unrelenting thumb. Either their choices are bad, cruel fickle fate intervenes, or the damn execution is just poor. But, somehow, they keep coming back to the place they desperately want to leave, and worst of all, the door to get in is starting to close.

I feel that door closing on me, too.

Seventeen
The Missing Twenty

IN DESPERATION, AROUND FIVE in the afternoon, he busts a pane of glass out of the window next to the back door, reaches in, unlocks the doorknob, and lets himself in. Pepe barks angrily, cautiously sniffs his leg, then wags his tail happily in recognition.

Danny has just broken into our house.

He carefully cleans the glass and readjusts the blinds, then exits the kitchen and closes the dog gate behind him. He lumbers down the long hallway, climbs into my bed, and blacks out from total exhaustion.

At seven o'clock the unwanted alarm rings loudly. He groggily shuts it off, re-smooths the blanket, fluffs the pillow, and heads back up the hall to our unused formal living room at the front of the house. He slides the large couch away from the front wall, backpack in hand, crawls in behind it, and pulls it as close to its original position as his lean body will allow.

I come in a few minutes later from football practice, make myself something to eat, and have no idea he's hiding there, sandwiched in tight like a squashed sardine in a tiny tin can.

He silently hides behind the couch for three days and nights, surreptitiously listening to the sound of us living our lives, only sneaking from the empty house in the afternoon to scavenge for food. But it can't last.

On the fourth day, Pepe nearly sniffs him out again—right before Pop and Helen head to work in the early afternoon. It's too close for comfort. If Pop finds him, it won't be good. So he slips from the house later that evening.

He sleeps outside that first night and survives for a few months afterward on the street until more frigid conditions force his hand once again.

On a snowy Saturday morning, Pop steps out on the back porch to put clothes in the washer and nearly trips over Danny's sizable feet. In desperation, he's sleeping inside the open laundry room on the concrete floor next to the washing machine. Like a stray dog curled up in a tight ball during an icy rainstorm, he's frozen half to death. His teeth chatter and his body trembles uncontrollably.

Helen steps outside with Pop and quickly ushers Danny inside the warm house. He passes me coming in through the back door, body shaking, head down, dark eyes staring at the floor, refusing to meet mine. And I'm stunned at his appearance.

I've seen my brothers leave—I've never seen them suffer.

Helen, who loves Danny dearly, is visibly upset. He probably reminds her of herself long ago when she was an orphan, unloved, and unwanted. She pushes Pop to give him the second chance that was never given to her.

And he gets it.

Months pass. Steady employment remains an issue for Danny.

And one day, there's an irreparable betrayal.

One Saturday morning after a long work week, Helen discovers a twenty-dollar bill is missing from her purse. She quizzes Billy and me about it first thing and is convinced of our innocence. Danny's not home early on, but I hear him and Helen talking later about stealing and shoplifting in my parents' back bedroom—and Helen sounds upset.

We have a small garage behind our house with a basketball goal attached to its rear and that afternoon I decide to peel off my T-shirt and put up some shots. Helen comes outside too—suns herself on a worn and white bedspread in the warm summer grass.

A few minutes later, the back door opens again and I hear my brother tromping down the steps. He approaches Helen gingerly. I dribble, shoot, and listen.

"Helen, I just want to tell you again, I didn't take that twenty," Danny starts.

"Well, if you didn't, who did? Are you saying David did?" Helen lifts her upper torso off the blanket and plants both hands behind her on the white bedspread, looking my brother directly in the eye.

I wait for the answer.

"No, I'm not saying David did."

"Well, are you saying Billy did?"

"I don't know. No, I don't think so," he offers weakly.

"Well then where is my twenty?" she pushes back.

"How do you know you had a twenty? Are you sure? Maybe you lost it."

"Danny, I already told you. I got paid yesterday afternoon. I cashed my check and gave everything to your Daddy, except for a twenty, which I left in my purse on the dresser in my bedroom when I got in from work last night around eleven. I checked at ten this morning and the twenty was gone—and so were you."

"Well, I don't know what to tell you, but I didn't do it."

"Danny Wayne Pruitt, you're lying to me!" she shouts, her face reddened by her widening blood vessels and the damaging rays of a welcome but unforgiving sun.

She pauses, then pushes further.

"How many times have I stood up for you when your Daddy was after you?"

"A lot."

"And haven't I given you money out of my own pocket, even when you didn't ask for it?" she continues.

"Yes, but Helen, I didn't take the twenty. I swear! I didn't do it!" he responds, more desperately this time.

I stop dribbling and make no further pretense about shooting. He's emotional, pleading his case. He *needs* this good woman to believe him. It hurts me to think about it, but I don't believe him myself.

Helen continues. I sense her desperation too.

"Danny, I love you and have always stood up for you, more than your brothers. Maybe even unfairly so. David's taken a lot from your daddy, but you've taken even more. And I've always defended you. I've always stood by you. Haven't I?"

"Yes," he says through suddenly glassy eyes.

"So I'm giving you one more chance. Just tell me: did you take that money out of my pocketbook?" she asks more softly, gently cajoling him to step up and take responsibility.

Danny hesitates.

In the years to come, I'll wonder what would've happened that day if he'd confessed. I do believe he would've held on to Helen as a staunch protector in the battle to survive Pop. Maybe he could've stayed at home and somehow worked things out, even stayed in

Greensboro. Instead, in some ways, we all lost a little of her support that day.

Danny shuffles his feet, straightens his back, and loudly proclaims, "Helen, I swear on a stack of Bibles, I didn't take that twenty!" The softness in her spirit is now gone and the empathetic orphan becomes a stern Mother Superior.

"Okay, Danny. I'm done defending you. Look into my eyes. You lookin' into 'em?" she demands.

"Yeah?" he says, not knowing where this is going.

"When I'm dead, lying in my casket, and you're standing over me, looking at my dead body, I want you to stop and think back to you and me right here, right now, and know one thing." She pauses. "I want you to know that I knew you stole that twenty from me, and then lied to me about it. You didn't love me enough, and you weren't man enough, to tell the truth. Do you hear me?"

"Yes," he answers with head hung low. He doesn't swear to his innocence again—but he doesn't confess, either.

"Now get out of my sight. I'm done with you."

He turns and walks back inside. Shoulders slumped, he looks dejected, like someone who just lost the best friend he ever had—the kind of loss that might be hard for a man to come back from.

The next day, Pop kicks him out of the house for the last time. He will not be back.

Soon after, it's Billy's turn. He loses a job at a local convenience store. Pop kicks him out too. He goes now to live in the woods near US 29.

Not too long after, I fight with my parents about help with college, bad things are said, and I become the last of the three of us to leave.

Eighteen
An Epiphany

A SUDDENLY HOMELESS HIGH SCHOOL graduate, I drive my car west up Cone Boulevard and try to settle myself down, to quiet my mind from the emotional reckoning with Pop. Hard but true things were said, and I desperately needed to say them. They cannot be taken back, and now I must pay the price: I'm on my own.

I now stand in my siblings' shoes, and I, like them, have very few options. I can see if Mama will take me in, but her decline continues and our estrangement has grown. I'm honestly not sure where she is right now. I also don't consider Billy or Danny—where or how they are living at the moment is a mystery to me. All I have is my Chevy and a few clothes.

I could drive until dark and try to find a quiet spot to park, sleep out the night, then figure things out in the morning.

But for the moment I need to conserve gas, so I park in a local shopping center and collect my thoughts.

The first thing I think about is my friend Kevin, a teammate from my high school football team. He and I are close. He's one of my beer-drinking, car-driving buddies, and surprisingly, I get on well with his parents and deeply respect his mom. She's one of the few adults who's been kind to and seems to have an interest in me.

With some reservation, I drive to his house and suggest we go for a ride. He prefers driving his tank-like Pontiac Catalina, so we each contribute four dollars, gas up, grab a six-pack, and head out of town. We talk for a while and I open up about what happened.

Kevin does not hesitate. He invites me to stay with his family until I can work things out with mine.

There are four kids and two parents living in their small, single-story brick house, and my entry makes already tight living quarters even tighter. It's down to Kevin and me sharing the same twin-size bed. He and I are both big guys, so it's tough sledding. After a while, and with encouragement from Kevin and his mom, I meet my parents at a local diner and we work things out. I also get into college.

Acceptance into UNCG changes the trajectory of my life. After our fight, I no longer have aspirations of getting help from Pop, but I'm still going to find a way to take classes in the fall. I'm not truly interested in academia just yet, but I'm definitely not interested in following the twisted, unforgiving path my brothers have taken. I'm also walking around with a sizable chip on my shoulder, bucking against the limitations the world seems to place on me.

For the first time in my life, I make plans—somewhat blurry and not fully formed, but plans nonetheless. Pop and Helen allow me back in the house as I pursue my studies. With the help of financial aid from the government, I begin to attend college.

That first semester proves to be more difficult than I could have imagined.

On a winter morning, I awake in a cold sweat, my white T-shirt stuck tight to the damp skin on my shoulders and back. It's just after Thanksgiving in 1979, a few weeks before first semester finals, and it's not going well—I have mostly Cs and Ds for grades and even an F in math. I lie in bed, pensively silent, and my mind's eye conjures a desolate scene: I see myself flunking out, hitting the barren, brutal, open roads of the homeless just like my brothers, with nowhere to lay my head, and the sound of my father's voice ringing in my ears— "Boy, I done told you. You flunked out, and you ain't worth a shit for nothing!"

I crawl out of bed, get dressed in an anxiety-filled haze, and feel growing desperation as I head out the back door. It's a frigid morning and sparse snowflakes land on ruddy skin as I scrape dense ice from the front window of my junker Vega. I slide into the driver seat, turn the defroster on full blast, tap the gas pedal to ensure the engines warm, then drive to my first class of the day: advanced algebra.

The professor hands back my poor grade on the prior week's quiz, and finally, *finally*, I realize I have to make a change. My future is at stake. It's just that simple. For the first time in a long time, I understand I've going to have to buckle down. It's some sort of miraculous epiphany, or perhaps I've simply suffered enough apathetic failure in both academics and life, but I suddenly realize that whatever I can be, whatever I hope to be, will be determined by the intensity of my effort to change my downward slide.

I take a last look at my shitty grade, stuff it in my backpack, decide to skip my remaining classes, and run—full speed—through the melting snow back to my car. I drive home in a near panic, plop myself down at the kitchen table, exhale deeply, and open a textbook for the first time in nine years.

It's impossibly difficult at first. Still, I hustle home after morning classes and study for a few hours before work, then return home at night after work and study some more. While slow and steady normally win the race, my opportunity to be the persistent tortoise in my studies has long since passed. Instead, I have to be the hare. I've got to study as hard as I can, as fast as I can, for as long as I can. So, I do it—all day and most of the night for the next few weeks. When Pop and Helen come in from work around midnight each night, I'm still at the table, books spread around me, learning things I should've picked up months, maybe even years, ago. But no matter, I've got to do this. I'm the previously idle and now suddenly desperate hare, and I'm gonna find a way to win this race—I'm gonna find a way to have some hope in my life.

Before I know it, final exam week comes, and I'm ready. I walk in and sit down to each one of them, and I am amazed at how easy they seem relative to the tests I struggled with earlier in the semester—and for the last nine years.

But the true defining moment is when I sit for the advanced algebra final.

I'm nervous. There are basic concepts I had to learn in a few weeks that I should've known long ago—and I have an *F* in the class. But I opened the book, started at page one, and read it cover to cover, completing all of the practice homework exercises along the way—homework exercises I had not turned in, as required, during the semester. It was grueling and mind-numbing, and though I have begun to pick it up, I honestly don't know if my efforts will translate on this final.

Exams are mechanically distributed, and once all the students are armed the professor gives his blessing to proceed. I flip over the test and go to work, completely focused—and to my disbelief, the answers come quickly and easily.

It's a full three-hour exam, and I've answered all the questions in less than forty-five minutes. I look up at the clock and can't believe it. I review my work one more time, and ten minutes later I walk up and drop the exam facedown on his desk. He remarks that he hopes I haven't given up—a reasonable comment, given my current grade—but I reply no, that I'm simply done and I studied hard. He turns over my exam, eyeballs it, looks at me quizzically, and then wishes me a Merry Christmas.

A few days later, I walk the halls of each classroom building, checking my grades on the exams in each of my five classes, including the dreaded advanced algebra. I aced all five of them, including the high *A* I scored in math. My *C*s, *D*s, and *F*s have turned into *B*s and *C*s for my first semester of college. I can't believe it. I'm now in a position to continue into the spring semester, something that seemed highly unlikely only a few weeks ago!

But something bigger than improved letter grades has happened in these three fateful weeks for me. I've not worked at anything academically since learning multiplication tables in the fourth grade. I've not fought for anything I've wanted for myself, other than surviving a hellish existence at home, in years. I've been knocked to the ground when stray crumbs missed the trash can, ridiculed for the way I looked, put on the streets for speaking my mind, and seemingly cast aside by the walled-off cliques of my peers. I've fought back against it all with impassioned words—but never with action. In the last three weeks, however, I've put myself out there and given everything I had. I took action!

It's an incredibly scary thing to give everything you have to something, or someone, you want. After all, if you give it all you have and still fail, or are rejected, where do you go from there? The unknown answer makes us afraid to reach for the coveted prize, to take hold of an opportunity, to make the try. But isn't that the underlying predicate to achievement: the courage to try—and a willingness to accept the possibility of failure in the attempt?

Herein lies a burdensome weight to those of us who are abused as children—one that has far-reaching implications in the trajectory of our lives. Like most, our willingness to try is initially derived from our realistic belief in the possibility of success, our belief in what we're capable of—can we somehow really do it? As abused souls, the strength of *our* conviction must hold against one single and contemptible fact: those we loved and believed in most when we were young didn't believe in us.

It is incredibly hard to find faith in yourself as an adult when you didn't have it given to you as a child. But for those who have been abused, it is undeniably sweeter, far more satisfying, when the brave attempt is made, success is found, and the poisonous voices from the past are silenced.

But first, we must find the courage to try.

I could easily fall back on the excuse of my upbringing and never know what I'm capable of achieving. I've done it for nine years. But no more. I've done the work and been rewarded. Maybe I *can* have a say in a better future. Maybe I *can* control, with the good Lord's help, the direction of my life.

One thing is clear: Nothing is going to happen for me while I'm sitting on my ass. It's time to get to work.

Nineteen
Out of the Woods

ONE DAY, BILLY GATHERS his meager belongings and decides to leave the woods off US 29. He catches the bus at the mall again and soon winds up in a halfway house near the Salvation Army in downtown Greensboro. They take him in but make it clear he'll have to work. With my father's words echoing in his head about "a man having to work for a living," he takes a job at a local Hardee's and walks the five miles each morning to arrive at his shift by 5:30 a.m.

After a few months, he moves to a room in a small house with a man he met at the plasma center. For now, he escapes the homeless streets, but it's a perilous reentry into society.

After a while flipping burgers, he finds a new job as the night manager at a local Shell convenience store. He works the register inside and stocks shelves with candy and potato chips when customer traffic allows. Though he's working now, in his free time he still reads his New Age books and smokes marijuana—lots of it. He also has a coworker, Mike, who is not only smoking it but selling it—directly out of the Shell store.

At 2:45 a.m. on a Thursday, working a joint shift, they decide to fire one up at the store. Although Mike sold some of his pot about an hour ago, no other customer has been by in the last few hours.

"Billy, try some of my latest," Mike says as he pulls a very large bag of pot from his backpack behind the counter. "I've got some banana kush here that will really level you out."

"You know, Mike, I appreciate it but I brought my own stuff," Billy responds as he pulls his Bic lighter, a small bag of pot, and rolling papers from his right pocket.

He takes a three-finger fold from the bag and drops it onto the rolling paper resting on the counter. He puts the remainder back in his pocket. He has just enough left for the joint he'll smoke at home before he crawls into bed later this morning.

He distributes the product evenly on the paper, positioning it close to the near edge. Using his thumb and fingertips, he rolls it tightly before he licks the excess to seal it in place.

Joint and lighter tucked discreetly in his right hand, he moves around the waist-high counter and stands quietly in front of the entry door as he surveys the nonexistent traffic outside. If it were 9:00 p.m. on a Friday, the roads and the store would be wall-to-wall with cars and people. But it's totally quiet now.

Looking left, then right, he sees nothing and decides it's safe. He walks back behind the counter to the right of Mike and lights up. He takes a deep draw, holds it briefly, and exhales slowly. He's never lost his taste for the stuff since a friend introduced him to it back in the day. It relaxes him and helps him forget bad things. At the same time, he keeps one eye on the small open window to his right that he uses to monitor customers at the gas pumps. Seeing nothing, he takes another draw and waits patiently for the anticipated buzz.

"Damn, Bill, that smell is rank. Who'd you buy it from?" Mike asks as he stashes his goods on the floor behind the counter. He's expecting another customer around 4:00 a.m.

"I'll keep my sources confidential, thank you. I guess your stuff's better huh?"

"Well, what do you think? You see 'em linin' up in here to get it, don't ya?"

"Yeah, I do. But Mike, I gotta say, I don't like you selling it here." Billy shakes his head. "You're gonna get us both in trouble. If the owner finds out, I'll lose my job. If the cops find out, it'll be bad news for you. Can't you do it somewhere else?"

"Oh, come on man, we already agreed on this. If anything happens, it's on me. Relax and enjoy your toke—even if it's just some cheap shit."

"It's good enough for me. You just need to be careful, man."

"Never had any problems. Speaking of that, I've got this guy coming in around four, and . . ."

The door bursts open. Two plainclothes officers rush in quickly. A uniformed officer comes in behind them. His weapon is visible but un-brandished.

"All right, you two, it's the police, get your hands up over your heads now!" the first plainclothes officer announces loudly.

Billy thumps his joint out the open window and Mike kicks the bag of reefer down the aisle where it comes to a stop comfortably near Billy's feet.

"I said get your hands up and don't move," the officer exclaims.

They comply. He moves around the counter and surveys the area. When his eyes lower to the floor, he spots the large bag of weed resting near Billy.

"I told him not to do it!" Mike exclaims. "He offered me some of the stuff in his bag there but I said no. Dammit, I'm just trying to make a living here! I knew there was gonna be trouble!"

Shocked, Billy turns toward Mike—Mike, who said it was on

him and is now trying to push blame his way. He quickly makes a decision. He'll confess to the lesser crime.

"Okay, I was just now smoking it," he says truthfully. "There's a half-lit one I tossed out the window. But the bag isn't mine. Mike kicked it over here when you guys came through the door."

"Officer, that's not true. I'm not the one smoking it. It's not on my breath, and he just confessed to smokin' it. You heard it, just now. And he got it from that bag at his feet. His bag!"

The uniformed cop steps outside and finds the joint on the ground, just as my brother said. He walks back in and shows it to his superior behind the counter.

"That proves he was smoking!" Mike says.

"Look, I have a small bag in my pocket, along with rolling papers and my lighter. Come check if you want, that's the pot I'm smoking, not his!" Billy exclaims loudly, increasingly anxious over how this might go.

"Okay, you, just stuff it," the officer behind the counter says. "Get your hands behind your back. I'm gonna cuff ya. You're under arrest." He grabs Mike's wrist.

"Why me? It's his! What are you doing?" a worried Mike asks.

"We're arresting both of you," the officer says. "You for selling it; him for having it. And stop the blathering. We've been casing this place for weeks and have pictures of you, your buyers, and cash changing hands." He begins to read him his rights.

And Mike starts to cry.

The uniformed officer moves behind the counter, cuffs Billy, and reads him his rights as well. He walks him back around the counter toward the door, places him in line behind Mike. Billy can see the blue lights flashing from the two cop cars parked parallel to the storefront.

"Hey, buddy, where's the key to the front door?" the cop asks. "I also need a phone number for your boss."

Billy points him to the drawer just below the register. The cop grabs the key and a slip of paper with a phone number on it, and also takes the bag of pot as evidence.

Finally, both Mike and Billy are taken out. The one officer locks up and sticks the key under the mat right outside the door. While Billy waits, he sees Mike get put into one of the cars, his head shoved down as he's ushered into the vehicle. His eyes are red and teary. He knows he's screwed. He'll pull real jail time for dealing.

Billy is scared too.

They arrive at the station. Billy spends a few sleepless hours in a cell with three other rough-looking men. Mike isn't one of them. These hours are spent in both regret and fear. *I should've never smoked pot at work. There goes my damn job—and what are they going to do to me?*

After a few hours, they take pictures and prints. He later speaks with a public defender who informs him since he's a first-time offender, he'll most likely get a misdemeanor drug possession charge and rehab. He'll also be required to pee in a cup for at least three months. "A summons will be coming in the mail," the lawyer says. "We'll talk again."

As he exits the jail and steps outside, he looks down to see his hands trembling slightly. While it looks like he won't go to prison, he could have, especially if Mike's lie had held.

I got lucky, but I'll have this on my record and there's no sense in even calling my boss. Hopefully, he'll still send me my last paycheck. God—I screwed up.

Weeks pass. Billy remains unemployed, and now the rent is due. He doesn't have the money, so his plasma friend unceremoniously asks him to leave. He packs up, then dodges around the Greensboro streets for a few weeks, eating and sleeping where he can. He thinks about going back to the woods but then he'd be right back where he was not so long ago—so he swallows his fear and pride and makes a different decision. Desperate, his feet carry him back to Pop's house late on a Friday evening.

The doorbell rings and I'm the only one home. It's mid-summer and I'm living here while working to save money for my sophomore year in college. Pop and Helen are taking a weekend trip to visit family. I answer the door and a quick look at Billy's face tells me things are not going well. He looks exhausted and hungry. Knowing I can get in trouble, but also knowing Pop and Helen will not be back until Sunday evening, I let him in.

We talk for a while, with Billy sharing as much as he will; then it becomes dark out, and now I'm at a loss. If Pop finds out he's been here and I let him in, there'll be trouble. If he finds out he's spent the night, there'll be hell to pay. Maybe he'll even kick me out again. Still, I can't do it. I can't put him out. He sleeps at home that night, and I don't ask him to leave the next day either.

But Sunday comes, and Pop gets back sooner than expected. I've been wrong not to respect his rules. My brothers are going to have to make it on their own and Pop is trying to force the issue. Me caving while he was gone has now put him in the uncomfortable position of kicking Billy out all over again. He solves this by telling Billy to get his things together and directing me to drop him wherever he wants to go.

My father has no ambivalence as he issues his directive.

We climb into my car and sit in awkward silence as I back out onto Cone Boulevard. I tell him I'm sorry he can't stay, but we both know Pop's mind is made up. I ask if he has any money. He shakes his head no. I have $60 in a savings account that's outside the money I'm saving for tuition so I withdraw $30 from a local ATM and pass it to him.

"Thank ya, David," he says.

We exit onto Battleground Avenue. General Greene Elementary School is minutes away. It's early evening when we pull up in the vacant parking lot.

No one's around, and there's a patch of scattered woods off to the left that runs downhill for a half-block before tying into a residential neighborhood. Billy steps from the car as we say our goodbyes. I tell him to take care of himself. He nods, slings his backpack over his shoulder, and closes the door. Tears well as I watch him waffle uncertainly between the playground and the woodline. I blankly stare for another moment, then lean forward, close my eyes, and rest my forehead atop the narrow steering wheel. In my mind's eye, I'm seven years old and I see Herman, the soft-brown weenie dog, ears flying, chasing behind me in that old Rambler. I lean back in the car seat and my chest heaves as I watch Billy cut between the oaks and maples and step gingerly past a few prickly brambles. *How can this be?* I ask myself. And my heart hurts.

There've been some hard things in my life, but nothing else has been quite like dropping my brother in the streets, knowing he has nowhere to sleep for the night.

I pull out of the parking lot, gather myself, and swallow it all down. This memory will become a reminder of how easily *my* life can go astray. It will be added fuel to pursue something better, and I'll use it on those late nights of studying to remind myself why.

The next day Billy exits the woods and checks into a local dive hotel. He gives them a credit card for what will be an indeterminate stay.

After several weeks of searching, he finds work in a local engineering business and, after completing their training, becomes part of their land survey team. He now has a decent job but needs a bit more help to get back on his feet—the hotel tab's growing daily. So he calls Pop, who picks him up at the hotel (I ride along) and pays off the unpaid balance. Pop takes Billy in for a few weeks and, with Helen's agreement, makes a deal: they'll help him get an apartment and sell him their old Toyota station wagon on the cheap.

Two weeks later, we help him move into his new place.

Pop unquestionably played a large role in the tumult of Billy's first twenty-three years. He helped put him in those dark woods off US 29 for six long months but he also helped save him, to finally get him off the streets. This is the dichotomy of my complex father's personality and behavior—one that leaves a permanent mark on each of us, like a fiery hot branding iron on a bellowing calf.

Still, Billy, who maintains steady employment, keeps a roof over his head, and eventually gets married some twenty years later, is the lucky one. He escapes homelessness and the streets for the balance of his life.

Danny will not be so lucky.

Twenty
The Mother Question

I POCKET THE MONEY I make from my summer job, my monthly government checks (low family income, mama's illness) and other savings I have from the theater, and apply to live on campus at UNCG for my sophomore year. The college was founded as a women's college in 1891, but men have been admitted since 1964, and today nearly ten thousand students live on campus.

It's the fall of 1980 and this place is quite a step up for me. My application is accepted and I'm placed in a coed dorm at the south end of campus. On the appointed day, I pull up an incline to the small parking lot in front of Phillips-Hawkins dorm and, amazingly, find a parking spot right up front, about twenty yards from the front entry door. I move my few things in, park my car at a nearby lot, and have a slice of pizza on nearby Tate Street later that evening.

That night, I sleep soundly. I have no worries—no one's going to come through the door to confront me over a dust bunny in the kitchen or pubic hair found on a bathroom floor.

Walking to class the next morning, I note the beauty of the campus: the staid but sturdy brick three-story dorm buildings, the newly built Bryan School of Business building (where I will take many of my classes), and the central bridge in the heart of campus, which flows from leafy sidewalks that connect living space to classrooms. The large cafeteria—a vibrant place where students meet for the burgers, pizza, and casual observation of the opposite sex—sits just off the bridge; it's a social mecca and a welcome respite from the nine-story library off to the right and farther up the hill. The highrise book repository feels almost solemn to me—a place of solitude where silence and intellect come together in determined partnership and contemplation. I'm a bit apprehensive but also excited at the thought of the experiences that lie ahead.

Within a short time, I find my routine: I'm an early riser and like to start classes at 8:00 a.m. I look forward to my time with friends, which often happens in the cafeteria, whether it be a quick bowl of cereal or a drawn-out dinner where we talk about girls, parties, or an upcoming difficult exam. I also find my spot at the library—the back of the ninth floor, under a wall of windows. I like to see the people walking outside below me and feel the warm sun on my face as I study. Running or some form of exercise calms my mind, and making that a priority of my day helps me process and do the required work. I like the structure.

It's funny; unlike high school and home, I feel accepted here. I'm just short of six foot three inches now, making me taller than most of my friends. My face has cleared up for the most part and I feel like I've finally achieved what it means to be normal. Things are shifting for me, sometimes without my realizing it. Girls have started to notice me in class. I frequently see them looking my way and there are times when I look back, but I never say a word. Honestly, I don't know what to say.

My roommate and I are getting on well, but I have to admit it's surreal listening to him talk to his mom in the middle of the week, asking for additional money, telling her about the big date he has for the weekend. I'm imagining her unconditional love on the other end of the line—all wonderfully normal, but hard to relate to.

I come in from morning classes on a Wednesday mid-semester. It's a clear, crisp, October day. I've just eaten lunch and I decide to change and go for a run. I walk down the hall from the shared bathroom on our floor and have just stopped for a moment in my room to check my notes from a marketing class before heading outside when the phone rings.

"Hello?"

"David, this is your mama."

Mama and I have not spoken in any meaningful way for at least a year. She called a few times while I was still at Pop's, but our words have come less naturally as our time apart has grown more frequent and prolonged. Despite it all, I still love her. Our emotional bond is fragile but maintained by the simple fact that she's my mother.

"Hey, Mama. How are you doing?"

"I'm not doing that great, son. Your mama is struggling."

"I'm sorry. Uh, how did you get my number?" I query curiously.

"I looked up your Daddy's number and he gave it to me."

"Oh, okay. Well, I appreciate you calling."

"I hear you're in college, son. Mama is happy for you!"

"Well, thanks. It's a lot of work, but I'm getting it done."

"Good for you."

"What's going on with you? You taking care of yourself?"

"Well, son, I'm not doing so well. You know I'm not able to work. I'm getting some help for rent and food, but it's not been easy for me."

She must be getting help from the government. I assume, due to her mental illness, she is considered disabled and gets financial assistance as well as food stamps.

"I'm sorry to hear that, Mama."

There's a temporary silence on both ends of the phone. I search for words—none come. Mama often complains about her plight but always seems to muddle by.

Today, however, she says, "I need your help, son."

My stomach flutters. "You know, I'm in my sophomore year. I'll be out in a few years. I don't know what the future holds, but if I'm in a position to help you, I will."

Unsatisfied, she responds, "I heard you're getting money from the government too. Your Mama needs that money, son. I can hardly make it right now."

To the left of the phone on the wall, there's a mirror. In it, I can see pursed lips and eyes that close and then slowly reopen. I see my chest expand fully, then contract in resignation. I see a slowly dawning awareness of an unfortunate truth.

"Yeah, Mama. I get $130 a month. It helps pay for my books and gives me a little money to live on."

"Well, you work hard son, and I know you'll be okay. But Mama's not able to work and I have to eat, pay utilities, and pay my rent. So I need you to help me get the government to transfer that money over to me."

"I don't understand. What is it that you want me to do? You know I'm using that money to help me get through college, right?"

I hear my voice rising as my indignation builds.

"Mama needs that money, son."

My mind races. What does she want me to do? Is there some piece of paper she wants me to sign? Does she want me to call the Social Security Administration and tell them to give the money to her? Does she care that I need the money to get through school? How bad off is she?

"Well, Mama you're getting help from the government now, right? You're in a house and you've got food to eat, don't you?"

"Yeah, but it's tight, son. I need more help, and that money you get will make the difference."

"But still, you have a place to stay and you have food, right?"

There is silence on the line.

"Mama, you know I'm using that money to help me get through school. I'm working a bit at the theater and working factory jobs during the summer. But that money is a big help to me."

"You'll find a way, son."

That's it. She does not care what I need. She only knows what she needs.

"Mama, you know what's happened with Billy and Danny? They're struggling. For me, college is my escape. It's my way out. I want a better future. I'm working hard here, getting good grades. That money is helping me realize my dreams. Do you get that?"

She laughs.

"Oh, you'll be all right son. You know what you need to do. But your Mama needs that money to get by right now."

"Mama, is that what you called me about?"

"Well—it is. Can you help me, son?"

I pause for several seconds, taking a deep breath. I feel my jaw clench. My teeth are moving back and forth against each other, grinding even and slow. Thoughts of the past come flooding into the present. She didn't or couldn't stand up to the tyrant that was my father when the unrelenting blows rained down on us. She didn't comfort us, even when the withering storm of his anger passed. After the divorce, she seemed to forget all about us. Why?

When she came to see us after leaving Pop, I was glad and tried to show it. As much as an adolescent rough-and-tumble boy could,

I gave her affection—told her I loved her when she hugged me good-bye after a visit, and meant it. I'd seriously considered going to live with her and leaving my brothers.

But over time she stopped coming around. *Was it my job to seek her out? Wasn't she supposed to help me reach for my dreams?* This all leads me to the deciding question: Is her mental illness a get-out-of-jail-free card in this sorrowful game of a dying relationship between a damaged mother and a resentful son? My head drops. Once again, I look up at my anguished reflection in the mirror and my heart hardens towards my mother forever at this moment.

I have my answer: it is not.

"Mama I'm not signing any forms or helping you take this from me. On my end, understand, I'm not throwing the money away. It's helping me get a college education. Neither you nor Pop is helping me do this. I'm on my own. Just me. You have your own money coming to you to help with your situation. So I'm not going to help you do this. If you can take the money on your own, and that's what you want to do, then go for it."

Pause.

"Is there anything else you want from me?"

My final query is met with silence.

"Bye, Mama. Take care of yourself."

I place the phone back on the receiver. I do not slam it down. I'm not angry. But I am hurt and resigned, and I fully understand the significance of the moment. I turn and walk slowly over to my bed. Head in hands, I sit quietly, thankful for the solitude, for the chance to process what has just happened.

Even at nineteen, the idealistic concept of love is clear to me. I've seen enough in life, at least in the world around me, if not in my own world, to know how real love is supposed to work. I mostly saw it on the TV shows I watched as a kid. In that world, there was caring, support, and sacrifice. The love given to me, in contrast, has been nonexistent at worst and unevenly applied at best.

But there is no gray area in what I've just heard. My mother doesn't care about me—even a little. She's only looking out for herself. And after this it will be hard for me to trust anybody going forward; after this, I'll be prepared to walk away from anyone at any time. On this day, I'm walking away from my mother. In the end, I'm just not a big enough young man to be slapped down by my father, deemed irrelevant by my mother, and still rise to my feet with a smile on my face. But I stand up now and walk outside, and then, ensconced between the weathered brick buildings and tall oak trees, I take off running.

I run hard and fast and long. I run in the cool October air and cut through that bitter wind, tears building in the outer corner of each eye. I run until my lungs feel like they will burst. I run until I can no longer stand up straight. I finally slow in search of recovery but instead find myself kneeling, low and desperate, in the graying fall grass, eyes closed, seeing nothing.

As I kneel there, a plain reality comes flooding back to me: What has changed, really, after this conversation? What I already knew in my heart was simply confirmed: in terms of family, I am alone.

I sit for a while and let the low sun warm my tired body. But salty sweat and scant tears are soon dried and cast aside. I rise to my feet and begin the slow walk back to the dorm. I shower, gather my books, head to the library, and walk back later that night under the faded stars of a cloudless, pitch-black sky, resolute and alone. But my shoulders are pulled back and my head is up.

The months roll on and I try to put my break with Mama out of my mind, but my damaged family continues, persistently and painfully, to invade my life. Danny is still in town, though where and how he's living is unclear to me.

I get a page at the dorm one night telling me I have a visitor. It's him. And one look tells me he's upset.

We sit down on a couch in the downstairs common area and he tells me he's found Mama and she doesn't look good. He went to see her at a run-down house she's living in but she wouldn't open the door and talk to him. Not only that but he saw her in there, sitting in an old recliner and staring at the wall like she was in a daze.

I tell him she'll be fine; that I'm not going to worry about Mama anymore. Besides, I have a big test in the morning.

He says okay but mentions there was a large knife on the kitchen counter near the chair that looked scary just sitting there, especially given Mama's mental illness. "I knocked several times and she just told me to go away," he says. He asks me to come with him to see for myself; together, maybe we can get her to open the door and make sure she's all right.

I take a deep breath, give him one last, rueful glance and say okay, let's do it.

Somehow, when I think it can't get any worse with my family, it does.

When we arrive, I see that she's in a small, single-story, vinyl-sided home in a seedy neighborhood. Is she renting? I have no idea, but somehow she has a roof over her head. We park, I climb the steps to the front porch, and knock on the door with Danny trailing behind me. We get no answer.

There is a window to the immediate right of the door. Through gossamer curtains, I find her.

She is naked, sitting upright and stiff in a well-worn recliner.

Glazed-over eyes stare straight ahead. A bathrobe rests haphazardly on the table beside her. Then I see it; a chef's knife with a brown wooden grip and a large blade with a serrated edge sitting just a few feet away on a counter in the small kitchenette to her rear.

Mama never cooked a lick when we were kids. What's she doing with a knife like that?

My eyes return to her motionless, naked body. She doesn't move but her mind—her mind is clearly preoccupied. The voices, it must be the voices, she still hears them in her head, calling to her, criticizing her, the voices that keep her from hearing the call of a family that once needed her but now, having been ignored and rejected, accepts her absence and disinterest as a fact, a given, a trivial matter for a once-broken but now hardened heart.

Still, I'm here, and this doesn't look right, so I ring the doorbell.

"Mama, it's David and Danny," I call out. "We just want to see how you're doing."

No response. No movement. I ring again.

"Mama, it's me. Are you okay in there? Open up."

Her head lifts and turns, and she looks, for a moment, toward the front door, but I sense no real recognition. She seems irritated, distracted.

Danny and I exchange glances. He remains quiet.

I move farther right on the porch and check each of the two window frames for accessibility, but there is no easy give. I jump down off the porch and check the right side of the home. I see two more windows—options for possible access.

I decide not to check them. I walk back up to the front door instead and ring again.

"Mama, it's David. Let me in. I just want to check on you," I repeat.

She looks up but does not get up. I'm a gnat, an irritant. An empty voice distracting her from the more important voices in her head. She finally speaks to me, not out of desire but out of necessity.

"Go on and leave Mama alone now," she directs in a calm, reassuring tone as she continues to stare straight ahead. There is nothing in her line of sight except a bare wall.

"Mama, let me in," I push back a bit more aggressively. "I'm not going to bother you. I just want to make sure you're all right."

She ignores me and gives no response this time.

"Mama, you need to answer me," I implore her.

No answer. I lose patience.

"Mama if you don't let me in, I'm gonna kick this door open."

Nothing.

"I mean it, Mama."

She slowly looks up as I peer inside at her from the window. She stands up, seemingly unaware of her nakedness.

"Leave that door alone. I'm fine. I've told you."

"Mama, it's cold out here and you're in there with no clothes on. Are you all right?"

"I'm fine." She leans over, turns away from me, picks up the robe, pulls it over her shoulders, and ties it loosely at her waist, much to my relief.

"Mama, let me in or I'm coming in on my own," I say with finality, the tone of my voice deliberately loud and firm.

She faces the front door and I finally have my first clear view of her. As her head lifts slowly, I see a look in her eyes I've not seen before. It's frightened rage, like a penned-up dog that's been abused sidling to the back of a narrow metal cage. And I'm the untrusted keeper reaching out with a tentative hand to provide previously denied comfort and care—but to no avail. For the first time I can ever remember, Mama is showing me her teeth.

"No, you're not. You're not coming in here. I want you to leave now," she says in no uncertain terms. If looks could kill . . . and I see again the knife sitting on the counter.

I take stock for a moment. She is now clothed. Yes, there is a knife, but it's been there, I assume, for some time. I'm not fully confident that she won't use it on me if I try to force my way in, but I'm reasonably sure she won't use it on herself. I didn't like the sight of her naked, slight, and catatonic in the chair. But I saw so many things in my youth that a little boy shouldn't see. This, while a first, is not that shocking in the context of my dysfunctional family life. She is a lone apparition now, not walking the crowded halls of Dorothy Dix or the Cone Hospital mental ward but wandering on her own, lost in fractured, damaged thought. Fortuitously, however, she is cocooned in a warm house. She has a place to sleep. And she does not want me in her cage.

I look over at Danny. He is noncommittal. I change my tone.

"Mama, are you telling me you're all right?" I ask.

"Yes, I'm all right," she offers.

"Well, if you're not going to let me in, I'm going to leave you alone. You take care of yourself, you hear?" With that, I move with resigned deliberation away from the door—but before I go, I look through the window one last time.

She heads toward the chair, her back to me, and resumes sitting, but at least the robe is still on and tied at the waist.

Danny and I walk back to his beat-up Impala, and I tell him I'll call the police from the dorm later tonight, but for now I need to get back to the dorm in a hurry, I've got a test tomorrow.

As we drive, he has more news for me. He says Billy is in jail for loitering; that he's homeless; that he called him yesterday and asked if he would come to bail him out. It's going to cost $50 and he only has $15. He asks if I can cover the rest. He'll drop me at the dorm, he knows I have a test; he'll take the money over and bail him out.

I don't respond at first, because I know it's a lie. I know where Billy is. He's in the apartment that Pop helped him get. I helped him move in a few months ago, for God's sake! Danny's been out on his own a while, doesn't know this, and is flat-out lying to me. And now my heart is broken again. Danny, the family member I'm probably closest to, is just like Mama. He doesn't give a shit about me other than what money I can give him!

I angrily confront him and he admits to his lie. After an emotional discussion, I give him twenty-five dollars. I even tell him I love him, because I still do. But I exit that car a little less trusting and a lot more jaded. I go up to study for my test.

I call the police about Mama, as promised, and they agree to check on her. When they call back, they acknowledge the strange behavior but also remind me she is committing no crime. They offer no further assistance.

After tonight, I will not see Danny or my mother again for another nine years.

I have my ups and downs over the next few years but I manage to complete my studies and become a first-generation college graduate with a dual business and accounting degree. I also meet new people who become close friends. Some of them are just as dedicated to their studies as me, some not as much. Some of them are friends I'll be close to for the rest of my life, while some will not even make it to graduation. But we're all part of a common community: all of us, in some way, are looking to better ourselves. I see it in so many of them and it lifts me up, keeps me working, and I manage to make it through. In time, my very closest friends become my family. I don't tell them about the earlier times of my life, but they begin to heal me anyway without even knowing. We choose to spend time with one another because we want to and when we do, there is trust, support, and a lot of laughter. And it means everything.

I'm slowly learning: the things I could never find in my home as a child can still be found in the world.

Part IV
Rising and Running

Twenty-One
Getting Down to Business

IT'S 1987 AND POP calls me at work one day and says there's a letter for me from the North Carolina Association of Certified Public Accountants. I took the CPA exam a few months ago and they've sent the results.

At lunch, I drive by his place to open it. To my surprise, I passed all four parts—I'm on my way to being a CPA!

I'd been in the working world for a couple of years when I realized I needed the CPA credential to move ahead. But there was too much drinking, partying, and girls for me to get it done in Greensboro, so I left town and moved an hour north to a rented house on seemingly deserted Hyco Lake, pretty much in the middle of nowhere. Alone, I worked a job during the day and studied late nights and on the weekends. That's all I did for a year. The lesson I learned during my freshman year in college about putting in the work stayed with me. And it paid off.

Since coming back to Greensboro, I've taken a job with a manufacturing company called Kayser Roth (KR) as an accounting supervisor with their retail division, Rolane. I've served under an incredible mentor, Terry, for the last couple of years. But he recently gave his notice and his boss, Sally, the controller for the division, needs to fill his position of accounting manager.

To my surprise, she agrees to interview me for the position and offers me the job. It's an increase in pay and responsibility, and I accept. But Sally and I are not a great fit. I'm inexperienced and because she transferred in from another division of KR directly into the lead position of controller and relied on Terry, who already knew the ropes, she never learned the detailed reporting requirements of my new position. When I ask her in-depth technical questions about how she feels something should be handled from a reporting standpoint, she directs me to the accounts payable supervisor. It's not unfair for her to do that, and with a more seasoned professional, it would probably be fine. But while I'm still training, it's a bit of a struggle. It's the first time in my still-young career that I've felt a bit in over my head.

But there are also larger problems with the business that demand my attention.

Our division has struggled in the last few years. Our general manager (GM) is a volatile, autocratic boss who leads by fear and intimidation. Management by fear is not my style (not surprising, given my background) and, in my opinion, is not the right way to go. I know some have made it work, but our GM isn't one of them.

Business results are not good, and the heat is on from the higher-ups at KR. We're now putting together the annual budget for the upcoming year after coming off a bad year. The budget is to be presented in a couple of weeks to the CEO and CFO of our $800 million parent company.

As we're compiling the budget data, I notice that profit is planned down from the prior year (which was not a good year) while capital expenditures are planned to be significantly up. Capital expenditures are money spent to improve or maintain the business; for example, it might be new register systems for the retail stores, or the funds required to open a new store. Unless financed, this usually means cash going out the door pretty quickly. Capital expenditure dollars can be scarce and it is a difficult sell to have a bad year, project worse the following year, and still ask for more money. I know this is going to be a difficult budget to get approved.

I express my concern directly to Sally, who simply shrugs it off and says Jim, the GM, is driving the bus. On a larger scale, I'm more concerned about the direction of the business in a way that I've not been before. I'm starting more and more to focus on the business as a whole in addition to the debits and credits of a mid-level accounting position. I'm beginning, for the first time in my young career, to see a bigger picture.

We complete the budget on Wednesday and with the presentation scheduled for Friday at KR headquarters, there is plenty of time for Sally to prepare. I'm there to provide any support she needs in the meantime.

But Sally does not show for work on Thursday. She calls me late in the morning to tell me she has the flu and won't be in today or tomorrow. Within minutes, Jim is in my office, looking nervous as a cat.

"Have you talked to Sally yet?" he asks as he walks in and closes the door behind him.

"I just got off the phone with her. She didn't sound too great."

"Well, we've got this budget meeting tomorrow. You good with the numbers?"

"Yes, I know the numbers that are in the budget," I reply mechanically.

"All right, you just make sure you're ready to go." He quickly gets up and heads out the door.

My head is now spinning. This has all happened in the space of a short fifteen minutes. Sally calls, the GM walks in, and now *I'm* going into a meeting with the CEO and CFO of this large conglomerate defending a budget that looks to me to be indefensible. If I were a few years further along in my career, I would stop Jim and tell him the budget is a problem. What's the game plan for explaining it? What will our strategy be going forward? Are these capital expenditures going to turn things around next year? Why is our profit down? Is the broader market an issue? Can we raise margins to offset the soft topline sales we're budgeting? And what about sales—is our ad spend correct? But at this point I'm not yet experienced or assertive enough to ask those questions and even if I'd asked them, there's no time to change the course we are on. The meeting is in twenty-four hours. I assume that Sally has asked all those questions, the GM has all the answers, and it's my job to simply recite the numbers we're presenting.

I study the details behind the numbers that afternoon and the following morning. Jim's assistant calls me at one thirty that afternoon and asks me to come down, saying Jim's ready to go over everything.

He tells me to kick it off by going over the income statement first and the meeting will flow from there. I have to admit I'm nervous as we ride in silence in his silver BMW, but I'm ready to hold up my end. This is his show, not mine.

We arrive at the elaborate Corporate HQ offices and, after a brief wait, are ushered into a large conference room where five well-dressed people sit around a rectangular conference table, waiting for us. Coffee and water are sitting on a small table at one end and a window with an open view to the large and full parking lot below sits at the other. The CEO and CFO are there, along with three of their able lieutenants. I offer to pass out copies of the budget, but they are already armed. Jim attempts to make small talk, but they push to get started. He cuts his eyes at me, signaling me to get underway, so I do.

"We appreciate everyone's time in allowing us to present the Fiscal Year budget," I begin. "Why don't we get started; if you'll turn to page three, we'll get into the P&L." I wait for them to get there, then continue, "If we take a look at sales, we are budgeting down to the prior year. We're also budgeting to add two new stores, which are part of our capital expense request."

One of the lieutenant's pipes in quickly, "David, our group has reviewed the budget in detail already and there's no need to cover the individual line items."

"Okay?" I look at Jim and then back at the group across the table, looking for more information.

"Well frankly, we just don't get it," he continues.

I sit silently, as does Jim.

The CFO now takes over.

"What we don't understand is how you all can come in here and budget profit to be down 40 percent while your requested capital expense spend is up 150 percent. How in the world can we possibly support that?"

I turn to Jim, looking forward to hearing his response. To my surprise, he's looking back expectantly at me. He wants me to provide the answer!

I don't like this. I don't understand this.

Think, dammit, profit down 40 percent and capital expense up 150 percent—is there any reasonable explanation?

Jim continues to look at me.

"Well, uh . . ."

"What the hell is going on over there?" the CEO demands hotly, glaring at my boss in a none-too-happy stare-down.

I attempt to respond. "Well, uh, if we look at pages 1 and 2, we can talk about the strategic issues that . . ."

The CEO slams his fist down on the papers before him, shaking the entire conference room table. Coffee spills from a thick paper cup and a victimized staffer slides his chair back to avoid the spillage. My mouth agape, I look on in shock as the CEO rises angrily, storms out of the room, and slams the heavy wooden door behind him.

The CFO and his team look across the table at us. For a moment, there is complete silence. He gets up from the table, tells us to sit tight for a minute, and steps out, presumably to talk with the CEO. We all sit quietly and stare at one another. Jim finally speaks, saying something about how we need the capital expense to improve the stores, but it's too little too late. Time drags by for a few minutes; then the CFO calls out one of his guys for a quick conversation, after which the lieutenant sticks his head back in and says, "That's it for today."

"Walt will get with you next week," he ends, looking at Jim, before closing the door behind him.

The others get their things and depart, leaving the two of us alone. We then gather our stuff, slide back our chairs, and see ourselves out of the building. I note the strain on Jim's face as we conduct our chastened exit. He is livid.

"What the hell just happened?" he asks, talking to himself, as we get back in the car, somewhat stunned.

"What the hell just happened?" he queries again, looking at me this time.

I sit silently for a moment. I'm mentally still a trained seal. If he were to backhand me right now, I wouldn't be surprised.

"Well, I tried to speak . . ." I start, then pause. "They didn't like the budget or our results."

"I just had the wrong person in the room with me, that's all," he reassures himself.

I don't respond to his assignation of blame. I assumed that the GM of the business would be prepared to speak to the strategic reasoning behind our budget. Sally told me as much. But he was not. Assuming anything was a big mistake—one I won't make again.

I go home that night and guzzle down several beers. My thoughts are focused on the last few days, and suppositions begin to form. The meeting itself seemed, at first, shocking, particularly given my inexperience. I've never seen anything like that before. But upon reflection and after several Miller Lites, it almost seems like it was scripted—the fist pounding the table, the door slam, the group walkout. Was this all pre-planned beforehand, with Sally being excused from the experience? Did she hang me out to dry? I'm now concerned the GM will walk in on Monday morning, go straight to her, and demand my head.

I spend the weekend drinking heavily and thinking about what happened, what I might've done differently, and then let my paranoia begin its work, preparing me for the worst. Fear, self-doubt, and recrimination kick in. I'm a fake. What the hell am I doing in the corporate boardroom of a multimillion-dollar business, dealing with the best and the brightest? Have I been found out?

I sleep fitfully that weekend and dream about long-ago things I wish I could forget.

"David, get in here, NOW!" Pop shouts.

It's the day after Christmas on Huffine Mill Road, and I'm in the back bedroom playing with my new Batman action figure. Billy and Danny are preoccupied with their playthings but Billy cuts his eyes at me apprehensively as I drop the caped crusader and rise to meet Pop's call.

I turn the corner from the bedroom and head up the hall; there he is, hands on hips, staring at me while alternately looking down at the floor to the right and out of my sightline. He does not look happy.

I reach the front of the house and see the metal cars and race-track lying in a mess on the living room floor.

"What did I tell you all about your toys yesterday morning after we opened presents?" he demands angrily.

"You told us to put them away if we weren't playing with them," I correctly respond.

"And what about last night, when you all were playing before bedtime? Did you hear me remind you then?" he continues, seeming to get angrier the longer this conversation goes on and the offensive vehicles lie idle on the floor. His eyes narrow.

"I did. I'm sorry, Pop. It was late. I got tired and just forgot. I'll pick them up now." I say this knowing my opportunity to do so independently has passed.

He slaps me in the face. The heavy-handed blow hurts, but not like it has in the past—when the hit came unexpectedly, when I was shocked that I'd been struck, when my head snapped back as if I'd been blindsided by an unseen tackler on a frozen football field. This time, my head does not even turn. The element of surprise is now gone. I simply look at him as he admonishes me to pick everything up. I drop to my knees and begin to disconnect the pieces of the track. I slide the bottom half of the box over and begin to fill it. Pop moves back into the kitchen to continue preparing breakfast.

"Yeah, I left a mess, but does he have to get so mad?" I mutter under my breath. "Why does he have to slap me? I'm having a good Christmas. I'm in my bed not bothering anybody, and he has to slap me around," I continue, louder now, and I feel my eyes begin to water.

He hears me, and I guess I want him to.

"What? What are you saying in there?" he asks, my challenge not fully registering.

I foolishly speak up. My anger, my indignation, cannot be swallowed down.

"I said I left a mess but do you have to get so mad? Do you have to slap me?"

"Boy, I told you to keep it picked up and you didn't do it," he says, still working in the kitchen.

"I just forgot. I didn't do it on purpose."

"You'd forget your hind end if it wasn't tied to you," he offers.

"Well, why can't you just take them away from me? Why do you have to hit me?" I hear my voice rising.

"Boy, you live in my house, under my roof—I'll whip your ass if I want to," he says in a voice now rising in return.

"You didn't whip me. You hit me in the face. And I don't like it." I can't stop myself.

"What did you say?"

He walks over. There is no going back.

"I didn't leave this stuff on the floor on purpose. I don't understand why you have to hit me!" I say defiantly. The tears begin to glisten on my cheeks.

"Boy, I'll take this belt off and really tear your ass up. Is that what you want?"

As he prepares to do just that I look up at him, feeling incredibly defenseless but determined nonetheless to show my ass.

"As soon as I get old enough, I'm gonna get outta here," I say, glaring at him.

"You do that, but for now, you better get that shit cleaned up if you know what's good for you."

He turns to walk away. I should keep my mouth shut. I should finish picking up and hump it back to the bedroom. It will end here. But I can't. Still, the answer to his question is no. I don't want him to whip my ass. I want him to stop and say he's sorry, that he shouldn't have hit me, that he's made a mistake. He can say I disobeyed him, that the cars will be taken away, anything, just stop hitting me in the face.

The hits to the face are more jarring, more humiliating, more punitive, more dismissive. When he whips me with the belt, my back is turned and I cannot fully see the anger, the simmering hatred, the unleashed frustration, the unrelenting determination to extract tears, compliance, and submission. But when he hits me in the face, he stands in front of me, and it's all there to be taken in. I know he'll never apologize or back off. So the older I get and the more times it happens, the more resentful I become—the more my anger, my hatred, my frustration grows and I have to let him know it, let him feel it coming back from me.

"Yeah, I know, you'll beat the shit out of me, just like you always do," I say, fully aware of the price I will pay for speaking those words.

He turns and comes flying toward me, uncinching the damned black belt as he comes.

"PICK IT UP!!" he screams as he stripes my back and shoulders.

I gather the cars quickly, knowing the time spent until the job is complete will equate to more blows, more damage. I beg him to stop, to no avail. Mama does not come. Billy and Danny are in the back, not moving, waiting to comfort me if I make an intact return. I opened my big mouth. This is my punishment to absorb.

"I'm doing it! Stop, please stop," I cry through falling tears but he continues to stroke.

Through the adrenaline, I can feel flash stings like pissed-off bees thrusting sharp stingers into my neck, shoulders, back, legs, and arms. Thin stripes marking my defiance will be visible for days. It's done. I slide the box in the corner beside the couch, stand up straight, and back up against the front wall of the house. I do not stay down on the floor.

"The next time I tell you to do something, you do it and keep your mouth shut. Do you heah me?" He stares me in the eye, looking for confirmation of his absolute authority.

Silence.

"Do . . . you . . . heah . . . me?" he repeats as he clutches the two ends of the belt, still doubled up in violent preparation, and at the same time jabs the point of his index finger firmly into my chest. "Boy, are you gonna make me . . . ?"

"Yes sir," I say, finally, with reluctance and a subtle trace of defiance still masked on my face.

"Now get outta here. I'll call you when breakfast is ready."

I leave my dreams and the weekend behind. I get to work Monday, early as usual, and see Sally's door is closed. I sit in my office quietly, working but preoccupied with the potential consequences coming my way.

In a few minutes, she stops by—and, to my shock, has no bad news for me. I tell her what happened, she takes it in, albeit without surprise, and it's back to work as usual. But the disastrous budget meeting is a precursor to a new day at Rolane. The GM is let go a few days later and Sally leaves, voluntarily, a month or so after that. She is a decent person, but I will continue to believe forever afterward that she deliberately sent me into that meeting in her stead, already informed as to the outcome.

Painful as that experience was, however, I was lucky to be in that meeting. The simple lesson is that when the numbers are not good and you're in a senior leadership position, even with competent, talented people that report to you, *you* are accountable, period. More importantly, you are accountable to yourself and to your organization to deliver results. I internalize this.

Personnel changes are made. Terry, my former mentor, comes back to take the controller position. Joe, who was a senior guy under Jim, becomes the new GM of the division. With Terry in place and Joe doing good work, the business gets better. I watch closely and absorb their approach to improving our results. It's all about the right talent, proper planning, strong execution, and consistent accountability. As a young professional in my mid-twenties, I've already seen the wrong and right way to move a business forward—what a tremendous advantage!

However, while I learn on the job, I continue to engage in licentious behavior in my personal life. Many times, I wake up bleary-eyed and soft-headed on a Sunday morning after a night of drunken debauchery. Some of this is careless youth in action, blowing off steam. I'm busting it during the week, so I deserve the time to cut loose and relieve the pressure. But at times, it's too much. There is alcohol, insecurity, and depravity—hidden at work and mostly from the view of friends, but turbulent and roiling inside me on the black nights and then defiantly fogged over by a relentless drive that pushes the demons down once a beckoning light sneaks through the blind-covered window behind my bed on another Monday morning.

Still, push though I may, the demons always seem to resurface— my abusive upbringing, failed relationships, my missing brother, lost opportunities—I carry it inside me without fully realizing how negatively dwelling in these past moments may impact my future.

Admittedly, it's hard to let go of bitter memories when we feel we've been wronged, or to forget a serious mistake when we've done wrong. But no matter the magnitude of the difficulties of the past, if we're thinking about them *after* their occurrence, it means one very important thing: we survived the experience. And since we survived, it might suggest we survived for a *reason*. Maybe it was our fate to endure *and survive* our past trials because there's something we must accomplish in the future—a reason for being, a purpose moving forward that is more important and relevant than anything that's ever come before.

I have not yet begun to consider this possibility. But I do sense there's more for me to do.

I need to get to it.

Twenty-Two
Running Down to the Riptide

Aт SOME POINT, IT makes no sense to stay. He is a broken young man who takes off running. In the early months of 1982, a decision is made, and in a fateful, fractional moment, Danny Wayne Pruitt becomes firmly and inexorably homeless.

The Department of Housing and Urban Development (HUD), a cabinet-level agency in the federal government, is charged with helping Americans meet their housing needs. They support homeownership and community development and help prevent discrimination in gaining access to affordable housing. In defining who is eligible for HUD-funded programs they include four broad categories in the definition of "homeless":

People who are living in a place not meant for human habitation, in emergency shelter, in transitional housing, or are exiting an institution where they temporarily resided.

People who are losing their primary nighttime residence, which may include a motel or hotel or a doubled-up situation, within fourteen days, and who lack the resources or support networks to remain in housing.

Families with children or unaccompanied youth who are unstably housed and likely to continue in that state.

People who are fleeing or attempting to flee domestic violence, have no other residence, and lack the resources or support networks to obtain other permanent housing.

The HUD definition explains when people are homeless. But it does not explain the individual stories or circumstances that place them there. It can be the sudden, unexpected loss of a job or an increase in expenses with insufficient income, leading to eviction. In many cases, one can be evicted by a family member. There can be abuse or mistreatment in the home. Prison time and the uncertain employment future after time served can lead to homelessness. Physical sickness, disability, or mental illness can easily put you on the streets. Drugs and alcohol can also play an important role.

Danny's path to homelessness all seems so clear, almost preordained. He's the unfortunate son of abusive and mentally ill parents. Because of this and his erratic behavior, he was evicted from the family home. He'd tried to make a life for himself on his own, but his untreated illness and the occasional cruel twist of fate have repeatedly led to failure in his quest for independence. He feels he has no control over his life. He is scared and ridden with anxiety. Unemployed and defeated, he lost hope—and with his lie, he lost Helen. Of course he ran. What other option was there?

Not long after I give him the twenty-five dollars for Billy's "arrest," Danny makes one final stop at the Salvation Army shelter in Greensboro. There he meets a man named Jimmy Payne. After a few days of getting acquainted, they decide to head to Charlotte together.

Later, Danny will have adopted the effective tactics of a seasoned hitchhiker. He will move through and across various cities and states quickly and efficiently. He will learn to travel alone, maintain personal cleanliness, keep a little money in his pocket, hold up a visible sign with a specific destination, stay off the main highways, and take a good look through the window before he climbs in the car.

But he and Jimmy know none of this when they set out on the road to Charlotte.

Danny and Jimmy have each other, but after a while, the dirt and wear of the road clings to them like fleas on a stray dog. Speeding cars carrying distracted drivers fly past their outstretched thumbs. So, they keep walking.

It's an hour and a half from Greensboro to Charlotte by car—approximately a 100-mile jaunt. Packs on backs, a hot sun beating down or a wet rain pouring, Danny and Jimmy end up walking those miles.

Soon after arriving in town, they find themselves standing in line, hoping to scrounge a bed for the night in a local Salvation Army. As they talk, a scuffle breaks out several people ahead of them. A loud discussion between two irate men grows more heated and confrontational by the minute. Suddenly, they begin to push and shove, hell-bent fists are thrown, and a knife is pulled. They dance briefly, circling each other, looking for an opening, jabbing and feinting, and then, in an instant, it happens: with a quick swipe, the smaller man slices vertically down the cheek of the larger one's face. The poor soul falls to the ground, his hands pressed to the wound, as blood gushes between his fingers. The line uniformly steps back as he lies there moaning and screaming.

A local shelter official calls the police and the medics arrive on the scene quickly. The assailant runs and the victim is carried off by an ambulance. The line mechanically reforms and two fewer people stand between the remaining shelter constituents and a bed for the night. Five minutes later, it's as if it never happened. But Jimmy and

Danny eye each other warily and another lesson is learned: Time your arrival to stand in line for shelter. Get there early, lie low while waiting, and know that sleeping outside might be a better alternative than fighting to keep your spot.

Within months they leave Charlotte and move onto Jacksonville, Florida. There, they sleep under an overpass for the first time. Danny learns that a cardboard box placed under a sleeping bag keeps you warmer than sleeping directly on the cold concrete. He also learns that many cities have temporary gathering places—labor pools where those willing to work congregate and, if lucky, find employment and desperately needed cash. Often, the work is physical and demanding.

After a brief stay in Jacksonville, he and Jimmy separate. Danny continues farther south to West Palm Beach. He learns there is Palm Beach and West Palm Beach, and they are different. There is no beach in West Palm Beach, only the Intracoastal Waterway. The beach and the "real money" lie in Palm Beach, where the rarified billionaires reside. One of three bridges must be crossed from West Palm to get into Palm Beach, and Danny walks wearily into town, looks to the east, and crosses one. He wants to see the beach, see how the rich folks live and swim in the ocean—and so he does.

There are signs up that day instructing swimmers to stay out of the water. Hot, weak, and exhausted after walking innumerable miles, he ignores them, drops his backpack, jeans, shirt, and shoes, and dives in. His body slides under the waves and the sweat and dirt of his travels are washed away by the cool rush of salty water against baked skin. Swimming just above the sand beneath him, his hair flows free, as the back of his hands touch, then separate, and he moves out farther into the deep, hidden from the red sun beneath the cover of the waves. He rises from the bottom and his head clears the water as his feet clip the sand. Temporarily refreshed, he takes a deep breath, dives back under and continues parallel to the shore, enjoying the peaceful silence, the weightlessness of his body, the passive float of tired legs. Then he rises a final time—only to realize that he's drifting backward, away from the white-sand beach and his belongings. He's caught in a powerful riptide.

Panicked, he fights his way back directly against the driving current. He fails—he was exhausted before he got in. After a vain struggle, he relents and the eastward flow carries him out even farther. Now spent and terrified, he begins to falter and sink, in the process swallowing mouthfuls of aqua-colored, salt-filled water.

But he gathers himself. Using his limited strength, he rises above the waves again, and looks toward the elusive shoreline. He sees a male and female lifeguard who, upon spotting his distress, wade out bravely, intending to help. But he's drifted out way too far, they're not going to make it. His life is his own to save—or not.

His legs nearly spent, he summons his remaining composure and dog paddles laterally for a few desperate seconds that feel like an eternity. After several strokes, he turns back toward the distant shoreline and this time finds that the current will allow him to paddle in. Yet he hesitates; his body is cramping, faltering badly. His chest and shoulders are nearly immobile, his heart is pounding, and he can barely catch his breath. But with the threat of death tugging at his wet heels, he manages several determined breast strokes while his legs hang lifelessly below the waterline.

With a final spread of his arms and a chest push forward, he reaches down with a fully extended left toe and finds shifting sand; the rolling water, at least between the waves, is now, miraculously, below his upturned face. He sucks in the salty air and with a final push forward off his left foot, extends his right leg—and suddenly both feet stand firmly atop the sandy seafloor. His neck clears the rushing, insistent waters.

He stands motionless in the churning waves, gasping for air, his insides burning from the saltwater resting in his gut. His body offers no further movement, though his feet remain anchored to the gritty sand. The lifeguards come out to meet him and together they carry him in to shore. He staggers from the water, scantily clad in his jockeys, and, exhausted, collapses to the ground.

He remains there for a few hours, occasionally sipping the bottled water the satisfied lifeguards have left behind. Eventually, he rises on still shaky legs, puts on his clothes, grabs his bag, and moves on, having survived his first brush with death.

He heads farther south, to Fort Lauderdale. There, he begins to learn skills that will help him survive his new life on the road. He learns how to do general carpentry work like cutting, drilling, nailing, fastening, and planing and how to handle tools such as chisels, saws, routers, drills, and hammers. Measuring, framing, leveling, and good old-fashioned painting are all things that allow him to work, and therefore feed himself, when he needs to. Over time, he will also add plumbing, electrical, and landscaping skills to his resume. But right now he's early in this nomadic journey, and those skills are still to come. In the interim, he takes whatever work he can find.

One week, in the dead-still air of a sweltering Florida summer, he's hired as a general helper on a commercial construction site. He works his ass off, carrying two-by-fours and bags of Quikrete and doing some rudimentary painting throughout several ten-hour workdays. The local shelter only allows a single-night stay, so he finds a vacant lot behind a local business to sleep before rising early the next morning to do it all over again.

At the end of a third particularly brutal workday, he finds an outdoor shower on the beach, washes, wolfs down bread and a can of pork n' beans, and under dark skies rolls out his Walmart sleeping bag next to the deserted building, and passes out.

In a quiet, deep part of the night, he is abruptly awakened by a hard tug at his foot. He rolls over, looks up through bleary eyes, and is jarred awake by the sight of a leering man standing over him who then turns and takes off running toward the city sidewalks.

Oh shit, he thinks, *he's got my backpack!*

He groggily and much too slowly gets to his feet to give chase.

They're running full speed down side streets when the man turns left, heading further away from the ocean and deeper into urban sprawl. There's little noise except their footfalls touching asphalt. Danny is sure he can run him down and persists in the effort for what seems like at least a mile, but the man, simply too fast, turns a sharp right and is gone into the night.

This is trouble. He still has his sleeping bag but everything else he owns is gone. Most importantly, he's lost his driver's license and social security card. After this sorry episode, he'll learn to keep his wallet (with cash and ID) in his pocket. But for now, he's got a problem. Without identification, jobs are hard to come by.

He goes to the local Social Security Administration to get a new card, but to get it, he needs ID. After a few days, he swallows his pride and calls Helen. He assures her he's all right but needs his birth certificate. He says he'll keep in touch and asks her to send it to a local mission where he can pick it up. She does so, and, along with Pop, is simply happy to know he is alive and well in Fort Lauderdale—at least for now.

Twenty-Three
The Second Speech

ONE DAY AT WORK Terry walks into my office with a new challenge, one that feels daunting and well beyond my capabilities. It's time for our annual meeting with the district and retail store managers across the country. All field personnel and home office staff, including our GM and, possibly, the CEO and CFO of Kayser-Roth, will be at an off-site conference at a local hotel. In the past, Terry, as our finance head, has presented our financial results from the prior year. He's stood confidently on stage, spotlights bearing down on him, to make the hour-long presentation. But he wants me to give the presentation this year. He's a great boss—giving a young subordinate a chance to lead. But I've never stood up in front of people to speak before, and it's the most important meeting of the year for the business.

In the retail world, there are home office personnel who are bright and competent in their own right, but then you have the people who do the real work of retail—those who work on the front lines in the store, interacting with the customers on a day-in, day-out basis—and one way many retailers and their leaders serve these key associates is to bring them into the home office on an annual basis to review the results of the prior year and discuss the game plan for the upcoming year. It's a wonderful—and important—opportunity to get the team on the same page, lift morale, build camaraderie, and inspire future performance.

Thus, with great nervousness, I begin to prepare the numbers and my thoughts. I don't know what I'm going to do with the presentation, how I'm going to approach it, but I do know I'm not going to stand up there and mechanically regurgitate numbers. I've seen this done before and it's a slog, an exercise in monotony that is forgotten within minutes. If I can get the words out without my voice quaking in fear—and it's a big if—then I need to find words that will inform my colleagues about the past and at the same time focus us on our future. I need to deliver a message that will stay with the team and direct activity in the new year. This much I know.

But I'm completely terrified at the thought of doing it. I go to Terry and try to back out, suggesting weakly, but sincerely, that the company will be better served if he takes the reins. He ignores my request and pushes me forward.

The challenge of effectively commanding the spotlight, of believing I have something important to say, sets me thinking about how incredibly difficult it is for those of us that are beaten down to rise up. Some people have a gift, a natural comfort level with public speaking. But most of us don't. And really, does anyone not think that a child who is told they can be anything or do anything is better equipped to do just that? The alternative is a child who's told they'll never amount to anything. Overcoming detractors, particularly a parental one when you're young, is jarring and difficult. At an early age, you have no life experience to define any truth other than the one you're told. So you believe it. Breaking past that negative self-belief is the first mountain that those of us who are abused must climb to better ourselves.

It's not easy. Self-doubt creeps into key life-changing

decisions—still critical choices must be made. Are we willing to risk failure in the search for success? Will we put ourselves out there and give it our all, or remain hidden and safe from the damning judgments we've been trained to expect? Do we believe in who and what we can one day be?

While the well-loved child hears a cheering section saying, "Yes, you can, you can do anything, you can be anything!" we the abused run the race of life carrying the inner echo of damning voices that persist and hiss, "You'll never make it, you can't do it!" Because of this, some of us don't even run; we just step aside, ignore the starter's gun, and settle for an easier, less descript, less accomplished road to the right, or we weakly attempt the race and then die on that mountain of self-doubt.

In the end, positive self-belief is tethered to meaningful life accomplishment like a horse to a buggy, and until that first hoof moves the wheels will lie still.

And me? I've been fighting the urge to step back, to hide, all my life. Under the abuse of my father, I didn't feel I belonged up there on the mountaintop, looking down on the dark valleys I've left behind, and I'm not sure what has changed—even today. It's as if I'm hiding some big secret that's about to be discovered, I'm a pretender trying to run up this hill and the real truth—the one hundred or so people will see tomorrow afternoon—is that I ain't worth a shit for nothin' and I oughta take that lower, easier road to the right.

It's 4:00 p.m. on Tuesday. Our GM speaks at two—setting the tone for the next few days, outlining the specific goals for the meeting, and sounding off on the critical themes for the upcoming year. He's followed by our Director of Stores, who begins to narrow the scope, laying out the important tactics and the general role of store personnel in helping the team reach its goals for the year.

Finally, it's my turn.

I'm perched low and far in the back of the slope-floored, multi-rowed theater auditorium. My eyes are bleary from a sleepless night and seem to be above me looking down on my trembling frame, my shaking hands. My mind is functioning but only on adrenalized fear. I look around and see it's a packed house. Unfortunately, I have a good, long walk before getting to the steps at the foot of the stage that lead up to the bright lights.

I make it without tripping, thank God, then it's three steps up and onto a wooden platform, upon which the podium sits stage right. There is silence as I stride forward, but once I climb up on stage the GM chimes in and suggests the group take five while my presentation is readied on the screen.

This leaves me fiddling with the remote, checking the visuals, and mulling over what I'm about to do on the stage. I shuffle papers and stew in my anxiety for what seems like the five longest minutes of my life—I feel like the second man up at a French guillotine. I look down on the audience, at that moment milling around, grabbing food from tables set up in the back, and chatting in casual conversation, many greeting one another for the first time in a year. I can't say I'm reflecting on my life path to this point or making a mental list of my many inadequacies; in fact, I'm trying very hard not to do that. Instead, I'm mechanically making sure I have all my notes in order and making aimless conversation with my coworker who is there to troubleshoot any technical issues that might occur with the remote, the microphone, etc. God help me if that happens.

The GM calls the meeting back to order and introduces me. As I look up from my notes, I see all eyes on me, and I pray my fear is somehow hidden from the audience's attentive gaze. Feeling those eyes and the weight of my responsibility leaves me with a dry throat and, unfortunately, a blank mind. I'm wearing a white button-down shirt, a red tie, a blue jacket, and khaki slacks. I'm most thankful for the T-shirt I have under my button-down that masks the flop sweat rolling under my arms and gathering on my back and stomach.

"G-g-good afternoon and w-welcome," I stammer.

My fear is no longer a secret. They know.

"I'd like to mirror Joe's comments and tell you how happy I am to see everyone, p-p-particularly those who've traveled a long way to be h-h-here," I continue with visible uncertainty. "What I want to do in my time today is walk you through our results from last year, give you a f-f-flavor for what went right, what could've gone b-b-better, and have us talk through some of these issues as we think about the t-t-t-task in front of us for the upc-c-c-coming year ahead."

Dammit! I can't get a hold of my nerves.

My face betrays my genuine discomfort, and I can see the audience shifting in their seats. My internal struggle and unabashed fear lie clear and naked before the group. I can see the pained expressions on the faces, some of which I know quite well, including Terry's. How bad, how uncomfortable, is this thing going to be?

I turn sideways to the audience, look to my right and over my shoulder, and as I study the numbers on the company's profit and loss statement, comparing our actual results to our budget and the year before, a funny thing happens: I remember that I love this business, I love retail, and I love the numbers, because I believe, if properly explained and understood, they tell a story that should be heard, particularly by those who impact the results—*and* I'm extremely well prepared. I begin to lose myself in the narrative. It's an amazing life moment because when I need it most, I find the latent but resolute strength of my conviction. My voice stops quivering. My knees stop knocking. My sweat dries.

As a team, we did tremendous work last year. But there is more work to be done. It's my job to help focus our efforts and it all starts with our sales results, our only negative. But I do not want to go in that direction right away. A better story is our margins, which are up significantly. We cut our inventory, refined our product assortment, and improved quality throughout our stores, from display work to customer engagement. I congratulate the team on these gains.

I next focus on the dramatic variability in sales performance by store, mainly due to our high turnover in the store management position. I make the case that if we can reduce the turnover, fill that critical leadership role more effectively, we can attack our sales problem. This is our biggest challenge—the pivotal problem to be solved if we want to open more stores and begin to grow the business more rapidly. I see heads nod in unison. Our HR Director gives me an affirmative thumbs up.

In preparation for this presentation, I analyzed the business thoroughly, strengthened my understanding of some key areas, and identified a few business levers we can pull to make a difference in the upcoming year. I proceed to share what I learned from that exercise now. I'm confident no one expected me to have this level of strategic and tactical understanding. But in this moment—my coming-out moment—I decide to show everyone who I am: a dedicated member of the team who is also a student of the business; someone who can paint with a small brush, providing both detail and insight, but can also, given the chance, wield a roller and impact the larger picture. Point by point, my shared insights create immediate questions and stimulate conversation about possible actions to improve the business.

At times, I stand quietly on stage as thoughts are exchanged by the group. I interject when clarity or support for a proposition is needed. After a while, critical discussion ends. I summarize my final thoughts, issuing concise reminders of the key issues we've just covered, and then end my presentation.

The group gives me a large, well-sustained round of applause. I exit the stage and return to my seat in the back. During the break, several members of the team come up to congratulate me, to ask other questions. I feel the acceptance, the respect of my peers. I feel a self-worth that is strange and new to me. It is also intoxicating. And amazingly, the thing I've feared professionally perhaps more than anything else is done, and I'm pretty sure it's been done damn well. I've just started my run up the mountain.

As far as my career goes, I will never again look back to the flat, easy road on the right. I don't know for sure if I will make this climb successfully, but I for some reason suspect that I might. In that hour I just spent on stage, I learned the strength of using an analytical mind, the value of contemplated preparation, and the power of informed, sincere, direct, and aspirational communication.

Later that evening, I drift off peacefully into a deep sleep—no nightmares, no bad memories—knowing a big corner in my professional career has been successfully turned. Screw it, I may be worth something after all.

Twenty-Four
Meet the Family

HER FULL NAME IS Paula Ann McClenny, and while she was born in Rantoul, Illinois, she was brought up primarily in Goldsboro, North Carolina. She actually lived in several different places during her youth—her dad was a master sergeant in the Air Force and mobility was part of the job. But Goldsboro was her home for several years before she was accepted at UNC-Chapel Hill. Four short years later, she landed in Greensboro, mainly because her older brother lived there.

Her mother's family are mostly from Texas, ranging from San Antonio in the south to farther north in Dallas, and all are of Mexican or Spanish descent. They are a large, loud, proud, welcoming clan—a family unit that values each other and their time spent together. Her father's family are farmers from the rural area of Turkey in eastern North Carolina. They are simple country folks, but what they lack in sophistication they make up for in their kind nature. She has two older brothers, Doug and John, who are seven and eight years older than her, which means she was raised as an only child for a portion of her adolescence.

Her parents are warm, kind, intelligent people who raised their children well. They love unconditionally and exerted a positive influence on the trajectory of their lives. They are sincere in their religious beliefs and are always there when they are supposed to be—on birthdays, graduations, anniversaries, and the arrival of new grandchildren. Paula grew up in what seemed to be an idyllic situation. This, of course, was a bit different from what I experienced in my youth. But somehow it doesn't matter. She is smart, kind, honest, and a good listener. She is also strong and beautiful. She has a propensity for doing the right thing. And while the right thing might be unclear to some, with the values she's been given it is not unclear to her. She has a definite perspective and a firm point of view. She believes what she believes and lives her life accordingly. There is no falsity or hypocrisy to her.

From our first date, I sense her strength and resiliency. I'm also very aware of the baggage I carry with me—the painful memories of ridicule and abuse, the emotional scars. I will not be a walk in the park to deal with. It will be constant work for me to move my life forward. I know I need someone who can step up and face the challenges of life with me and shoulder their portion of the load.

As I look into her eyes, I wonder, *Can I keep my demons down and be the strong and true husband a good woman, maybe this good woman, most definitely deserves?*

The truth is, I don't know.

Before proposing, I'm a wreck. Hiding from her, dodging her calls, wallowing in my fear that I can't give her what she wants, needs, deserves. It has been two years and I know she is the one. Paula calls me one day, upset by my absence and sudden distance. She thinks I want to break up, when in fact all I want is her. I propose, and thankfully, she accepts.

But I have a shame I carry about my past that has to be managed.

She has already met Pop and Helen, who have both been on their best behavior for the most part during our courtship. I've told her just a few stories of my youth with Pop, and she knows it was very different from her own, but she doesn't entirely understand the implications for both of us. And now there's more that she must learn: it's time for her to meet my mother.

It's been nine years since I saw Mama standing naked in that lonely house, staring back at me, daring me to come in. I find her number, call, and set a time for her to meet with us on a Saturday afternoon. The initial phone conversation is brief and awkward. Neither of us knows what to say. I tell her that I'm getting married, that I'd like her to meet my fiancée. She is amenable and quickly agrees to the meeting. She wants to know the exact day and time we're coming by, telling me she has to get her hair ready. I don't share any details of my life—where I am, what I'm doing—and she doesn't ask.

I also don't ask about hers. I assume she will tell me how bad things are, that she's barely making it, and I have no room in my heart or life to hear it, no desire or willingness to try and help. I don't know what that makes me. I want to be a good man, but I'm clearly not a good son. I wish I felt something, but I don't. I hang up the phone and think about what I'm trying to accomplish by bringing the woman I love to meet the mother who didn't love me. The truth is that part of Mama lives inside me and, if God so blesses the two of us, may one day live in our children. *Full disclosure*, I think. Paula has a right to know who I am, where I come from. She is strong and she loves me. *She'll understand*, I tell myself.

On the appointed day, we hold hands as we walk up the pavement and turn left into the small stucco building that houses Mama's apartment. Hers is the first one on the left and the complex itself, while not run down, is low-income housing. It's clean and quiet out-side as I step forward to knock.

After a moment, I hear feet shuffle to the door. There's a small peephole in its upper center and I suspect she gets a look at me before I get to see her. Finally, she opens it up with a smile on her face and issues an enthusiastic invitation for us to come in.

Paula steps inside first, and I follow. A few feet in, I turn to see my mother immediately lock and deadbolt the door behind us. The first thing I see is fear. Then I take a closer look. She's aged a bit beyond her years, and her height has been stunted by the passage of time. Her posture, formerly erect and upright, is now tilted. Her shoulders slope forward but her neck and body remain thin, except for a small pot-belly around her middle. Her brown hair is darker, thinner, and more wiry than I remember. It's also dyed and coiffed, but unkempt at its edges—her appearance and her reality are one and the same.

She's wearing white pants and a striped blue-white blouse and looks a bit like the nurse she never became. Her eyes have retained their vivid blue and her skin has paled whiter due to age and, I sus-pect, some level of reclusiveness.

My mother appears to live quietly in a narrow rectangle. From right to left, there is a small, square kitchen partially enclosed by a breakfast bar. It flows into a narrow sitting area where a loveseat and easy chair rest snugly in front of a nineteen-inch Phillips. The love-seat has a tear in its fake leather arm, though it's partially covered by a white afghan with a red rose in the center surrounded by a narrow green border.

Paula and I each take a seat on the red rose. Mama sits in the easy chair across from us.

Right away, my mother notices herself in me: "Look at those purty blue eyes," she says.

I acknowledge the compliment and then introduce her to Paula.

Mama is cordial but continues to focus her attention on me. "You've gotten tall, and your hair's just as purty," she says. "And your face is all cleared up."

I shrug off her words, a bit embarrassed, and she finds my modesty funny. I hear the familiar cackle, "Hee, hee, hee, hee"—a laugh that is a bit too loud and goes on too long.

"Is your Mama embarrassing you?" she asks.

Paula and I exchange glances, and I can't help but note the rather large steak knife on the kitchen countertop by the sink, just past the dead-bolted door to my right. It reminds me of a similar sight nine years ago: her sitting naked and alone in the chair, the knife resting on the countertop. *Am I afraid of her?* I ask myself. *No*, I decide. But I can't discount her range of possible behaviors.

I recall the story of her hitting Billy with a dust mop, putting a gash in the side of his head all those years ago that required three stitches. Sadly, there is some part of her that's just off; I've seen it. And I've accepted it. I also have Pop's pragmatic instincts. If she goes for the knife, for whatever reason, I won't be surprised, and I'll be ready to deal with it. I refocus on my mother and try to connect.

I tell her about Paula, how we met, when we're getting married and even ask if she'd like to come to the wedding.

"Oh no," she responds. "I have nothing to wear, and your mama looks a sight."

I tell her what I do for a living—that I'm a licensed CPA, that I work at Kayser Roth—and that I'm about to buy a house in the central part of Greensboro for Paula and me to live in. None of it seems to register. It's as if I never told her my story because she's preoccupied with her own. She talks about the apartment we're sitting in, her general living circumstances, how the government doesn't provide quite enough for her to make it. She doesn't even have enough money for her makeup, she says.

But she doesn't ask for my help—not this time. Does she remember the last time she asked back in college, when I refused, when I hung up on her? I'm guessing she doesn't. Watching and listening to her, I'm beginning to understand now. It's not about me. It was never about me. She doesn't have it in her. And because she doesn't have it in her, I no longer have it in me. I'm simply checking this off my list, making sure Paula understands and is okay with this part of who I am.

She makes her attempt to talk to Mama, but the answers she gets are stilted and the lingering silence is uncomfortable and awkward for both of us. Mama doesn't ask, but I tell her that Billy is fine and lives in an apartment just a few miles from her. I tell her I think Danny is somewhere down in Florida, though I don't know exactly where. This elicits little reaction as she continues to stare at me. She doesn't seem angry or dismissive. She's smiling. But why does she keep staring? Is she curious about what her tumultuous time with Pop wrought? Is there pride in what she sees? No, I remind myself, that's false hope. Whatever part of her brain that hears voices and sees imaginary visages replaced the part that feels the deepest human connection in the world, that of a mother to their child. I'm now convinced of it. And there's no cost to her, no note of the loss of this part of her humanity. She doesn't even know it exists.

In the end, the loss lies with me, the child. But I don't mourn or feel pity for myself. Wallowing in that emotion will destroy me. Sitting here, right now, with my vacant, empty mother, I reach a pivotal understanding: Her love for me is missing. But that won't stop me from loving Paula or being who I'm meant to be or reaching the goals I set for myself. Her absence can't be a crutch, an excuse, or a roadblock. The world is still mine, open and available. I have to work hard, be assertive, use my talents, trust my abilities, and encourage the inner voice that tells me I can be special in my own way, that I can achieve and succeed. The same God that gave Mama her damning voices seems to have given me one of my own, one that dominates and drowns out all the negative voices from the past that tell me I can't do it. It's a gift, this singular voice. I don't know why it's been given to me—or why, it seems, my brothers don't have it. I only know I have to use it, cling to it, act on its calming rejoinders, push any other weaker impulses aside. I have to act on behalf of myself, my soon-to-be wife, and a possible larger family to come. And I do so, now.

I rise from the loveseat and pull Paula up with me. I thank Mama for seeing us, and I remind her to take care of herself. She doesn't ask if she'll see me again, and I make no effort to falsely reassure her. I don't know the answer, and right now, it doesn't matter. We see ourselves to the door. I stop to hug her—not without some feeling, some recognition of the possible finality of the moment, but my inner voice quickly sweeps it aside.

The door closes behind us, and we head to the car.

In the short walk, I'm lost in lonely, contemplative thought—and then I feel Paula's hand reach for mine. Our eyes meet and she smiles, and I know she's still with me. I know she understands what it all did to me—how it's still a part of me now, even today—and with that one heartfelt touch, I get back a little piece of what I've been missing for all these years.

Twenty-Five
Peach Field

DANNY'S OLD PALS JIMMY and David are in South Carolina and he decides to make his way there now. They find work in the labor pools in Columbia, but nothing that will add real dollars to their empty wallets.

One early morning in the pool gathering area, a large, brown-toothed gentleman—a no-nonsense, thick-necked brute in a rickety, old-model F-150 pickup truck—pulls the three of them aside and says he has plenty of work picking peaches. It's a four-day job, and meals, showers, plus sleeping quarters are provided as part of the deal. He assures them they'll each get paid well when the job is done. It sounds good, so the three of them throw their bags in the back of the truck and hop in. They ride a long way, for over an hour, down winding, rolling, aged country roads, before eventually turning right onto a long, sticky, dirt-clay trail in the middle of nowhere, green fields of thick vegetation spreading out to the left and right.

It's the kind of unrelenting day you find in early August in the south. The heat rises from the pock-filled dirt path in shimmering waves that reflect off a white-blue sky. Danny hangs his arm out the front window as the truck rumbles down the dirt path and the sun reacts harshly, punishing the skin on his upper arm. He drops his pink limb back inside the truck. The trail widens now and he sees the beautiful salmon, yellow, and green of the linear peach fields open up before him. Its beauty, however, is deceptive. The fruit sits high and delicate in the trees but one must extend far and grasp gently to steal it from the branch, all under a merciless sun that does not reward the effort.

The truck finally stops, and after getting instructions from the driver, they join several others already hard at work in the orchard in picking the mostly ripened peaches. There looks to be twenty-five to thirty mostly Black and Latino workers in the orchard, on their feet or up on ladders, gently dropping peaches into baskets as the irrigation sprinklers intermittently line the trees and fill the air with a wet mist that heightens the scent of the fruit and mixes with the salty sweat of the laborers.

Danny moves to his assigned row, cradling the ladder on his right hip. He sets up on level ground beside the first tree and climbs up five steps, moving higher and closer to the heat, less hidden from the sweltering sun. He pulls his cap low and tight on his head to spare his face from the burn. Still, he must diligently reach highest for the fully ripened ones and his face absorbs the brunt of the effort. Sweat pours off him in thin but persistent streams.

He takes the occasional break to gulp ladled water from one of the tin tubs scattered throughout the field, then climbs back up his ladder to continue the work. He makes his way down the row, one tree at a time.

Progress and time move slowly. By early evening, his shorts and T-shirt cling to his dehydrated, sunburned limbs. At 7:00 p.m., work is called.

He staggers over to check in with the boss man, who is talking to the crew by the building just north of the fields that Danny assumes will be their accommodations for the night. The man says that inside the building they'll find several bunk beds along the back wall; they are to pick one of their choosing. Showers are located in the building as well, so help themselves. Food will be served at 8:00 p.m.—they'll eat at the picnic tables outside.

Danny heads inside, showers quickly, then goes back out to fill up on beans and tortillas. He sees David and Jimmy and plops down beside them to share his meal. As they talk, he takes note of the large pots and burners where the bosses are gathered, and for the first time notices that each of them is carrying a gun. He ponders this troublesome fact for a moment, then heads back inside and climbs up on the bunk bed he chose earlier. Exhausted from the heat and effort of the day, he's out before his friends can even get back inside. He sleeps fitfully.

In his dream, he is brought back to a long-ago Saturday evening in Greensboro. Daddios, a local disco bar, is open for business. He's a divorced man now and for some reason the damn girls have always liked him. He likes them back. He finished his shift at the pizza parlor a few minutes ago and he's ready to party now. He's meeting his buddy over at his house at eight, and they'll make the drive to High Point Road and Daddios together.

As he heads inside to clean up, he considers how much he hates that he's back home with Pop. But it'll have to do for now. And recently, there's been a change in the rules. Due to Helen's positive input, he's now allowed to take a shower instead of a tub bath, though he has to do so quickly. And he does—the water runs less than five minutes, he's sure of it. It feels good to get the smell of work off him after a long day of cooking pizza.

He puts on his underwear and jeans and, shirtless, heads back to the bathroom. He plugs in the blow dryer in the outlet above the sink, cranks up the heat, and begins to style his hair. His thoughts wander to a blonde he met the other night. They hit it off, and he thinks he might have a shot with her. She had beautiful brown eyes and man . . .

BAM!! The blow dryer is slapped out of his hand. He watches it crash to the ground, and suddenly Pop is on him.

"Boy, you been running that damn blow dryer for at least fifteen minutes!" he screams.

Shocked by this sudden, out-of-nowhere assault, he backs up.

"Pop, it hasn't been that long. I'm almost—"

Pop's sucker punch hits him under the left eye—a straight right that staggers him backward. His butt bounces against the sink and the back of his head smacks off the mirror. He is stunned, unable to respond. He instinctively puts his hand to his eye.

Pop reaches over his shoulder, unplugs the cord, and tosses it onto the floor underneath the sink on top of the fallen dryer.

"Boy, you're back in here, living off of me, running up my damn electricity, and I'm putting a stop to it."

Danny stands, back to the mirror, taut but with a slight tremble, in the close quarters of the small bathroom.

Pop steps forward, lifts his balled fist, and puts it, knuckles first, directly in his face.

"Boy, you might be too old for me to whip your ass, but I can use this instead. You keep that dryer on for less than five minutes, ya heah me?"

Danny nods his head yes.

Pop exits the bathroom quickly. Danny picks up the dryer, wraps the cord around its neck, and carries it back to the bedroom. He puts on his shirt, runs out the back door, and goes to meet his buddy. He gets too drunk that night at the disco. The blonde never shows. He sleeps at his friend's house and comes back late Sunday evening, when he knows Pop is already back in his bedroom asleep. He sneaks back to his room quickly and closes the door. He closes his eyes, including his bruised left one, and hides under the blankets from his father.

Another day in the peach field passes. The work is slow but progress is steady. Sweat and dirt cover Danny's body at the end of the day. There are no dreams on the second night; his mind and body won't allow it.

On the third day, at it again, bright and early, he goes hard until 10:30 a.m., when they're given a fifteen-minute break. He gulps down ladled water, sits for a couple of minutes, then decides to relieve himself and hoofs it quickly to the building.

As he unzips, he becomes aware of loud voices by the open window behind him on the back wall of the bathroom. It sounds like an argument. After zipping up, he walks over and discreetly peeks out the window. He sees two men standing tautly, face to face, toe to toe.

"Your pickings were small," one says. "And you screwed up—you picked a bunch of green peaches."

The other man angrily calls bullshit. As instructed, he pulled only those that gave slightly when gently squeezed. The peaches he picked and dropped off looked like all the other peaches in the barrels, he maintains.

He hotly demands his money, but the other man coldly suggests he might think about calming his skinny ass down. In fact, the man says, since he's done such a shitty job, picking the unripe produce and costing him money in the process, he'll have to stay overnight again tonight and pick more good ones tomorrow, just to break even! And don't forget, he says, you owe me for room and board—"That shit ain't free," he reminds him.

As he delivers his rebuke, his fellow henchmen stand close by, ready to step forward with bad intentions.

This bullshit is rigged! Danny realizes. They're going to work the piss out of them, then nickel and dime their way out of paying. *I'm just frickin' slave labor!* He moves to the sink, rinses his hands and face, then slowly rubs cool water on the back of his reddened, scorched neck. *Think, dammit*, he tells himself. He steps out of the john, looks into the blinding sun, and briefly considers a drastic, risky move, like grabbing his backpack and getting up out of there right now.

Then, pragmatically, he takes a closer look at the other pickers and his desolate surroundings. Six trucks are parked just off the peach fields, and at best guess thirty pickers are heading back up the hill. Only he is left behind. If he goes inside to grab his backpack, he will be confronted, stopped, just like the other poor sap. Plus, these men are armed, and he has David and Jimmy to think about. No, he's stuck for now.

All of them are captives in a labor trafficking operation. He was tricked into coming here and working his ass off just like these other poor bastards. He eyeballs the bosses, most of them milling around the trucks, while simultaneously eyeing the straggling crew as they head back up to the peach trees. He locks eyes with the brutish driver, who quickly returns his glance, and the look that passes between them tells the story of his betrayal and their captivity.

"Better get your ass up that hill, time's wastin'," the man says.

Danny turns and slow-walks the nasty incline through the late morning's wavy heat, inundated by the foul smell of the dirt and sweat sticking fast to his body.

He gets back to the trees, climbs his ladder and begins to pull off more peaches. But he now has one thing on his mind: grabbing David and Jimmy and getting the hell out of there—tonight. *This is the occasional shitstorm of life on the road*, he thinks. *Some people are kind to you, some will just plain shit on you, and some might even be willing to kill you.*

The question is: Is he just being shit on here, or is it something worse? The best thing he can do, he decides, is to work his ass off the rest of the day while attracting no suspicion. He'll talk with David and Jimmy at lunch break and do some further intel tonight.

They exit the fields a bit before seven and as he glances around at the dirt-laden, motley bunch of fools, he sees a few eyes looking around with the same restlessness he feels, while the rest are vacant, droopy-eyed, resigned, ready for blessed sleep, still willing to deal with the prospect of picking peaches in the hot inferno that will be their fate early tomorrow morning.

The sun is setting as daylight begins to fade. He grabs gym shorts and a T-shirt from his bag, clothes a man can sleep or run in, and heads over to shower. He talked with David and Jimmy at lunch, told them what he heard in the bathroom and suggested they feel out a few other pickers to see what they know. Time to find out what they learned.

The reports they share over dinner tell the same story: There's a lot of work and, so far, no money. They agree—they'll sneak out tonight. He watches the armed bosses pull out one by one that evening as he sits quietly at one of the picnic tables. All six trucks leave, and he thinks—though he's not sure—that the men and the guns leave with them.

It's now almost 2:00 a.m. and pitch-black outside. One dim overhead light remains lit, on the ceiling at the far-left corner of the bunk area, which is why he perched himself near the door on the far right. He does not know who, if anyone, is keeping an eye on the workers as they sleep, but he assumes there might be someone. He lies quietly on his lower bunk, never closing his eyes. He stashed his backpack under his bed earlier. He's deathly afraid. But he pushes the fear aside, gathers himself, then quietly rises from the bed, reaches under it, grabs his bag, and makes his way to the door on the right.

Cautiously, he steps outside. There's a floodlight at each corner of the building. This is the moment, if someone is watching, that he'll be stopped and confronted. He turns the corner and moves to the side of the barracks to escape the light. He holds his breath but sees no movement, no response—all remains quiet and still. He snatches up his backpack, puts each arm through a strap, then pulls the drawstring on both until the pack rests tightly against his back. *Dear God,* he thinks, *what have I gotten myself into?*

He considers moving to his left, heading out into the tall grass, dropping to the ground, and crawling on his belly until he escapes the floodlights. Instead, he peeks around to the front of the building, sees the coast is clear, takes a deep breath, and, after muttering to himself a quick "fuck it," darts up the hill to the dirt road. There will be some visibility for about a hundred yards but the farther he gets from the floodlights the blacker it will become.

He continues sprinting down the dirt road. When he reaches what he believes to be a safe enough distance, he looks back to see if he's being pursued. Nothing. He turns and runs some more until minutes later, in complete darkness, he stops and pulls out his small flashlight. He flips the switch and, thirty yards up, sees two poor bastards that are running up out of there same as him. They look back but keep moving, heading toward the same country road and the same freedom he's looking for. *Nobody will believe this shit,* he thinks.

The plan is to find Jimmy and David in Columbia tomorrow. Hopefully they'll make it out fine too, but he'll worry about them later. For now, he keeps moving, and a half-hour later he makes it to the country road. He turns left to make his way back toward the city and hopefully shelter. But he won't make it tonight.

Twenty-Six
Lima Beans and CFOs

PAULA AND I MARRY on October 14, 1989. We get back from our honeymoon and settle down in our newly purchased home. But I quickly become restless in my professional career. I like Rolane, and the people and possible opportunities in the larger Kayser Roth Corporation. But I'm a married man now and may be a father in the future; I need to find a job that I'm passionate about, a job where I can give my best efforts with the possibility of achieving real success and security for my family.

I hear about a retail controller position for a company called Performance Bicycle. After college, I bought a high-end, carbon-frame road bike that I pedaled all over the streets of Greensboro for about a year, and I thoroughly enjoyed it. Bikes seem so much more exciting to me than socks and pantyhose, the main products made and sold at Kayser Roth. I also like the fact that it's in Chapel Hill, not Greensboro. I have a lot of memories in this town and not all of them are good. So I update my resume and apply for the position.

I don't hear anything for a while, but one day at work I get the call to come for an interview. I have my chance.

The company is located on the southern outskirts of Chapel Hill on US 15-501 South, heading toward Pittsboro. It's much smaller than Kayser Roth ($30-40 million in revenue vs. $800 million) but they're a young company, and they're growing. I drive up and meet the head of accounting and we hit it off—her questions are straight-forward and direct. After we talk, she sends me to the founder and CEO, Garry Snook. Garry is an average-size man, with heavy pepper and light salt hair. He looks fit and solid and has bright eyes that give me the sense that wheels are turning rapidly behind his direct, if preoccupied, stare. Within moments, I know this is a different ball game.

His rapid-fire delivery of questions signals that he is smart, asser-tive, tough, and no-nonsense. He suffers no fools and gives off a vibe of being the stereotypical "smartest guy in the room." It's actually no vibe—time will prove his smart-guy status to be legit.

Garry tells me the company has a problem and he wants to know if I can help him solve it. They're having tremendous shrink prob-lems—that is, inventory is being lost or stolen in the stores and it's killing profit. I tell him I'm sure I can help. He tells me he wants to be the largest cycling retailer in the US, then maybe sell the company or take it public sometime in the future. I learn he isn't a hard-core cyclist but is very financially astute. As a finance guy myself, he will be my toughest critic. Before starting the bike business, he was head-ing for his Ph.D in finance at Duke University.

Reflecting later that night at home after the interview, my gut says Garry is good at what he does. I might want to work with him.

A month or so later, I get the call and accept the offer. I say a respect-ful good-bye to Terry, my first and probably most important profes-sional mentor. I'm now twenty-nine years old.

I begin my new job as controller of the retail division of Performance Bike in March 1990. Performance has roughly ten stores in just a few states and is just getting that part of the business off the ground. Meanwhile, the direct mail side of the business is growing rapidly, with management expertise already in place. Right away, I sense the difference between Performance and the prior companies I've worked for—an energy and enthusiasm that I haven't seen before. The growth and leadership are inspiring. The retail operations are a bit of a mess, however, and I know that Garry is expecting me to fix it—the exorbitant shrinkage has to be stopped. It's costing the company a fortune. I put my focus there.

With the support of the retail operations team, I begin to implement change. Culturally, these changes are a big deal for our bicycle-riding, non-traditional retail store managers—and they fight me, hard. But with the support of retail leadership and my face-to-face persuasion skills, after we bring in all the managers to Chapel Hill for our annual meeting, they gradually buy in.

Within the first year, the shrink results get significantly better— down to about 1 percent of sales from almost 5 percent of sales. Dollar-wise this is a huge savings for the company, and store managers are now making more money as well since they are partially bonused on shrink results. It's a win for everyone. I have a store manager tell me he has never seen so much change implemented so quickly and successfully. Our director of stores, who fought me on a lot of the changes, calls and apologizes. He becomes a full supporter as we move forward.

One day, Garry, who is a little bit of a mad scientist operating effectively behind the scenes, comes down to my small corner office, shakes my hand, and congratulates me for the great improvement in results. True to form, he also asks how I will get it below 1 percent in the future. It's a lot of pressure, but I'm having a ball at Performance. I'm adding value and gaining a real sense of accomplishment.

But then, one day at work, I get a phone call from Kayser Roth. Terry has decided to leave and move to a CFO position at a freight company. The controller slot is now open. They tell me it's mine if I want it. They send me an excellent offer in writing.

I have a big decision to make.

I inform my immediate boss in accounting and the head of the retail stores of my situation. I want to stay at Performance, but from a dollar standpoint, it makes no sense for me to do so. Not wanting to lose me, they arrange a meeting with Garry, who not only offers to exceed the salary I've been offered by Kayser Roth but also to cover the loss I'm taking on that sale of my house in Greensboro.

I happily accept his kind offer. But now I have something to prove to Garry Snook. I will make it my business to do just that.

Paula and I decide to sell our home and move into an apartment in Chapel Hill. With this decision, I fully commit to Performance.

My talented peers in accounting and I find a way to reduce the time to close the books from thirty days to five and produce a sophisticated financial model that allows Performance to triple the size of its line of credit with the local bank. This provides critical capital needed to fuel high growth in the years ahead.

One good day Garry promotes me to director over the entire accounting area. Fully empowered, the team and I renegotiate various large contracts, significantly cutting expenses, and institute a new annual budgeting process, along with monthly departmental budget review meetings—cutting more costs. Over time, other areas of the business—including our distribution center and our small manufacturing operation, where we make our own branded cycling clothing—are placed under my wing. The team and I begin to drive effective change there as well.

There are things I still need to learn, but I'm on my way. Things are going well and I believe I'm capable of doing even more. I also think I can help us grow the business. So I ask to meet with Garry.

I tell him I love working at Performance and am demanding nothing, but I think I can and should be the CFO. I then lay out my case, citing what I've done and what I think I can do in the future. My only ask is that if he decides to say no, he tells me why and lets me know which specific areas I need to target for future growth. He gives me a good listen but does not commit.

That night at home as Paula and I finish our dinner, I think to myself, *If he'll just give me a shot, I know I can do it*—and immediately I wonder where this unshakable belief in myself in the business world comes from. Yes, I've had some success in my still-burgeoning career and have fought my way to a better place from a pitiless, desperate early life, but in the quiet, ink black hours of a fretful night or in the unwanted light of an early-morning advance, I'm still plagued by self-doubt and bad memories. Yet somehow I always wake up, a new day arrives, and straightaway I'm at work, focused, intent, looking to get the job done—no obstacle too big, no challenge unachievable.

Maybe, I think, *I'm just a driven man guided by a rigid work ethic born from a father who lived it.* But no, it's not that simple; in truth, I'm more driven by his words—words that were intended to ridicule and humiliate but have instead become fodder for relentless intensity, energy, and commitment. Still, there are a lot of driven, talented people in this world. For me, I think, there must be more.

And there is.

There is a merciful God who I go to in prayer, and it helps. Aware of my insignificance, I still trust that, for whatever reason, he is with me. He has to be. How could I understand my journey to this point without sensing his guiding hand? I prayed for normalcy as a teenager—that's all I wanted, all I aspired to. Over time, I learned to simply pray for support—not for some miraculous outcome in life. And today, at this moment, I just want to be a good husband, a good son—heck, I just want to be a good man. I want to work hard and do my best, and whatever hand God deals me—well, it's His will. It's simple: I pray, I mean it, and prayer calms me, focuses me, and reassures me. The irony of the contrary roots of my confidence and ambition strikes me: a faith in a heavenly Father and a desire to prove something to my worldly father. I put the thought aside, cross my fingers on the CFO opportunity, and rise from the table to help Paula clean up after dinner, thinking, *We'll be fine. Whatever Performance decides—CFO or no CFO—Paula and I will be fine.*

Garry makes me the CFO of Performance. It's 1997. I'm thirty-six years old. He gives me a healthy raise and seems genuinely happy about his decision. However, I know this is no gift. I'm sure he likes and respects me, but he also expects me to perform, to help him grow the business. He will settle for nothing less and will fire me if he doesn't get it.

I wouldn't want it any other way.

Soon after making me CFO, Garry makes Bob, our VP of merchandising, our new COO. I like Bob—he is a high-energy guy who executes well. This, to me, is an excellent move. With the three of us running the business, I feel we now have a real team that can grow the company. Now it's time to make it happen.

But at night, at least on the worst nights, the damned memories linger.

"EAT IT!" he screams.

I'm seated at the kitchen table to Pop's right. He sits at the head of the table, looking down on me angrily, tongue sticking out of the right corner of his mouth, hand raised, braced to strike if I do not comply with his demand. It's dinner time, and there is no vote for what is put on the table, no chance to object or not consume the contents placed in front of you.

This is not to say that Pop deliberately puts food on the table that we won't want to eat. He's rushed. Mama is unable to help out with cooking meals or grocery shopping. It's all on him and he gets it done. But he does consider our refusal to eat something an insult, as well as an opening to the possibility that we will come back later on and want something else that might cost him time or money—neither of which he is willing to provide.

"EAT IT!" he screams again.

All noise ceases as my brothers look up from their plates and put down their forks.

"Eat it, David," Billy says, almost whispering.

"Yeah," Danny says, "you gotta eat it. You can do it."

"You-all stay out of it," Pop says. "You better eat them beans, boy."

I try. The only beans I eat are pork and beans, straight from the can. I do not like green beans, hate pinto beans, and simply can't stomach lima beans. Small and green, their firm texture rests stubbornly in my mouth until my teeth break the seal on the slimy, buttery, yet grainy interior, a combination that makes me gag.

I see the hand raised and know there will be no hesitation in bringing it down on the back of my head or the side of my face. I put the green limas in my mouth. The hand goes down. I chew and chew some more. I swallow, but nearly throw up. Involuntarily, I heave, and tears begin to well in my eyes. Attempting to wash the dreaded green curd from my mouth, I desperately take a bite of beef stew.

My brothers' plates clear quickly, but the remaining beans on my plate are not moving. This fact does not escape my father's notice.

"Boy, put some more of those beans in your mouth," he demands.

I begin to whimper. "Pop, you know I hate them. Why do you put them on my plate?"

"Boy, I have to work hard to put food on the table. And you're gonna eat it. Besides they're good for you."

"How are they good for me? I hate them."

"They're good for you because I say they're good. Now you better eat them beans, and I mean now." His voice lowers and his eyes harden in that clear signal he gives when shit is about to go down if instructions are not followed.

I scoop a single bean up and into my mouth, and he stands up, sending his chair flying back from the table.

"Get a forkful of those beans and put 'em in your mouth, NOW!" he yells as he leans over me, hand raised again, breath on the back of my head.

I begin to cry, and I now know I'm going to eat them or he's going to beat the shit out of me. The one bean floats in my mouth as I refuse to bite down. I reach down with my fork, scoop up three more and put them in my mouth. I do not bite down. He sees it as he angrily peers down at my jawline. The menacing hand remains up, firm and high.

"CHEW IT UP!" he screams.

Billy and Danny reflexively slide back from the table. I'm on my own.

I know I have to bite. I don't know if I can get it down, but I have to try. So I bite and begin to chew. I have no other food to blend in to help get it down; I procrastinated on the beans as I ate everything else on my plate, vainly hoping he would let me slide on the despicable fare, and now I have nothing but water to help me wash it down. I reach and sip. It goes, but just barely. I shudder at the vile taste in the back of my throat. Several beans remain on the plate and there is no way I can get them down.

"GET SOME MORE UP OFF THAT PLATE!" he yells, unmoved by my suffering.

"Pop ain't that enough? I ate some of 'em—I can't—"

He doesn't let me finish. Similar to how he'd snatch up our dog Herman by the nape of the neck, making him whine in pain, and angrily throw him outside when he pissed on the floor, he now grabs me by the back of the neck and pushes my head down toward the plate, toward those damn nasty-ass beans. He will not relent. My nose is directly over the beans. The smell nauseates me. I have no room to get my fork under the beans and my face.

"Pop let me go," I mumble, "I'm gonna eat 'em. I promise. I can't get 'em up."

He backs away but waits. I scoop the last five beans off the plate and put them in my mouth. He watches me chew for a moment, then, convinced I'll find a way to get them down, begins to take the plates off the table for deposit in the kitchen sink directly behind him. I reach for the water to help me wash them down. The beans go mushy mixed with the water, and I spit them out onto the table.

I don't have time to react. He turns from the sink, sees the spit-up mess, and delivers a full, swinging forehand to the back of my head. The blow makes direct contact; I lose grip of my glass of water and water spills onto the table as the glass rolls off onto the floor, somehow without breaking.

Still in the chair, I holler that I tried. He screams for me to pick the glass up. He follows me and slaps at the back of my head, tongue protruding, all the while ordering me to pick it up. I skitter away from him and quickly stand straight up, the glass now firmly in hand. I stand, crying recalcitrantly, while my unsteady eye pieces together his livid figure. But I do not look him in the eye—I look only at the belt around his waist, because I know what's coming next. I put the glass on the corner of the table.

Billy and Danny watch, mouths agape.

I say I'm sorry, then stand back fearfully and begin to beg. Begging is not unusual for any of us. We all do it. We can't fight back—we're helpless and defenseless—so we beg, unabashedly and unashamedly. Fear, not pride, is the dominant emotion of my childhood, and also in this moment. So I cry and stutter and beg, saying I tried, I got several of them down, I didn't mean to spit them up on the plate, that I will clean it up, all through heaved sniffles.

"Please Pop, don't use the belt," I beg. "I tried. Please don't hit me, Pop."

On this day, the hand goes down to the belt but the strap is not loosened.

"Put that damn glass in the sink and scrape that shit off the table into the can. If you spill one drop of it on the floor, I'll really give you something to cry about," he says, eyeing my still-falling tears. Knowing him as I do, there is no doubt that he means it.

On the rare occasion when we were very young and given a pass, we ran to fulfill the command without question—no wounded pride, no visible resentment, only hustling compliance.

When we were spared the pain of the swinging black belt, the pain of battered pride and shattered self-worth was minuscule by comparison. There was a shared relief among us that the beating had been forestalled, but also a corresponding awareness that there were only so many rods that would be spared in the Pruitt household, and at any moment, for any reason, your ass could be on the line next time.

This uncertainty, the perilous question of personal safety some of us live with when we're young, can create a deeply rooted fear that changes us for a lifetime. As adults, it can lead us toward feelings of anxiousness and a sense of worthlessness that needs to be disproven almost daily by tangible accomplishment or the love and assurance of family and friends. Some of us don't make the causal connection between the anxious feelings of today and the brutal uncertainties of the past. Understanding that link and recognizing that our circumstances have changed for the better can free us from the fear—and the difficult memories. We must understand that we're no longer helpless, no longer defenseless, and that we can now protect ourselves—and are worth protecting.

Newly crowned Senior Vice-President-CFO, I toss fitfully in my bed, as usual, my back turned to Paula.

I always face my dreams and memories at night alone. They're mine and only mine to bear—to recall, to relive, but also to move beyond.

Twenty-Seven
Sunset in Savannah

IT IS THE JOB of the homeless, at least the ones who want to make their lives easier, to manage society's perception of them. We see them and we label them—quickly. The poor soul lying in a makeshift bed of paltry, haphazardly gathered possessions on a city sidewalk; the baseball cap–wearing, sign-carrying panhandler walking up the hill then back down again in the road median on a well-trafficked street corner, hungry-eyed, staring insistently at the passing cars, seeking acknowledgment, seeking sustenance, offering gratitude in return; the hitchhiker toting a heavy load, mechanically striding, face forward, almost begrudgingly reaching back and offering a raised thumb but not conceding any sense of a desperate need—the ones not yet broken by the rigors of the road. We label them "homeless" as if the only successful conclusion of their state of being, their perilous journey, is to find a home, a final destination.

Society accepts this sweeping label of "homeless" as being appropriate and has us aggregate all souls lacking permanent shelter under that humbling label. The truth is, among that population some plights are shared and others, of course, aren't. But there is one common predicament those labeled "homeless" do share: getting and staying clean.

For many that means disconnecting from drugs and alcohol—in some cases, the instruments of their dire circumstances. But that isn't always the case. Danny does not smoke weed, snort coke, stick needles in his arm, or drink alcohol. But he still needs to get clean—to wash his body. All of the homeless share this dilemma: they may not want or need to find a home but they damn sure need to find a shower or a sink and wash themselves, as well as their clothing. When the homeless are clean, well-rested, and reasonably presentable, they are potentially employable and less likely to be kicked out of public places. Being clean can also help in searching for and finding a home, either temporary or permanent.

Cleanliness impacts day-to-day things we take for granted, like entrance into a convenience store or gas station, walking unaccosted down a city street, entering a public library, stopping for a meal at a local restaurant, or walking into a supermarket. Staying clean is a matter of survival for the homeless population. The more they blend in, the easier their life becomes. But it is, of course, a circular challenge. To get clean when you don't have a home of your own, you generally need access to public places. To get access, you generally need to be clean. It is not easy. It is a skill that must be mastered—and Danny has managed to do it.

Shelters, of course, are the easiest answer. Shelters have showers. But the shelters aren't always available. It's a supply and demand issue. Neighborhood parks, beaches, and local camping areas offer places to bathe as well. But they are less private and secure.

Laundromats with bathroom facilities are an effective option that Danny employs on occasion. They serve the two-pronged purpose of allowing both clothes and body to become relatively clean in a short time. He enters in the early afternoon when the crowd is thinner, pulls his dirty clothes from his backpack, tosses them in the washer, enters the bathroom, and locks the door behind him. He strips down, pulls a washcloth and hand towel from his backpack, and uses the hand soap dispenser and the bar of soap/shampoo he keeps on hand to wash up in the sink. If the sink is large enough (and clean enough) and no one knocks on the door, he sticks his head under the spigot and washes his hair as well. By the time he rolls on deodorant and steps out, he's pretty damn clean, and his clothes will be clean and dry soon as well—an efficient venture. It isn't as good as a shower, but it meets an acceptable standard.

If he knows he's going to be in a city or town for a while and shelter access is limited, a local gym membership is quite helpful. The month-to-month memberships with showers are great and if they operate 24/7, even better. If he finds work during the day and plots his nightly accommodations accordingly, he can enter the gym locker room after 9:00 p.m. and get a hot shower in relative privacy.

The local YMCA or recreation center, a charitably minded church, or other forward-facing community service centers are possible options as well. The gift of gab and persuasiveness are huge assets in getting clean—and luckily, those are attributes Danny possesses in plenty.

But sometimes there are no easy showering options. When this is the case, public restrooms become the next option. Like the laundromat restrooms, they provide an incomplete but helpful experience. And there are degrees of acceptability concerning public restroom use. Local grocers, even Walmart (if he can get past the greeter), are pretty good options, particularly if the restroom is in the back and used less frequently. They tend to be pretty clean, although locking the door can be problematic and there is nothing worse than a father bringing in his kid as Danny's standing in front of the sink, shirtless, cleaning under his armpits. A fast-food joint is okay sometimes.

Some shift managers are completely obliging. Others, if he does not make a purchase and sometimes even if he does, move him quickly toward the exit.

Gas station and convenience store restrooms are a bad option. If that becomes the only option, it's best, for his purposes, if the restroom is a "walk-around"—that is, outside and around the corner of the building. While these sometimes require a key, they also give him more time. He can lock the door (usually a deadbolt) and quickly strip down, wash up, and put on clean clothes. The problem, of course, is the lack of cleanliness in the bathroom itself. The unflushed toilets are disgusting, and the idea of putting his bare feet on the filthiness of those black-and-white tile floors is a hurdle for him. But then again, he's gathered meals from trash dumpsters—he can manage.

Sometimes he's living under an overpass in the middle of nowhere and bathrooms or showers are simply not available. His secret in that situation is bottles, or other containers, of water. He always keeps water in his backpack—it's a necessity to manage both thirst and hygiene. He can wash himself, including his hair, with a bottle of water. He uses a bit of water and soap, along with baby or hand wipes, to wash his body first, then pours the bulk of the water over his head to rinse. It's not as good as a shower, but it's relatively effective.

But even if he finds a way to keep himself clean, Danny, as in the case of any homeless person, remains a direct challenge to the caring capacity of those he encounters. He has no home. He has no job. For the most part, he has no money. In maintaining his perilous state, he presents a firm barrier to societal acceptance. Preconceived notions are often formed as to any value he retains in our frequently black-and-white view of the world. "I'm making it, why can't they?" we ask. Mistrust, sympathy, concern, confusion, disgust, apathy—it's all there. We're not looking at ourselves, we're looking at something that we tell ourselves is completely different from us. Sometimes we're looking past them. But even when we're moving ahead quickly, we do—for a fleeting moment, as we pass—see them. We feel them. When we react, however we choose to react, what does it say about them? More importantly, what does it say about us?

Danny's breaking his rule today. He's heading south toward Savannah, Georgia, late on a Saturday afternoon, walking down the hill of a freeway ramp about fifty miles north of the city onto I-85. He has to be careful hitchhiking on the interstate. Painful experience tells him that cops and freaks are sometimes poised at the end of an anxious thumb. But I-85 is the quickest way into town and there are only a few hours left before dark. If he gets lucky, he can catch a ride into the city. There's a shelter he's heard good things about, the Old Savannah City Mission on Bull Street, somewhere near the downtown area. Food, and perhaps even clothing, are part of the services offered, and Savannah is big enough for him to get off his feet for a few days, find work, and get some money in his pocket.

He looks up, his eyes mostly hidden beneath the tattered latex bill of his Dallas Cowboys baseball cap, and sees blue skies, the sun perched steadily over the horizon with the soft yellow-orange light of the blue hour held in abeyance—but only for a while longer. It's 5:30 p.m.

The last few months have been happily uneventful. After spending time in Boone, North Carolina—work eventually dried up there—he decided to move farther south. Even after all the years, the miles traveled and sights seen, the excitement of targeting and then pulling out for a new location remains real to him. He enjoys traveling and is anxious to see Savannah, a historic city, and what he can do there.

He walks slowly down the ramp to I-85, one foot in front of the other, pushing steadily to the highway, when the abrupt sound of shattering glass explodes violently a few feet behind him to the left. He spins quickly and sees what looks to be a truck, or perhaps an SUV, out of the corner of his eye.

It blows straight past him—it's an SUV, a Jimmy, red and speedy. As it flies past, he hears the sound of adolescent laughter. He looks down at his feet and sees the broken remains of the Budweiser bottle lying in the gravel and grass.

"Damn stupid kids." He shakes his head. "Idiots, they could've really hurt me. This is the kind of shit I have to put up with: cops pull me for just walking along, minding my own business, and these kids run wild trying to lay me out with a beer bottle. There's no damn justice in the world." He puts his head back down to shield his eyes and slowly plows ahead, lost for several minutes in indignant thought.

With shocking suddenness, he hears abrupt acceleration again, and as he lifts his head, he catches sight of the red Jimmy for a second time and what looks to be three teenage boys—a driver and two passengers, both armed, throwing backward toward him as the car passes. One misses wildly but the other heaves his bottle straight at him. He instinctively turns away, and the second bottle catches the back of his left leg. It does no harm, simply bounces off his jeans and then falls easily in the grass, its remaining contents spilling onto the ground. He's just been pegged with a full Budweiser. He hears their laughter and, this time, muffled cursing including the words "bum," "tramp," and "dumb fuck loser." They accelerate and speed away.

This time, he does not put his head down. Instead, he watches them speed ahead and takes note of the next off-ramp roughly a mile up the road. This is where they must've turned around before, he thinks. He follows their progress and sure enough, when they reach the exit, they get off the highway. *What the hell, they're coming back!* Anger and resentment well up in him. *What the hell do these assholes think they're doing?* He watches them speed up and, now back on I-85, move over to the right lane. They're going to exit off and come at him again.

He bends down and looks for any loose, sizable rocks he can gather. *Let's see how they like it—the dumb bastards.* He finds three good-size rocks and sheds his backpack, dropping it behind him but keeping himself between the bag and the road. *I'm gonna peg these sons of bitches.*

But as they head back toward him, he stops a moment to consider his options. If he throws a rock or two, he might gain a moment of satisfaction, but he'll also immediately escalate the situation. They're having "fun." He's their patsy. If he fights back, he becomes their enemy. He is demeaned by their audacity, their willingness to dismiss him as a person of any value. He feels like the lowest of the low—these little bastards do not even think of him as human. Still, he drops the rocks and picks up his bag.

They exit again, take a left at the stop sign, cross the overpass, take another left, and now they're coming down the hill again, back at him. He can see them inside the truck but does not look at their faces. He follows their hands as the truck slows to give them a better shot at their target. They pass and two bottles come flying. Both throws are short and crash on the hard gravel in front of him; broken glass splinters off onto the side of the road and into the thin grass. He looks at the front passenger in the eye, who mouths, "Fuckin' A." The truck speeds off again.

They're coming back for sure. He didn't throw a rock, but he made out like he wanted to. If they saw it, they're going to be meaner now, maybe even ready to fight. He looks around considering his options.

There is only one. There are woods to his right. And he has to go now.

He turns and runs, legs pumping, over the low-cut grass, backpack in hand. Farther down the hill, he slows and steps high over uncut weeds, then jumps a small ravine and breaks through the spare trees and bushes leading into the deeper woods. He makes his way into the thick brush, drops his bag low and flat on the ground, and places himself behind a sizable oak. He doesn't want to go too deep; he wants to hide, but he also wants to see the on-ramp, see them pass. He squats low and waits.

Sure enough, the red Jimmy comes cruising down the ramp again. They slow, look around for him—to no avail—and then gas it. He figures it will take a couple of minutes for them to loop past again. So he waits some more. Again, they come, but in frustration speed away quickly. He thinks that might do it. He times them and sees nothing; he slowly steps from behind the oak.

Humanity has pissed on him again. He might be a homeless bum, but at least he isn't an asshole, and he's just been attacked by a carload of them. Now he'll never make it to the city shelter in time tonight.

He looks around. The brush is fairly thick—trees large and small, leaves and pine needles at his feet—but the ground is dry. There's been little to no rain recently. He's thankful for that. There also looks to be a little more space deeper in to get his blanket spread out on the ground. He's got some trail mix and cookies in his bag, and water. It's past 6:00 p.m.

The hell with it. He pulls the trail mix out of his pack. *I'll just sleep here.*

Part V
Life, Death, and
the Relative Distance

Twenty-Eight
T-shirts

THERE IS A CHANGE in how he looks at me now.

I work for a living, just like he did. I take care of myself and my family (Paula and I now have two young sons)—just the way he always wanted me to. He understands it, appreciates it, and gives me respect in a way I never knew he was capable of.

He sees that I do different work than he did. Pop worked with his hands; he was a union guy and once he fought with management for better pay and benefits. He knows, since I've been promoted to CFO, that I'm a member of management myself, one of the supposed bad guys. But he trusts me. He says I'm a good person, and he knows that I treat people the right way. The only time we argue now is when I don't call, or he doesn't see me enough. Strangely, he wants to be around or hear from me as much as possible.

I have a nice home in Chapel Hill and he, along with Helen, often drives in to see us and spend time with the kids. One day, while watching me on the floor playing with my youngest, he—for the first time—asks, "Well I guess I wasn't much of a father to you boys, was I?"

I hear his "sort of" question and it makes me wonder if he harbors any regret for the way he parented the three of us. When I probe and say, "Why do you ask?" I do so deliberately. Over the years, the thought of what hearing an apology from my father would mean has crossed my mind more than once, and it does so again now. *Would I forgive him?* I ask myself. Yes, I believe I probably would. But one thing is patently clear: as much as I'd like to, whether I get an apology or not, I can never forget.

We sit in silence as I await his answer.

When he says, "Well, your Mama went off and left you, and I raised you the best way I knew how," it's clear he's defending himself. He doesn't intend to apologize; instead, he wants me to reassure him. I dance. I tell him he kept a roof over our heads and fed us—we'd have been orphans if he hadn't—and that seems to be enough.

Danny's name comes up often. We both ask if the other has heard from him and the answer is always no. "Well, he's on the road some-where, I guess," Pop says. "That's what happens when you won't work for a living." I take the latter statement as an incomplete truth and I sense no guilt, no remorse, from him for Danny's travails. Whether he doesn't feel it or doesn't show it is a question. Sadly, I think it's the former.

He asks if I can get him Performance Bike T-shirts to wear around his neighborhood, so he can tell his friends who I am and what I do. He calls me a big shot, and I don't think he means it in a bad way. He no longer thinks that I'm not worth a shit for nothin'.

There has, indeed, been a change.

But not everything can change.

Twenty-Nine
The Stupid One

PERFORMANCE BIKE IS NOW off and running. Bob brings energy and drive that is infectious. I bring fiscal discipline, pragmatic decision-making, and strategic thinking. Garry brings vision and restlessness; he's always searching for growth, funding, and wealth. The three of us are a team—a team that values the employees we serve and focuses on one thing: getting results. And we do. Over the next few years, the company and its associates prosper as we deliver consistent results from a sales and profitability perspective.

With our rapid growth—and at the height of investor interest in internet-based businesses (the "dot-com" era)—Garry sees his chance and in 1999, after the successful establishment of our website, PerformanceBike.com, sells a majority percentage of the business to a private equity firm. When the deal is complete, the three of us have new bosses and twenty million dollars in cash on the balance sheet to help grow the company. Garry retains minority ownership and Bob and I are given promises that if we continue to perform well, we will be appropriately rewarded. Unspoken is the fact that if we don't, we will be terminated in short order. There is a lot more at stake and a lot more scrutiny now. Time to put our big boy pants on.

Yet we're in trouble almost immediately. The dot-com bubble

bursts. There'll be no public offering to sell the performancebike.com website to a ravenous investor community. That market no longer exists. The private equity team is concerned. The path to getting an acceptable return on their investment will not be easy because the world has changed—and there remains a large problem that must be solved for us to fully unleash our growth potential.

Performance has the broadest assortment of cycling products in the country, but we don't have the most prestigious bike brands. The most popular brands won't sell to us because we're seen as a chain. So, we open a store in a market and slog it out for a few years against the local mom-and-pops until the consumer figures out the best value proposition (us). We've got to mature our presence in these new markets more quickly.

Garry, Bob, and I get together to discuss the dilemma and arrive at a potential solution: instead of opening new stores and competing with the #1 and #2 existing shops in the market, why not buy them out, change them into Performance stores, kick out their bike brands, and put in ours? Will this speed up our ability to take local market share and grow the overall business more rapidly? Will taking the leading bike brands out of key markets pressure them into doing business with us? We need to find out.

As CFO, I lead my team in taking on the task of identifying the targets, negotiating the terms, performing the due diligence, finalizing the contracts, and buying up the stores. The first one works okay. But the next several do quite well. Garry and the board members are pleased, and since the deals are working, we aggressively move forward with the strategy. And I no longer doubt the validity of my presence in the executive boardroom. I know I belong.

Over the next five years, we make ten acquisitions, adding over $100 million in revenue and corresponding profit to the company coffers. And after running the gauntlet of adolescence under Pop's erratic dictatorial rule, tough back and forth negotiation with these strong-willed, hard-charging business owners is a task I can comfortably handle. In fact, it's not even the toughest challenge I face right now.

That challenge comes at home.

I desperately want to be a good father.

From the day my children are born, I've told myself that I will be better, do better than Pop did by me and my brothers—but it's not so easy.

My oldest son is ambitious, curious, and affectionate. He fires off constant questions about everything from dinosaurs to Allen wrenches and, in general, is a rule follower like his mother. We often read together, mostly about Harry, Ron, Hermione, and the other muggles, mudbloods, wizards, and witches in the Harry Potter books. And when the two of us are out and about in the family SUV, we laugh at ourselves as we sing along loudly (and poorly) with the music on the radio or the latest CD. When he grows tall enough to peek over the steering wheel, I put him in my lap and let him steer slowly through the quiet streets of our neighborhood—breaking most city ordinances and good parenting rules in the process.

My youngest is charismatic and has a good heart—but he's fiercely independent. When I read to his older sibling at night in bed, he chooses to sit on the floor playing with his Pokémon cards, seemingly not listening—but occasionally dispelling the myth of his indifference with a thoughtful question like, "Why does Draco Malfoy dislike Harry so much?" He will try new things—but only of his own volition. He doesn't follow the crowd or remotely care what they think. Unlike his brother, he's not much on sitting in my lap, but when I injure myself playing weekend warrior basketball, he breaks off from a neighborhood-wide kids' game of "Plant the Flag" and runs home to check on me.

My kids, like all kids, need discipline. Right or wrong, another thing I tell myself is that I will not lay a hand on them—not even a smack on their bottoms—and I don't. But boundaries must be set. When they do something wrong, they need to know it will not be accepted—there will be consequences. My approach is to choose my battles wisely and then, once I determine a line has been crossed, to use the look on my face, the tone of my voice, and the words I speak to get them to regroup, rethink, and get back in line. They tell me I'm scary when I get "the look." But they don't see it very often. I give "the look," for the most part, with deliberation and purpose—I want it to mean something when they see me angry. My words and demeanor are the tools I'll use to hopefully influence their good behavior. It's also true that I'm not always as pointed or strategic in my efforts to discipline them as I'd like to be—sometimes I simply lose my patience.

I'm no perfect parent.

My younger son and Paula struggle in my absence. After a long day at work, I sometimes walk into the house to their combative shouting. Paula, wearing a look of exasperation like a driver's ed teacher whose careless student just ran a stop sign, tosses the child-rearing keys to me. I try to dial things down by calmly questioning my son about the latest disagreement. Usually, I find that he's being obstinate, that he likes to push his mother's buttons, that's he's making his life more difficult by arguing about an issue that has no real importance to his life—and I tell him this. But he doesn't seem to care. I use a word to describe his behavior: stupid. I use it too often, until one day he looks at me with an expression of anger and hurt and says he doesn't like me calling him stupid. Though my face doesn't betray it,

I understand immediately the significance of the moment—the sins of the father being passed on by me, an ignorant, impatient son! My son's anger is completely justified. I'm dead wrong and, it turns out, the stupid one between the two of us.

Still, my saving grace is that I care deeply. I tell the boys I love them a lot—and I mean it. I think that's where good parenting starts, from a place of sincere, unconditional love and a selfless reprioritization of your life's purpose. It's no longer about you or me, it's about *them*.

And if the singular responsibility of child-rearing is teaching our kids right from wrong based on well-informed experience and good intentions, how we go about it depends on *who our kids are*. We must have our emotional and behavioral antenna tracking persistently throughout their development, so we can pass on our vision of right and wrong in a way they can understand. My two kids learn and react differently, so I will parent them differently. If my youngest requires a bit more patient explanation and gentle cajoling to get him to the right place, I'll happily do it.

One night while lying in bed, after a particularly challenging day on the parenting front, a prescient question rolls through my mind: Are we as parents responsible for the outcome of our children's lives? Of course, we're going to worry and we want the best for them—but are we *responsible*?

I lie quietly, stare at the tray ceiling above our bed, and ponder the question while Paula sleeps beside me—and a first thought comes quickly: The weight of parental responsibility is carried longest by the parents who fail their children when they're growing up.

As parents, we know in our hearts if we've raised and loved our children well—not perfectly, mind you, but well. We know—and our kids know too. There is no mystery about it.

A parent that has raised their child with grace, love, and self-lessness can take comfort in knowing that whatever mistakes—and successes, as much as we'd like to claim them—come later in life are the responsibility of the child.

But when the parent raises their child badly and the child later struggles? Well, if they're lucky the child will figure things out on their own, or God, in his singular benevolence, may choose to help that child—but if not, he'll have to absolve them as a bad parent.

I roll over, close my eyes, and resolve to do my best to seek grace, not absolution, in raising my two sons.

And I also know this: I'm never going to use the word "stupid" around my children again.

In 2004, I lead Performance Bike through a final acquisition, I believe the largest in US specialty cycling history up to that time, a multi-superstore concept based in Southern California and Arizona. Our business now boasts well over $200 million in total revenue and is, without question, the largest, most dominant specialty cycling retailer in the United States.

But one day, Garry calls Bob and me from Aspen and says that the private equity guys are very happy with what we've done with the business. And they're now ready to sell.

I sense that things in my life are about to change, big time.

Thirty
Dirty Face and the Law

THE HISTORIC SOUTHERN PACIFIC Railroad to Yuma, Arizona—which began its run in 1865—is the first train my brother jumps in his quest for efficient and inexpensive travel across the United States.

Train transportation for the homeless is a dangerous, uncomfortable, and dirty experience. The "freighthopper" will either go to a railyard and find a spot to hide and sneak on while the train is stationary, or jump on while it's moving—which is referred to as "Catching on the Fly." Sometimes, the rider will catch the train at a "sideout," a spot where there are two parallel tracks and trains pull aside for others to pass.

Once the train has been caught, hiding while they ride is the freighthopper's mission.

There are intermodal cars (shipping containers—usually forty feet long, with various contents), junk cars (mixed cars and literal scrap), and coal containers. Within these groups, some cars can be ridden, while others can't. "Open door" containers are welcomed by the un-ticketed rider. There is sometimes loose cardboard to provide cushion under a sleeping bag and, if the weather is right, a welcome cool breeze. But there is also danger in open-door rides. Many of these cars have sliding doors that can close and leave its passenger locked in the dark with limited airflow. Unlucky riders can and have died. The solution? Grab a loose railroad nail or spike and keep the sliding door from latching shut.

On intermodals, the passengers ride in the metal beds in front of or behind the containers. On coal trains, the riders often hop into Distributed Power Units (DPUs) or engine units that are remotely controlled from the leading locomotive on the train. The DPUs allow for longer trains and, in some cases, provide the unwanted traveler with some level of creature comforts. But many times, the traveler must hide in a dirty coal truck, drop down into the topless entry of a gondola car, or become a "pig in a bucket"—that is, ride under a tractor-trailer (when the trailer is on a metal platform with large holes cut out in the bottom) or even ride in the small exposed porch of a tanker or a truss-bottom well car. In many of these settings, the rider is exposed to the risk of falling off and getting hurt or getting caught by the railroad police (or "bulls," as they're known by practitioners of the ploy). And if they don't get hurt or caught, they will most certainly get dirty. The coal, the dirt, the terrain surrounding the track, and the rural environments that are passed through make staying clean impossible. Other homeless people know and/or recognize freighthoppers by sight and even have a name for them—"Dirty Face."

Danny travels up and down the East Coast for a time before returning once again to Florida. He works the labor pool in Jacksonville for a few months, until he and his pal Jimmy decide to hop their first train and go West. With backpacks in tow and a minimal food supply, they walk twenty miles west of the city to Baldwin, where a major trainyard resides. After casing a stationary, three-engine, seven-thousand-foot-long coal train in the open yard for an hour or so, they sneak quietly on board under the cover of darkness. They suspect one of the yardmen sees them climb into the open car, and are confused as to why he makes no move to impede their trespass. In time, they'll learn the yardmen are generally patient with the comings and goings of the homeless traveler.

They cautiously move from various cars to DPUs, both to avoid detection and to survey their temporary home. Soon, the train fires up and begins to pick up speed, at times going as fast as fifty-five miles an hour on its way to New Orleans. The two of them separate, and Danny carefully makes his way to the DPU at the rear of the train. There is a captain's chair up top and he makes himself comfortable as he watches the scenery change from small-town southern America, where dim street lights shine on local townships in the early-morning darkness, to backwoods areas with trees, creeks, and overpasses tightly positioned on either side of the tracks. The scenery is compelling, sometimes breathtaking, and he contemplates the occasional joys of his haphazard life as the train plows forward, unerringly, on its well-traveled route.

After a while up top, he takes the stairs down below to the bathroom and finds bottled water in a small refrigerator outside the bathroom door. He uses the urinal, grabs a couple of bottles, then returns upstairs and falls asleep in the captain's chair.

A few hours later, he's awakened by the engineer, who impatiently takes a long look at his dirty face and lean frame while considering his options.

"I need to ask what you're doing back here," the engineer says as he surveys the surrounding controls for any damage.

Shaken, Danny rises to his feet, gathers his composure, and attempts to explain.

"Oh, hey man—I was just getting some rest," he says, knowing this might be trouble.

"You're not supposed to be back here. This is for authorized personnel only."

"Okay, I'm sorry. I'm leaving right now. I . . ."

The homeless often see bad things as they move surreptitiously from city to town, overpass to underpass, mission to shelter, rail line to highway, but sometimes, on the ragged journey, they witness kindness and mercy.

The engineer raises his hand and motions for him to stop talking, then instructs him to keep his hands off the controls and graciously steps out the door, leaving him alone again in the DPU.

Exhaustion and relief overcome Danny. He gratefully moves back down below and passes out, his back against the rear wall of the small compartment. And he rides that end unit comfortably—all the way to New Orleans.

The train is scheduled to stay in New Orleans for a day and a half, taking on additional freight, before continuing its journey west. With supplies gone and bellies empty, Danny and Jimmy climb off, backpacks in hand, and head into town looking for food.

They spot a local pizza parlor on the outskirts of town that's just finished serving its patrons during the busy lunch hour. They sneak around back, quietly slide open the door of a green metal dumpster, and climb directly into the smelly refuse.

Any real hesitation is held in abeyance by their empty stomachs. They search hungrily for leftover, half-eaten pizza and find it in abundance. "You'd be surprised at how much good food gets thrown away," Danny will marvel aloud to other freighthoppers a few days later.

Bellies and backpacks full, Danny and Jimmy sleep under a nearby overpass the next two nights, then hop back on the waiting train to complete the journey west.

But the second half of the trip does not go as smoothly.

They run into trouble ten miles outside of El Paso, just north of the Mexican border and the Rio Grande. Customs Border Patrol has boarded the train in the form of a heavyset Latino gentleman in a green, tight-fitting uniform who approaches them aggressively shouting, "You don't belong on this train! I need you to get off right now!"

Danny and Jimmy, taking note of the man's firearm, size, and continued advance, are forced to make a quick decision. As the train continues to hum westward at thirty miles an hour, they toss their backpacks off the open freight car and, after hesitating for a moment, jump for it.

They land with a thud and tumble briefly on the open desert ground. Sitting upright now, they check for damage. Happily finding none, they get to their feet, dust themselves off, and run back to grab their backpacks.

That night, under a dark but cloudless desert sky, they use the railroad flares they took from the train to build a fire.

The next morning, they head into El Paso.

A few weeks later, Danny and Jimmy return to the desert, west of where they jumped off the last train, as a red sun begins its descent into early twilight. They're looking to finish their journey to Yuma. As the train approaches, they split apart, each looking to safely board. It's their turn to "Catch on the Fly."

Standing patiently, Danny spots an open freight car. He takes off running full speed, five yards away from the powerful train whizzing by and bellowing loudly in his left ear. Seeing an opportunity, he slows, rears back with his right arm, and throws his backpack into the passing open car.

He lands it safely aboard. Now it's his turn.

He accelerates full speed again, turns, and sees a hand-rail approaching hard on his left. It's connected to three steps leading to an open platform.

Left hand extended and feet flying, he reaches out, grabs the rail, and safely pulls himself up the stairs to the open platform, panting hard.

After recovering his breath he makes his way through several cars to retrieve his backpack, then finds Jimmy—who also made it safely aboard. Relieved, he wipes the sweat from his dirty brow and feels blessed that his first-ever jump went so well. He's heard some bad stories. Sometimes, men lose their backpacks when they successfully throw them on the train but aren't strong enough or fast enough to board themselves—and sometimes they stumble and even die in the effort. Though it was a little unnerving, he made it.

Several hours later, they arrive at their destination. The train stops for supplies and personnel and unloads its freight. Danny and Jimmy climb off and separate. Jimmy is heading northeast to Phoenix, while Danny's heading due west to San Diego.

But first, it's on to the California side of Yuma.

The relationship between law enforcement and the homeless is often complicated. The police feel burdened and frustrated by the presence of the homeless, while the homeless feel targeted and harassed by the police. Sometimes with no formal policy in place, the handling of the homeless by the police is left to the discretion of the individual officers. It comes down to human nature. Interactions can range from empathetic to merciless.

While hitchhiking on California I-8 West, Danny hears them before he sees them. The light flashes red, the siren wails, and the officer parks his boxy patrol car a few yards in front of where Danny stands motionless, watching, thumb down, his back to the oncoming traffic.

Two policemen step from the automobile, lights still flashing, as the cars continue to plow past—though their occupants slow a bit and crane their necks in an effort to better see the impending encounter.

"Hey fella, don't you know it's illegal for you to hitch a ride on the interstate?" the large officer inquires, continuing to move forward.

"Well, no sir, I didn't—this is just the quickest way for me to get to San Diego," Danny responds uncertainly, suddenly recalling why he normally avoids the busy highway.

"San Diego? What are you gonna be doing in San Diego?"

"I'm just looking for work and a quiet place to settle down for a while," Danny answers, confused by the question: what business is it of his why he wants to go to San Diego?

"Hey buddy, I'm sorry but you can't get to San Diego from here—at least not with your thumb up on I-8. I need you to drop your bag and get up against the car, hands on the hood." The officer points at the patrol car.

"But why, officer? I haven't done anything."

"I told you—you can't hitch on this interstate. It's illegal and dangerous for cars traveling at these speeds, pulling off the road—particularly if they do so at the last second. Now get up against the car like I asked you." He speaks more forcefully this time.

Eyeing the policeman dubiously, Danny drops his backpack to

the ground, walks over, and places both hands on the right side of the car—away from the cars flying past on I-8.

The second officer walks over and begins to pat him down with both hands, arms to ankles, and stops upon feeling a thin metal object in the left pocket of Danny's cargo shorts.

"Well, what's this?" he asks as he reaches in, pulls out the knife, and flicks the blade open to complete his inspection.

"It's a buck knife," Danny says evenly. "I carry it with me all the time. When you spend as much time outside as I do, it comes in handy."

"Looks like a concealed weapon to me," the officer replies.

"It's not a weapon, it's a tool. Sometimes I need to cut cardboard, rope, small branches, whatever. I've had that knife for years!" Danny responds indignantly.

"Well, not anymore. I'm afraid we're going to have to confiscate this."

"It's a tool. I need it—man, this is ridiculous."

The first officer steps forward. "What's ridiculous is you thumbing a ride on this interstate. As I said, it's dangerous. I'm afraid we're gonna have to write you a ticket." He begins to write it out, pages flipped back, a little black book in one hand and a blue ballpoint pen in the other.

"A ticket? Officer, you gotta be kidding!"

"No, I'm not kidding. You have sixty days to pay—or get yourself a lawyer and have your day in court."

Danny hears the sound of the officer tearing off the ticket and sees his partner place the buck knife in *his* pocket!

"Hey come on! That's not fair! That's my knife—and a ticket, too?" Danny cries, more loudly than he intended.

"We're confiscating the knife and yes, you're getting a ticket. You broke the law. Now, do you want me to take you in for loitering and resisting arrest? Do you want me to search that backpack? Hey, listen, we can take this as far as you wanna go. Or do you want to just take this ticket, keep your thumb down, get off this interstate at the next exit, and end this right now?"

Shit, I've had that knife for years! he thinks angrily.

But this is a no-win situation. The knife is already gone, and he could wind up spending a few nights in jail—and getting additional charges. No, he needs to cut his losses. He begrudgingly reaches his hand out and takes the ticket from the officer.

"Good decision. Now, do like I ask and get off the interstate—and keep that thumb down," the officer reminds him.

He and his partner head back to the car. Seconds later, the engine cranks and rocks fly under skidding tires. Danny is left standing there, knifeless, his backpack still resting on the ground.

He watches the officers drive away. The car bleeds into the westward sun and the onslaught of throbbing traffic.

Frustrated, he pauses for a moment, making sure the officers are well out of sight, then angrily tears the ticket into a thousand pieces and tosses it high into the air. The sensation of it raining down around his shoulders is better than a light spring shower in the western mountains of North Carolina—a place he's frequented in his wandering days.

Confiscated, my ass. They just stole my buck knife.

He takes one more look up the highway, then turns and doggedly puts his thumb back up.

It's been a tough trip west so far, but he's moving onward the best way he knows how.

Thirty-One
WTF

WHILE I FLOURISH IN the workplace, I struggle a bit in the heightened social strata of Chapel Hill, North Carolina. Life in Chapel Hill revolves around the University of North Carolina—professors and university employees make up a big part of the citizenry. When we make our move to a home in town, we end up on a cul-de-sac with two doctors from UNC Hospital and two tech executives from RTP (Research Triangle Park—the Silicon Valley of the southeastern United States). There are also professors sprinkled in several houses close by. Frankly, I'm a bit overwhelmed by my elevated surroundings.

My inherent skittishness makes things difficult for Paula.

We're invited to neighborhood gatherings with these seemingly important people and it makes me feel like a fish out of water, an imposter. While I have found success, my insecurities get the best of me. The people I am standing next to are the one-percenters, the glitterati of academia and tech, and they converse about topics that I am unwilling to share my opinions on. I squirm awkwardly and noticeably in the thinness of my fragile skin. My anxiety builds for days before we attend these events, and once I arrive, I falsely sense haughtiness, pretentiousness, and disdain from my unwitting neighbors. How can these highly successful people possibly know what it's like to be slapped brutally in the face over the inability to digest a lima bean?

Paula, who can talk to anyone, suffers as a result of my social anxiety. There are friends she should have, confidants she could enjoy, that she doesn't—mainly because I come as part of the package. I hate the weaker parts of myself that hurt her.

She's also blessed with a wonderful family that, in many ways, I've searched for and always wanted: a father who treats me with respect, a mother whose faith and support are a bulwark that I will, in time, come to rely on, and two brothers who are open and approachable and embrace me as one of their own. Still, it's not enough. I am, at times, overwhelmed by the loving crowd and the lack of space and time to manage the conflicted, tortured thoughts of my often-troubled mind.

It's hard for Paula to understand and accept. I know. I don't understand it myself. But I do know that in the back of my mind there is a fear of being found out, discovered—a paranoia that the truth about my past, about who I am, will spill forth, fully visible, before these seemingly unforgiving people. I also carry a narrow-minded view of family and what it means. My in-laws, though wonderful, are not my blood and I'm not theirs—yet they treat me much better than my own family ever has.

No, the problem is not that they aren't my blood. The problem is that in my head I'm not theirs. I married their wonderful daughter and gained, in my mind, contingent-only access to a sublime brood. Although I know the marriage will not fail, I allow myself occasional consideration of the remote possibility that the marriage will end, and when that happens the love and respect I currently receive from them in full measure will be withdrawn. I do not belong. I'm not good enough.

Much later in life, when my mother-in-law is dying in our home of inoperable cancer, I will finally address her as Mom. I will know then—I was a complete and utter fool, and poor Paula and our family had to put up with it for several years.

Paula, after a few years of successful employment, is now a stay-at-home mom, and her parents, now retired, participate quite a bit in both of our boys' lives. If there is a ball game, most of the time they are there. However, there is one problem with the strong relationship between my kids and my in-laws: Pop feels that we give them access and special treatment that are not available to him and Helen. As a result, Pop's relationship with Paula begins to break down.

It all comes to a head one Saturday afternoon when we have a birthday party for Matthew, my youngest, who is now eight years old. The attendees are, of course, our family of four, Paula's folks, Pop and Helen, a bunch of Matthews' school buddies, and a stray parent or two of the visiting kids. Pop has made it a habit, when it's one of the boys' birthdays, to not only bring a gift for the birthday boy in question but also for the non-birthday boy, so he won't feel left out. Perhaps his approach is derived from growing up in a poor family with many siblings—and few birthday presents.

Paula politely asked a few months ago, on Zack's birthday, for Pop not to do that anymore. She explained that she wants the boys to learn that the spotlight is not always theirs, that they should be supportive of the other when it's their time to shine. It seems like a worthy lesson in growth to me.

The disconnect occurs when we discover that Paula's folks have brought gifts for both Matthew and Zack today.

Before Paula can react and resolve the issue, my father goes ballistic. He challenges Paula right there in front of the crowd—why can they bring a gift for the other boy, but he can't? She explains, but he's having none of it. He turns, leaves the kitchen, and storms upstairs while we're in the middle of singing happy birthday to Matthew. I hear doors slam above my head and the sounds of luggage being haphazardly gathered and packed.

I walk over to Paula, get the sorry briefing, and immediately consider my options. Should I go upstairs and try to get him to calm down, listen to reason, and stay—or should I just try to get him out the front door as quickly as possible, ensure that his staggeringly blind rage is let loose outside the walls of our home and away from the prying eyes and ears of our guests?

As I start to head upstairs, the decision is made for me: Here Pop comes, stomping down the steps, bags in hand, Helen in tow. He looks at me angrily and says, "You, outside with me, NOW!"

As heads, including those of several little five-year-olds, turn in my harried direction, I follow him out the door.

He sets his bags down on my front porch. "You saw that bullshit!" he screams at me. "Your wife told me that I couldn't give them both presents on their birthdays, but she didn't say a damn thing about her mama and daddy doing the same thing!"

It's not a pretty scene. Parents are intermittently walking up my front sidewalk to get inside to pick up or check on their kids while my father is yelling. I don't like the sound of "your wife," and my mind searches for the right words.

"Pop, Paula didn't know her parents were bringing a gift for Zack. She was as surprised as you were. This is a little different, too. You were buying two gifts for every one birthday. Her folks have never done this before."

"All I know is, I saw both kids getting birthday gifts," he splutters. "I was told I couldn't do that."

"Pop, if you remember, we were at your house for Zack's birthday.

They never got to give him a present. They haven't seen him. So it's not like they always bring two. They owed Zack one, right? It was a late birthday gift."

"Well, how is he supposed to understand that? How is he supposed to cheer on Matthew for his birthday when he's getting presents too?"

"Look, Pop, neither Paula nor I knew they were bringing a gift for Zack. And they didn't know the rules because it's never been an issue in the past. It just happened. Come back inside and let's work this out," I cajole, casting a glance at Helen, who stands silently at his shoulder.

"Your wife don't treat us the same way she treats her own. We hardly get to see those kids. They get to see them all the time!" he says loudly, letting the real truth spill out. "And your wife keeps that road hot to her daddy's house."

"Pop, we might've been there one more time in the last six months than to your place. They're closer than you are down at the beach. The real difference in time spent with the kids is them coming here. You know I have a lot going on at work, so we don't travel that much. It's easier if you-all come to us—you're retired, just like them. They just come more often. You can come too."

A deeper, unspoken truth is that Paula is closer to her parents than I am to Pop and Helen. Another fact is that Paula and Pop have begun having confrontations over various issues in the last few years. We've already had a few "sit-downs" to clear the air between them and the two of us leave those discussions thinking all is well, but in Pop's mind, things have continued to fester. Paula speaks her mind—respectfully, but Pop does not take to being questioned or challenged in any way, even if it's done in a kind, reasoned tone. She's willing, he's not. And now the poisoned flower of resentment and estrangement is in full bloom. I'm looking dead at it.

"Your wife don't want me in her house. And you let her get away with it," he says in a low, guttural tone, head cocked down at a ninety-degree angle. His eyes glare at me, clearly, directly accusing me. I feel a steaming redness on the back of my neck and a hot fever rises in my body from toes to scalp—one that usually precedes an explosion of rage from whence there is no turning back. At work, I manage, at this point, hundreds of people, and there I always maintain my composure, even when handling hard things. I pride myself on that fact. But this man—this man is the only one who can so quickly take me over the top, beyond my limits, beyond any semblance of patience and rationality. I look back hard at those eyes—but then, fortunately, I catch myself. I see a mother walking up the street to our place, here to pick up her son, and I understand immediately: I better calm my shit down.

I take a deep breath, and exhale slowly.

"Pop that's not true. Paula invited you here for Matthew's birthday. She invites you for all the kid's stuff, you know that. And you know I want you here, too. This is crazy. Let's just calm down and straighten this out."

"When you think you can give me and your step-mama here a fair shake, you let me know," he says before turning and walking away, bags now firmly in hand.

"You know your daddy's right this time David," Helen admonishes, then starts to follow.

"Wait for a second," I call after them. "Helen, I don't. All the other issues we've talked about in the past and Paula has apologized. So have both of you. And this was just a mix-up with her folks on the presents. Come on, now."

"You know how it is when your daddy's made up his mind. You better talk to your wife." And with that, she's done.

As I watch them walk to their Toyota Highlander, throw their bags in, do a U-turn in the cul-de-sac, and drive away, not for a moment looking my way, I stand quietly and shake my head, thinking, *How ironic. Why am I fighting to hold all this together when any reasonable person who knew the circumstances of my upbringing would ask me—what the fuck am I doing it for?*

Thirty-Two
The Advice

DANNY FINDS HIMSELF SITTING in a local Salvation Army in Des Moines, Iowa, one evening in 2002, being asked, "How'd you get here?" by its director. He's tired but shares his story, as he usually does, providing a few low-light examples of the humiliating trials of his youth. The director takes note and suggests that he speak with a counselor who will be stopping in later that evening.

Danny agrees—if this is part of getting a bed and getting fed, then so be it.

Two hours later, after a shower and a much-needed meal, he feels up to the task. The director comes over and brings with him a woman he assumes is the counselor in question. She looks to be in her mid-forties and wears thick glasses. She has a lean build, an open smile, and a broad, pale white face.

They share introductions then both take a seat on a nearby, weathered sofa.

"So, Danny, where are you from and how long have you been . . . on the road?" the counselor inquires.

He notes that she does not use the term "homeless."

"I'm from Greensboro, North Carolina, and I left there when I was around twenty-three years old. It must've been late '82 or early

'83. Except for a few years, I've been traveling—I guess for well over fifteen years now."

"So, did you graduate from high school, a trade school, or college? I hope you don't mind me asking. I just want to learn a little more about you."

"Well, you know, I dropped out of high school in the eleventh grade."

"Why did you decide to quit?"

"They wanted me to stand up in front of the class and give a speech. I knew, uh, I couldn't do it, but the teacher, she made me anyway. I got up there, stuttered and stammered, couldn't get it out. They laughed at me. I left school that afternoon and decided I wasn't going back. My grades were no good anyway. I just couldn't focus on the stuff."

"Parents, any siblings? Tell me about your home life."

And the door cracks slightly.

"Uh, my mother was mentally ill. She was with us when I was very young, talked to herself and her imaginary enemies, but not much to us. She got shock treatments along the way and was finally committed to Dorothy Dix, a state mental hospital, when I was eleven or so. I saw her only a handful of times after that. My father pretty much raised us. We called him Pop. I have two brothers, one older and one younger. I haven't seen them in years."

"Tell me about your father."

And the door is thrown open wide.

No matter how many times Danny talks about that time, those days, and specifically Pop, it can quickly turn into an emotional experience. Feelings of shame, hurt, resentment, even pride, like a wounded soldier who's survived a brutal conflict, bubble up in his mind. He mostly swallows all of it back down, then speaks.

"Well, uh, Pop worked hard and kept us fed, kept a roof over our heads. But he was tough. One of the earliest things I remember is accidentally peeing in the bed. You know, I was just a little kid. He took off my underwear—I remember his hand wrapped around my leg—and whipped my ass with his belt. Then he made me stay in bed with my pissy jockey shorts on my head and my nose in the piss on the sheets. He wanted me to smell it. Made me keep my head down just above the piss and dared me to move it! Now that's the sort of thing you'd do when your dog pisses on the floor, right? Anyway, I don't know how long it was before he came back, but I remember him putting alcohol on the cuts afterward. God, it stung . . ."

"I'm listening," the counselor says.

"Uh, well, that kinda thing happened all the time when I was growing up."

"Did it happen just to you? What about your brothers?"

"Naw. They got it too. Though probably not as much as me. I screwed up some, that's for sure. The thing is—you never knew when it was gonna happen or why. There was no way to prepare. I got my head bounced off a stove. Got thrown in a trashcan for talking about our electricity bill with the neighbor. Hell, I got punched in the face for running a blow dryer too long. When we messed up, we got it. When we did nothing, we got it. You just never knew." He looks away, shaking his head, simultaneously disgusted and resigned to his past.

"You mentioned your mother was mentally ill. Did she also whip you and your brothers?"

"She did, some. She seemed to have it in for Billy—that's my oldest brother. She chased him around the house and beat him with a dust mop. She'd make us all stand in the corner for hours at a time. But mainly she wasn't around. She was nowhere to be found when Pop went off, that's for sure."

"Your dad was out of line. Were there any good times? Sounds like he fed you and, at least, kept a roof over your head."

"Uh, yeah, there were some. He played ball with us on weekends. Read us the Bible sometimes on Saturday nights. He told us he loved us—and he did, I think—but lots of times, that was right after he'd just beat the shit out of us and felt guilty about it. He'd get so mad. Just go crazy. He told me one time he beat me because I was just like him. Can you believe that? Told us all we were sorry as hell, that we weren't worth a shit. Boy, that made my little brother so mad. Almost got himself killed over that—just couldn't keep his mouth shut."

"How'd it make you feel?"

"What, him saying how sorry I was? Well, um, it didn't feel good. But I couldn't keep a job. Maybe he was right. Still I didn't like it. Couldn't do anything about it."

"You said you left North Carolina when you were around twenty-three. Were you still in your father's home then?"

Danny shakes his head. "No. I had been in and out of the house for a couple of years. Lost some jobs, had some bad luck. The best job I had paid good money, and I was doing good. But business got tough and they laid me off. If I could've stayed on there, things might've been different."

He pauses for a moment in reflection, in fleeting regret. It passes. He begins again.

"Course, now Pop stayed on my ass constantly about working. When I got too old to whip with a belt, he hit me with his fists. Yanked me out of bed late one night—he'd just gotten off second shift, I was in my teens—and dragged me down the hall by the ankle when I forgot to take the trash to the road, screaming how sorry I was, how I wasn't worth a shit. I didn't mean to not do it. I just forgot! He finally kicked me out of the house when I couldn't keep a job."

"You mentioned your mother was put away. Did your parents divorce?"

"They did. Pop remarried a woman named Helen. She loved me, treated me better than Mama did, even saved me from Pop a few times, but she let me go when Pop kicked me out of the house." Here, he chooses not to tell the full story.

"Why did you leave Greensboro when you did?"

"Uh, I don't know. I guess I felt unloved, laughed at, scared, beaten down—worthless, really. I guess Pop finally broke me. There was just no reason to stay. So I ran. The life I've had since has been hard—no question. I've gone hungry, I've slept outside in the rain and the snow. Um, I'm not ashamed to say I've climbed in dumpsters to find myself a meal. Ya gotta eat, right? I've had bad things done to me; truth is, I've done some bad things myself. But after I started traveling I also took control of my life, such as it is. I got street smart. Got a little braver. I've stayed off drugs and alcohol, and I've taken care of myself. Hell, Pop told me I couldn't do that—but I have, and that's worth something." He lifts his head a bit higher.

It's clear enough to him. He's learned some things, admittedly the hard way, but he's stronger than he was back in the day, and he knows it.

"Let's talk about 'Pop'—you talk about, and think about, him a lot," she observes.

"Hey, you know, I love Pop. He got it when he was young and just didn't know any other way. But yeah, I think about him and all that shit that happened a lot—even when I don't want to. Things just pop into my head. Things I don't want to think about, pictures in my head I don't want to see." Danny rubs his eyes. "They're always there. I ran from it. Uh, I've tried to get away from it. I have. But it never leaves me. I don't know that it ever will—no matter how far I go."

He looks the counselor in the eye for the first time, in silence, not without emotion but with wearied expectation.

"Danny," she says gently, "what happened to you back then is not your fault. You couldn't help that your father was abusive, that your mother was mentally unstable. You and your brothers should not have had to go through it, that's for sure."

He's heard this before. He knows it wasn't his fault. But it still happened.

"It was out of your control. The beatings, the yelling, your mother's absence. You had to live through it, but none of it was your fault. None at all . . . But to be honest, in my line of work, it's not a story I haven't heard before. A great many of the people that come through this and shelters just like it all over the world have a similar sad tale to share. Abuse, either violent, verbal, or sexual, sometimes drugs or alcohol, and also neglect are all different aspects of the same problem—a difficult, seemingly unfair upbringing that leaves its mark or scar indelibly on the recipient."

Hold it a minute, Danny thinks. Is she dismissing that time, that place, that man?

"Well, uh, I'm sure there's a lot of 'recipients' out there," he says, heating up a little. "But I'm guessing not too many got locked out of their house for the day when it was 20 degrees outside. And then did a group shit with their brothers in the woods, wiping their assholes with dirty leaves in the dead of winter. Or that had to crowd around and stand over top a damn trash can to eat a snack, praying that no crumbs—and I mean not one—would touch the floor, because if it did . . . well, shit!"

The sound of his voice rises now, even louder, and the truth, the truth of that time that's burned in his soul, the truth that made him run then and keeps him running now, spills out.

"I'm talking fear, man. Fear—all the time. Fear when you see him first thing in the morning and wonder what kind of mood he's in; fear when you come in from playing outside; fear when you step inside the house after school or work; fear when you're sitting at the dinner table; fear when you climb in bed at night. Fuckin' fear all the time." He snorts. "Hell, I remember hiding in the backseat of our car with my brothers when Mama was still at work, scared to death; coming home from the neighborhood bar at night in a weaving vehicle when Pop was drunk and complaining loudly about having to take care of my sorry ass, my brothers, hell, Mama—just waiting for him to reach back there, to turn on me. Uh, yeah, man, just normal, everyday stuff, I guess, right?"

"Danny, I'm not saying your experience wasn't unique to you. And I'm not saying it wasn't difficult, very difficult. I am saying what happened back then was not your responsibility. I am saying it was not your fault. And I am saying one more very important thing that you need to hear," she adds.

"Yeah?"

"You can't help what he did to you back then. But the direction of your life right now is your responsibility, no one else's. And it is your fault that what happened back then, as bad it was at the time, controls the outcome of your life now—today. My strong advice to you is to let no one, and I mean no one, but you and, if you believe as I do, God dictate the terms or the outcomes of your life!"

She says this with a firmness of conviction that makes him stop for a moment, sit up, and take notice.

"Point blank: your life from today moving forward—it's on you." She drives the point home with finality.

He remains silent. Over the years, most people have expressed sympathy and shock when he's given even a few of the details of his early life. And while it's sometimes been unspoken, he's usually been given the get-out-of-jail-free pass, the "oh, now I get why you're homeless" sympathy gaze, that exempts him from the responsibility of his aimless existence and his disparate state. It's bought him food, money, even a few nights in decent hotel rooms over the years. But this woman is having none of it.

The conversation ends quickly. He does not argue her point. He also does not change his ways—not today. But the great kindness he's been given in this moment, these frankly spoken words of wisdom, stay with him and begin to tug at his soul, forcing him, in moments of defeat or weakness, to consider the hapless direction of his life. He even briefly thinks of the possibility of making a change—the idea of stopping, of no longer running.

But he's not ready.

Not quite yet.

Thirty-Three
The Third Speech

IN MID-2007, OUR PRIVATE equity investors successfully sell Performance Bike—to another private equity firm. It's a time of tremendous satisfaction at past accomplishments—but also real uncertainty.

From a career perspective, I'd played a large role in the exponential and profitable growth of the business. I'd thrived under the demanding and informed scrutiny of billion-dollar investment firms and my early belief in my potential as an effective business leader is now fully supported by tangible results.

And the bitter recurring dreams of an abused child begin to fade as a strong work ethic and a determined pursuit of my responsibilities as a husband, father, and business leader take hold—my father's influence both wanes and waxes in the trajectory of my life.

But this purchase of Performance is different from 1999. When that deal was complete, we had millions of dollars in the bank to help grow the business. When I learn the specific terms of this deal (The Company will instead *owe many* millions of dollars to multiple lenders!), I forcefully express my strong discomfort. But there's nothing I can do. Garry has long since given up majority control and I'm simply a hired hand. Our new owners assure me they will be there to help us make it all work.

But the timing of the purchase is terrible. Within weeks, the great recession of 2007 (mortgage debacle, stock market crash, etc.) hits and our business, like so many others, is negatively impacted. Over a series of conference calls, the mounting frustration of our new owners is made apparent.

For the first time, our business struggles.

In December of 2007, only six months after the new investors bought us, Garry is relieved of his duties as the CEO of Performance. He calls Bob and me around the holidays and shares the distressing news. My heart is broken at the loss of my mentor.

That night, I share my concerns with Paula.

"What are you going to do?" she asks.

"I really don't know," I answer.

Later that evening, over a cold beer, I consider the dramatic turn of events and realize I have lived out my professional career just as I lived out my youth under Pop's erratic, unrelenting reign—with an ever-present element of fear. I never knew when Pop would come at me, hand raised or belt out, or why. There was no rhyme or reason, so I treaded lightly, always aware of his moods, always knowing the storm could blow in mercilessly, even on a sunny day.

Similarly, in my career, no matter the level of achievement—businesses bought, leaders developed, results delivered, departments turned around, capital raised—I live at work with the same silent but mostly well-hidden fear, constantly thinking someone will walk in and, with no warning, for no good reason, terminate my employment. And the fear has become heavier since Paula and the boys have come along and my responsibilities have extended beyond my personal well-being.

But my fear has always been focused on my employment, my performance, not Garry's. For some reason, I thought he'd be the CEO at Performance as long as he wanted. Looking back, that seems naive, particularly since the money guys took control. Still, I didn't expect his termination, and it has hit me like a sucker punch to the gut.

I take a final swig of beer and make my decision. Garry will be sorely missed in the day-to-day (he will, thankfully, remain on the board) and my future at Performance is more uncertain than ever. But for now, my family is happy in Chapel Hill—so I'm going to stick it out and see what happens.

Our owners hire a new CEO. He is a good and extremely charismatic man. He serves in the role for three years, while thankfully retaining me as his CFO, and I serve him to the best of my ability. But it doesn't work out. We simply don't get results. I consider it to be my failure as well as his.

Our owners decide to make another change at the helm—and they ask me what I would do if I were running the business. I answer them confidently and specifically, and in the first fiscal quarter of 2011, I am made the new CEO!

Though I'm the third CEO to lead Performance since our current owners took over in mid-2007, it's a role I believe I can handle, albeit not one I necessarily covet. Gratitude, not ambition, is the prevailing emotion I have about my life and career right now. Still, it is a huge moment, and a long way from where I started. My son Zack asks me, "What does a CEO do, Dad?"

I'm about to find out.

As I kick things off, I talk to key members of our management team, as well as our broader associate base, and things begin to crystalize.

From a financial standpoint, we have way too much debt and we do not get paid enough for the value of the goods we sell. The place to reduce debt is our high-dollar, slow-turning inventory. It needs to come down. If we can reduce that inventory, we can free up significant cash to invest in other initiatives to help our business grow. If we can cut inventory *and* increase margins *and* drive our overall top-line sales—well, that will dramatically increase cash and profit *and* reduce our debt, putting us on a much better road for the future.

But it's more than a financial overhaul to the company that must occur. Morale also needs a boost. We need a new message and rallying cry; we need to harness the formidable power of the talent of our great people. We start there, and within ninety days, after reviewing it with the board and getting key input from select members of our team, we've developed new vision and mission statements.

Our vision is aspirational and focused on improving the health of our customers and the planet—on contributing to a better world. It gives our associates a larger reason for working, and maybe for working just a little bit harder. Life is about larger things than the day-to-day grind of a job. Feeling good about what you're doing, why you're doing it, and who you're doing it with can be invaluable. It's also the right thing for us as a company to aspire to.

We've decided that our mission, which needs to be more concrete than our vision, is to focus our company on taking world-class care of our customers.

In the world of Amazon Prime and with the transparency of online retail, we can no longer win the pricing game. So, we will cement our position as the authority in the cycling space (still providing the same great pricing on our broad assortment of products), by giving our customers new and better services such as online training and product tips, in-store training classes, and also try to get more of them on bikes by hosting weekly rides from our stores. Hopefully that along with our drive to refine our inventory and raise our margins will be enough to motivate the team, win customer loyalty, and get our company back on track.

With our course now firmly set, it's time for me to pull the team together and communicate our new direction. I schedule a "town hall meeting" with our entire associate base across the country. It's set for a Wednesday afternoon.

I sleep well the night before the meeting. I know what we need to do and I know how to communicate it to our associates. I know the business, I know our customer, and I know who I am—both my weaknesses and my strengths. The experiences I've had throughout my career, both the accomplishments and the failures, have taught me that I have good problem-solving skills and an analytical mind, an ability to see a bigger picture and think strategically, and a sincere willingness to listen and learn, along with a relentless drive to create positive results and grow the talents of good people. My life journey also tells me I have stubborn resilience in pursuit of what I believe is right. No doubt I have innumerable weaknesses, but I've known about those since my days as a five-year-old running around that dilapidated old rental house. My career and life have taught me that I also have talent and ability, however—and, most importantly, when it comes to running a business—and my life—I'm not afraid. I'm simply no longer afraid.

I'm ready for this.

When I walk down the main stairs in our 120,000-square-foot warehouse at 12:55 p.m., approximately two hundred of our people are waiting for me. Just as importantly, our other 1,800 associates in retail stores, contact centers, and other facilities across the country are poised to hear my message and follow along with a PowerPoint on their computer or laptop screens. I wish I could be with all of them face to face. I wish they could see the fire in my eyes and the determination in my countenance.

I cross the floor purposefully and as I step up on the podium and adjust the microphone, the chattering stops and expectant eyes focus their attention directly on me. There is no shakiness, no fear—only focus. I have a job to do and the future of the company is on the line. We have a message to deliver and a direction to sell, so I'm going to give my full heart now, because I'm asking for their hearts and commitment going forward.

With optimism, passion, and the courage of my convictions, I communicate our proposed new direction. I field a few questions and ask for everyone's best effort and buy-in in support of our new mission. I believe I get it.

When we do our annual review almost a year later, in January of 2012, profit is up 5 percent and we've shaved millions of dollars out of our bloated inventory. A year after that, in January of 2013, profit is up a whopping 20 percent, more millions have been cut out of the inventory, and we've paid down many millions of dollars of debt. It might be the best financial year in company history! The lenders are thrilled, our high-powered board (including the former CEO of Vitamin Shoppe and President of Barnes & Noble, and the former COO of Whole Foods, among others) is pleased and so are the investors. More importantly to me, thousands of customers are riding their bikes with us on the weekends and attending in-store clinics, and our customer service scores are going up, particularly in retail. Our employees are also properly motivated and fully on board.

These are heady times, no doubt the best professional time of my life.

But while I'm feeling optimistic, I'm also wary. We still have a sizable amount of debt from the purchase in 2007, and I'm aware of larger macro trends that are already pressuring the business, stunting the momentum we've gained in the past few years. Customers are shopping less and less in brick-and-mortar stores across the country, and millennials are simply not embracing the bicycle like the baby boomers before them. Still, after such a great couple of years, I cannot possibly imagine the extraordinary challenges that lie ahead.

Everything I believe about who I am, and the man I think I've become, will be put to the test.

Thirty-Four
An Un-wasted Act of Kindness

His FEET ARE MOVING west from Omaha, Nebraska, on I-80. He's been on the highway for over three hours on a sweltering hot Memorial Day. The thickness of the heat feels like an inanimate, immovable, textured mist weighing down his clothes and weakening his legs. The highway is jammed with returning vacationers and impatient drivers who insistently move past his beckoning thumb. His pace slows to a near crawl—and suddenly he comes to a dead stop.

He's mentally and physically exhausted. His slumping frame is weary; his soul feels cursed; his will is broken. He prides himself on his fitness and physical strength—if he has food in his belly, which he does today, he can always go long and hard. But his legs are done and he stands immobile, forlorn, buried in the resentful thoughts of a troubled mind. His backpack feels oppressively heavy. So does his heart.

He lifts the pack off his shoulders and tosses it in the gravel at his feet. He drops down to his knees, lifts his arms, and buries his face into the folded shelter of trembling hands. His mind roils with memories. He thinks about an old girlfriend, Lisa, he had when he was just a kid working at the pizza parlor in Greensboro. He felt like he could do anything, be anything, when they were together. But it didn't last; she left him. He thinks about the day he left Greensboro with Jimmy—how excited he was to have a new start, how he foolishly thought he could find his rightful place in the world. But he hasn't found anything at all, at least not anything that's meant anything in his life. Now he's just outside Omaha—steamy, oblivious Omaha— kneeling beside a crowded interstate, hot, tired, and defeated.

"Why am I doing this to myself?" he asks no one in particular, completely insensible to the cars flying by just twenty feet from his left shoulder. He repeats the question several times, then asks, "What the hell is wrong with me?"

Quiet desperation presses in, weighing on him, a thousand times heavier than the load he just tossed to the ground. He's up and walking now, very slowly, back and forth, parallel to the highway, with the backpack serving as home base. He continues his one-sided conversation. Drivers honk their horns as they pass. He looks to the sky.

"I don't know what I'm supposed to do anymore, God. I don't understand. Is this all there is?"

Nothing. He keeps moving. Unanswered questions fuel bitter anger and resentment.

"I didn't ask to be brought here. I didn't ask to be born, to have to deal with Pop and Mama and all that shit back then. I didn't ask for any of it."

His hands wave maniacally in the air as he talks to God and himself. More cars are now blowing their horns—he's getting too close to the highway—but he doesn't notice or care.

"Well, what is it? What am I supposed to do? It can't be this shit." He points to his backpack lying on the ground. "Am I supposed to live hand-to-mouth for the rest of my life? Did I do something wrong? Are you punishing me for something?" he asks.

He looks to the sky. "WHAT DID I DO WRONG?" he screams, head thrown back.

God does not answer. The heat rises from the highway in shimmering waves. Danny's shirt sticks wet and tight to his back. He works up a lathered sweat as he continues his trek back and forth.

"Okay, I've stolen shit and I've hurt people. I know that. I'm not perfect. But I didn't do it when I was a kid, and still you let that man loose on me. I did nothing to deserve that! That's on you!"

He shakes his balled fist, arm bent at the elbow, then stares at his knuckles.

"I was just a stupid kid," he whispers faintly.

He turns his head from side to side. His lips fold inward; his eyes stare deeply into the passing ground at his feet as he continues to walk.

"Sometimes I can't make my mind stop, God. It won't stop! I feel restless, pissed off, fuckin' unsatisfied! I don't know why I couldn't stay with my first wife, with those other women. I don't know why!" His feet pound the pavement. "Tell me. Help me understand! Tell me what you want me to do, and I'll do it!" He looks to the skies again for instruction.

But there is no sign—just the oppressive heat and a hot wind hitting him in the face as speeding cars cut through the flat, muggy air. There is no thunderclap; no clouds roll in, filling empty blue skies. There are only angry drivers leaning on their horns at the sight of this strange man talking to himself and edging closer to their lane.

Nothing happens. Nothing at all.

"This is it then, God? This is the story of my life? Haven't I endured enough shit by now?" he asks angrily.

Suddenly, he stops walking.

"Haven't I?"

He lowers his head and breaks down. His hands drop to his knees as tears begin to fall, dropping softly to the scorched gravel. A merciless yellow sun snatches them up, confirming their irrelevance. He stands hunched over for a long minute, then takes a deep breath, stands up straight, and wipes his eyes with his forearm as sticky sweat replaces bitter tears. He turns and walks back to the resting backpack, ignoring the passing, honking traffic as his thoughts slowly tilt toward a final resignation.

"I'm getting close to fifty years old, and I'm fucking standin' on this highway in the middle of nowhere. I haven't seen my family in almost twenty years. I don't even know if they're alive. Hell, they don't even know if I'm alive."

And finally:

"Shit, if I died, it wouldn't matter. Hell, no one would even know."

Suddenly, he becomes mindful of the cars roaring past with heedless speed. Beaded sweat dots a burnt brow. And then—a desolate dread succumbs to a budding but resolute certainty rising fast in a fretful soul. He leans in closer to the highway. Time and motion freeze.

Fifteen yards in front of him, a silver Lincoln Continental gives its right turn signal and pulls off the crowded highway. Its flashers blink on, and it comes to a complete stop. He turns and glances up from the lonely solitude of his tormented mind. What looks to be an older, graying gentleman leans out of the driver's side window and shouts, "Can I give you a lift?"

Danny hesitates.

Over the many years, the cars that have stopped for his entreating thumb on interstates and winding two-lane roads have been piloted by people with varying degrees of purpose—both good and bad. Sometimes people stop, then hit the gas upon his approach. "Reach for the door handle only once"—my brother tells his fellow homeless travelers now. "Reach just once."

Some people try to help. But deeply personal questions are often asked: "What happened to you? How did things turn out this way?" And they always seem to have the same answer of the way to a better life.

Concealed evil has also met him in a stopped car. He had to run once from a man in Sioux Falls who said his wife was lying alone in a motel room and he needed him to make love to her on his behalf. He ran hard on that night.

Honest, non-judgmental outreach—neighbor helping neighbor, with no underlying motive—is a rare arrival. But the occasional driver allows Danny to breathe, relax, rest, and restore. He's not shamed; merely supported. In those times, he feels and expresses sincere gratitude and, most importantly, pulls into himself a revitalizing measure of faith and hope that can sustain and propel him onward for a day, a week, a month, maybe longer, lifting him for a time through his perilous journey on desperate foot in God's country.

But—there is always the moment: The moment when the door is open or the window is down, when questioning eyes meet, when words are spoken, when a decision has to be made—"Do I get in, or do I back away?" "Because once that door is closed, a risk is taken—on both sides—and two souls tempt a mutual fate. Over time, he has gotten better at the hitchhiker's decision-making process, asking the right questions and taking a hard look before he climbs in the vehicle. But he does not always get it right. Will he be right this time?

Danny stands there for a moment, unmoving, silent. He looks left to the killing highway for a final, ambivalent moment, then quickly makes his decision. He grabs his bag, shuts down his mind, walks slowly to the Lincoln, and looks thoughtfully into the open passenger side window.

"Where you headed?" asks the elderly driver with soft eyes.

"Salt Lake City, but mostly I just want to get out of the heat," Danny responds.

"Well, climb in," the old man says.

Danny opens the rear passenger door, puts his bag on the floorboard, unzips the top, and grabs his water. He opens the front door, plops down in the seat, and carefully closes the door behind him. He's relieved to get off his feet, to turn off the pain.

He looks to his left. He sees gray hair, bushy eyebrows, and a Leno-like chin.

"Thanks for the ride," he says. "Name's Danny."

"John," the old gentleman replies. "Buckle up."

John is heading to Henderson, Nevada, says he owns some sort of silver company there. Henderson is almost 1,300 miles away from where they currently are, outside of Omaha. It's roughly a nineteen-hour trip, and he welcomes the help in making the drive. Danny's goal is Salt Lake City, so they strike a deal: He'll do the bulk of the driving. In return, John will put him up in a room and buy him a few meals along the way.

They make it a good distance that afternoon before pulling off at a local restaurant called "The Rowdy Steer." Over a steak dinner, they share the stories of their separate lives. Danny sleeps that night showered, with a full belly, in a warm bed. He and John share the same small room—with two queen beds. He's a little nervous about this at first; he's seen too much over the years. But it's no problem. The man wants help driving and nothing else.

The next day, the food and the drive continue. Danny drives

while John periodically sleeps in the backseat—mouth hanging open, snoring loudly. They complete the trip late that afternoon when they spot a strip mall just inside the city limits of Salt Lake City.

"This is great, right here," the old man instructs.

Danny pulls into a parking spot and turns off the engine.

"Listen, I can't thank you enough for the ride and the food and the hotel room. Best night of sleep I've had in a long, long time. You really helped me out." He looks his savior square in the eye, says it, and means it.

"Hey, listen, you helped me," John says. "That drive would've been tough alone. I think I could've made it, but I'm glad I didn't have to find out."

On the road and over the course of a few meals, they've gotten to know each other a bit. Danny sees the good in this old fellow, and he seems to have found something he likes in Danny in return. A thousand miles back, they decided to take a chance—and each has been rewarded. John has gotten here safely, and Danny has gotten a lot more than John realizes he's given.

"Well, here's the key, let me grab my backpack out the back," he says as he puts the keys in the man's hand. After grabbing the loose strap of his bag and slinging it over his right shoulder, he walks around the back of the car, planning to head to the other side to shake the man's hand one last time. But the old man meets him at the rear of the car.

"Look, I hope you don't mind," John says. "I think you're a man who's had more than his fair share of bad luck. You helped me out, so I'd like to give you this to help you along your way. I hope it's all right?" He sticks his hand out, holding five twenties.

Danny looks down, sees the cash, then looks into the kind eyes of the old man and feels gratitude push up his chest and clench tightly at his throat. His heart thumps as he swallows it back down. He does not push John's hand away or falsely feign an inability to take that which is now so graciously offered. He needs the money. The man knows it, and so does he. He gives without expectation, with no agenda. He's not waiting for appreciation. He harbors no illusions and asks no questions about how the money will be spent. He does not view him through judgmental eyes or proselytize about what he should be doing with his life. He is simply helping because he wants to. Perhaps a benevolent God looks down with pleasure at the mercy and compassion the old man has shown. Perhaps this is all the man needs.

Danny takes the money. He thinks about hugging the old gentleman but instead extends a grateful hand. They vigorously shake and he slowly releases his grip—and, one final time, thanks him profusely. The man wishes him well, climbs in his car, and is on his way.

Danny walks across the busy street leading into town and enters a McDonald's. He grabs a cheeseburger, Coke, and fries, takes a seat in the back by the window, drops his bag, and loses himself, after all that's happened in the last few days, in a long, reflective moment.

In this long run, he thinks, *I've seen things I never thought I'd see, things I didn't want to see. But I saw them anyway. And I've come to know this plain fact: my pain is relative.*

He thinks about his time on the road and all the pain he endured, all the pain he saw: sallow-faced drug addicts lying half-dead on the streets as busy passersby tried not to trip over their prostrate bodies; young but sullen-eyed women prostituting themselves while carrying a baby on their arm; nights so cold he didn't know if he'd survive (on one snowy, 18-degree night under a dark overpass in Albuquerque, he almost didn't).

Then he remembers one particularly terrible night. He was staying at a YMCA in Des Moines on a bitterly cold day when he noticed an American Indian man with torn pants and no socks—he looked to be around fifty years old—hiding out behind the public library across the street. He had his cardboard bed, his few belongings, and his booze. He looked to be blind drunk and near passing out.

Danny stood in front of the Y quietly that evening, smoke escaping his mouth, and watched the man's chest expand and contract slowly, almost imperceptibly, wondering if he would survive the cold, black night ahead. He got his answer the next morning when he stepped outside to see the coroner take the man's body away in a van. That memory, one filled with regret, has lived inside him for years.

Yeah, I got no home and no family, at least not one I can go back to, but I've still got my good health, he thinks. *Still, it's damn wrong for me to take some kinda comfort in the struggles of others.*

Yet plainly, God has shown him, almost daily, that there are people in this world that have it worse than him. And, right or wrong, it's helped.

He takes a bite of his cheeseburger and savors his third good meal in a row. *Thank God for that old man*, he thinks again to himself.

Then other, better, memories come forward.

The old man isn't the first stranger who has stepped up to help him.

In Fort Worth, Texas, a woman approached him and told him to wait right where he was. After a while, he considered moving on, but just as he was turning to leave she suddenly reappeared and handed him a bag full of McDonald's burgers and a twenty-dollar bill. She asked for nothing in return.

A preacher in Fort Smith, Arkansas, picked him up and took him to Oklahoma City. They stopped and ate at Braum's Ice Cream and

Burger. He'd never forget the taste of that banana split—man! The price? He listened to what he believed to be a sincere personal witness to Jesus Christ. When he dropped him off in Oklahoma City, the preacher gave him his card, a twenty-dollar bill, and an invitation to call if he ever needed help.

An insurance salesman picked him up just outside of Columbia and gave him a good, honest conversation and a fifty-dollar bill.

He was even picked up by a group of college students on his way to Minneapolis, who left him with their best wishes and a $100 gift card to Walmart.

But the best thing anyone has ever done for him came yesterday, when he thought of bad things, things he'd never thought of before. He'd never felt so weak, so hopeless, in his entire life, not even when Pop got a hold of him back in the day. But the old man showed up, somehow, just in time.

Maybe God was showing him his worth—in the most critical moment of his life. He sits quietly, pondering the possibility, and a healing wave of gratitude slowly washes over him. He closes his eyes, then looks to the ceiling and mouths, "Thank you."

He rises from the table now. He looks in his left palm and counts out the four twenty-dollar bills and change. He puts it away safely in his wallet. He can make it go a long way. And his legs feel strong again.

It's getting late in the afternoon, but he has a little time to look around town before making his way to the local shelter before dark. He'll find work in the morning. It's around 75 degrees, and he's nearing the end of a perfect day. He steps outside and looks up at a yellow sun that doesn't burn quite so hot anymore.

He has no more questions for God—or the blue skies above.

Life on the road—his life—will go on.

Thirty-Five
Acceptance?

WHEN MY FATHER STORMED out the front door of our home in Chapel Hill, he had no plans of coming back. And in fact, he never has. There have been several attempts to reconcile, but all have been fleeting. Each time, when I've called later to check on him, he's been silent and sulky, almost non-responsive.

He continues to dwell on what he perceives to be his mistreatment at Paula's hands. Since I'm her husband, his son, and the man of the house, I'm complicit and just as guilty; I've allowed it all to happen.

After a while, Paula and I decide there's no way to make it work between her and Pop. If I want to continue to make it work for myself, to have a relationship with him and Helen, Paula will stay at home and I'll cart the kids to their house and spend the weekend in their company.

And I do for many years.

The good news is that Pop and Helen have done well in retirement. Pop's a saver who's built a decent nest egg. They also have a good income, between their two social security checks and two pension checks from Lorillard. They have a pretty brick patio home in an idyllic neighborhood fifteen minutes from Topsail Island in eastern

North Carolina. I could not be happier for them. Despite my lingering resentment over my brutal childhood and even now, with the troubles between Pop and Paula, I want him and Helen to be happy and comfortable—and they are.

I also desperately want my kids to have at least some exposure to my side of their family. It's part of who they are and who I am. But it isn't easy. My father's negativity, on occasion, bubbles to the surface in their presence. "How's your wife doing?" he asks. Then he proceeds to remind me of all the wrongdoing that's been heaped on him by Paula and my lack of "manning up."

Sometimes the boys are busy with sports or friends, and I visit alone. On those occasions, Pop feels free to share his knifing, needling opinions more directly with me. Those are dangerous times, because while I do my best to restrain my frustration with what I see as Pop's narrow-minded thinking, I'm less likely to keep myself from responding when my kids aren't there. One day he calls me over to his oval, glass-topped, four-seater dining table just off the kitchen to talk. The kids are back in Chapel Hill. We've been getting along well so far for the weekend.

"Listen, I want to talk to you about a few things," he starts.

"Sure, Pop. What's up?"

"Your mama and I have had our wills done, and we've put you in charge," he states plainly.

"Okay, Pop. I'll do whatever you want to be done. Did you state clearly what you want to happen in the will? That's important. I don't want to get into any arguments or confusion with Billy or Danny—assuming we can find him."

"Yes, I split everything evenly three ways," he says casually, as I expected.

"Well, that's easy. I'll make sure it happens just that way."

But I'm wrong. It's not going to be easy.

"I don't know what's going to happen with me and your mama when we get too old to take care of ourselves." He pauses. "I know she's not your mama, but she's been better to you than your real mama ever was."

"She has, Pop. You're right. You know, I've told you before—when you and Helen get older, I will help you. I'll make sure you're both properly taken care of." I've said this many times before when he's brought this topic up.

He looks at me dubiously, showing his cynicism for my promise, and sarcastically says, "Uh-huh." Then: "I don't think your wife is going to let that happen."

"Pop, Paula doesn't want anything bad to happen to you and Helen. And she's not going to have any problem with me helping you guys when you need it. She'll help too. I know it." And I do.

His face says he doesn't believe me.

"Well," he says, "I don't want to make you mad, but I think I oughta tell you: I thought about giving everything to Billy and Danny. You're a big wheel now. You make all that money. You and your wife don't need this little piddling amount I got."

I instantly feel resentful toward this man. Danny, God bless him, has not been around to deal with Pop all these years. Billy continues to stay in touch, though somewhat sparingly. But I willed myself to stay—and I stuck it out. When he takes shots at Paula, I keep coming. When he refuses to come to my home, I keep coming to him. When I work a sixty-hour week and get in late on a Friday night, I still pack up early on a Saturday morning and drive three hours to get to him. He insults me with petty comments, and still, I keep coming.

It's not about the money. At some level, he's right, I don't need the money. And I certainly don't want to take anything from my brothers. But I see myself as a dutiful son, and I'm hurt by the thought that he considered not including me. I don't want a penny more than my siblings, but I'm an equal son. I want equal acknowledgment.

"Well, Pop, it's your money," I say slowly. "You can do what you want. But I don't think that's right. I'm your son just like they're your sons, and I don't think I should be penalized for doing well. There are three of us, and I think you're right and fair to split it evenly three ways. I would not want it any other way. But again, it's your money. You can do whatever you want. Whatever's in the will, if I'm the executor, then that's what will get done."

"Now, David, you know your wife hasn't been fair to me and your mama in there," he starts in. "We don't get to see them boys nearly as much as your mama- and daddy-in-law does."

Oh my God, this is what he really wants to talk about. We're gonna do this again? I feel my anger rise. This is going to go in a bad direction in a hurry, and I don't think I can stop it.

"Pop, I work a lot of hours and have a lot of responsibility, but I take the time to bring the boys here every month or so. Despite the differences you've had with Paula, we've both told you, many times over, that you are welcome to come to our house any time you want. Matthew plays basketball, pretty well actually, and Zack is an excellent lacrosse player. They both play on traveling teams and have games a lot of weekends. That makes it tough for me to be here. But you and Helen can come to those games if you want to, I've told you that many times. You should come. You're missing it."

"Your wife don't want us there," he says stubbornly.

"Pop, you and Paula have had issues. All families do. I don't know how many times the four of us have sat down together and hashed things out. We've all apologized, and hugged, and said all is forgiven. But I call a few weeks later and it's like those discussions never happened. What am I supposed to do with that?"

"That's because I know she lets her parents see those kids more than us. She don't treat us the same. You know that."

"Pop, I'm dead on the weekends and the kids have stuff almost every weekend anyway. We hardly go to see her folks these days. But they come to us a lot. They want to see their grandkids, and they make it a priority. They're always welcome in our home, just like you are. And they take advantage of it."

"She let those kids both take presents on Matthew's birthday and she told us we couldn't do that. It ain't right and you know it ain't right, son."

"Oh my God. Pop, that was almost five years ago. We've apologized, and we explained the mix-up. They missed Zack's birthday. That's why they had a late present for him. We told you that, but we still apologized. Look, you're missing it. Zack is fourteen years old and Matthew's ten. They're growing up fast. I want you to be there. They want you to be there. Danny's gone and I hardly see Billy. You're all the family I have. You're choosing not to come. Can't you see that?"

I'm almost pleading now. I want to make it right. I want us to put it behind us. Paula will make it work. She'd told me that, and she's also told Pop that.

"I don't go where I'm not wanted."

I begin to lose it.

"Pop, Paula is my wife. She has told you herself, you are welcome in our home. She's been a great wife to me and a wonderful mother to those boys. And you won't even say her name anymore. How do you think that makes me feel?"

"Well, it's partly your fault. You don't stand up like a man and make her treat us fair—let us see those boys like her mama and daddy."

"That's not true, Pop. It's all in your head. They see the kids more because they come to see them. They make the effort. We don't go to their place much at all. There's no time. We have too much going on. I bring the kids to see you a lot more than I go see them, I can tell you that. You can come any time you want. We've both told you that."

"Your mama and I are not going to be mistreated, son."

Helen's sitting in the den off the kitchen as Pop and I sit at the table. I roll my chair closer to its glass-topped edge—and the loss of my sanity.

"*You're* not going to be mistreated? Are you kidding me? How about those times you mistreated *me* when I was growing up? Mistreated? You're gonna say that to me? Really?"

"Your mama and I have as much right to see those boys as they do."

It's as if I'm talking to the wall. The fact that I'm still here, trying to be his son, after all that's happened through the years, is, in my mind, unmitigated evidence that I still love them. Why would I then not be fair with them? What's he talking about?

"You do have the right, and you have the opportunity. You're choosing not to take advantage of it."

"David, you can't tell me she don't tell you what to do and that she don't take those young'uns to see them more than us."

My heart grows hard, my mind impatient.

"Pop, you bring me over here to talk. You tell me you almost wrote me out of your will. You tell me that I'm led around by the nose by Paula, that I'm some sort of a weak man, that I've somehow been unfair to you. Can't you see? That's ridiculous! You're doing this to yourself!"

"I'm telling you . . ." he starts.

That's it. The hell with this.

"No," I snap, "you're not telling me. You know what? You've underestimated me my whole life. I'm not a weak man. You're wrong. And I've been a good son to you. I bring the kids to see you. I tell you I'll help take care of you when you get old and you laugh—like I'm a liar, like I'm feeding you a load of shit. Well, *this* is a load of shit."

"I'm just saying your mama over there and I want to be treated fair! You know this ain't fair!!"

I leap from the chair and grab my side of the heavy glass table. I easily lift it off the ground and fling it up into the air. It drops back to the ground, the two legs at the far end hitting first and bouncing forward. The glass slides partially off the top and leaves my father sitting motionless, his two legs and criminal lunacy fully exposed.

"No," I cry, "*I* want to be treated fairly! For once, my God, please! You beat the shit out of me when I was a kid. You told me I wasn't worth a shit for nothing. You're telling me now I'm a weak man, and I know you're trying to poke at me, trying to get a rise, on the will thing. I know you are. Well, dammit, I've had it! I've tried. I've really tried. I've tried to put all the shit that's happened between us aside over the years, but you won't let me. Because whatever I did back then, and whatever I do now, even today, it's still not good enough. It's your insecurities. Can't you see that? You just conjure up bullshit in your mind. You sit around with dead time on your hands all day long, day after day, thinking about things, stewing on them."

"David, calm down. Sit down, we can talk about this," Helen cajoles. She's now behind me.

She places her hands on my right arm to hold me back. We've done this dance before.

"You just stew on shit," I go on, my whole body shaking with rage. "And you turn it into something bigger than what it is. But by then, it's too late, you believe it. Then it has to come out. You have to get it out of your system, somehow, some way. When we were little snot-nosed kids, our asses and our minds, that's how you got it out. The slap across the room, the drag by the ankle, yelling, cursing, standing over us screaming while we shook like scarecrows in the wind. We were your release back then. But you can't do that now—we're too big, or we're not around. But it still has to come out. You still have to dream shit up. So now you hold it in until I get here, and then you say I'm a weak, failing son, coming up short again. You turn Paula—my wife, the most important person in my life—into a bad person, a villain. Don't you see it's all in your mind? We'll come and see you. You can come to our house all you want, just like her parents! WHY THE HELL ARE YOU EVEN KEEPING SCORE ANYWAY?"

I step back from the table. I look once more, dead-eyed and exhausted, at my father.

"Don't you see? Granny, your mama, stirred up shit constantly when you were growing up. You told me once she kept your nerves torn up as a child. Do you remember telling me that years ago? Well, guess what, you do the same thing. You've done it all my life. You've torn my ass up, and you're tearing my nerves up now! And remember this: you ran my brother, your son, into the streets. Dammit! Don't think I don't know that!"

His eyes stare at me, big and cloudy. For once, he remains silent.

I step back from the disheveled table. "I'm through with this. I've had it. I can't take this shit anymore."

I turn and head back to the bedroom to pack my stuff. But before I slam the door behind me, I stop and look at my father, for what I expect will be the last time.

"I'm done with this. I'm done trying. And I'm done with you. It's over."

I slam the bedroom door behind me. I grab my backpack off the carpeted floor, place it on the bed, and put my clothes, my shaving kit, and my Kindle inside and zip it up. *Fuck this*, I think. I never had real parents to begin with. Mama only wanted what little money I had, and Pop abused us like dogs. The bottom line is, Mama doesn't feel love, and Pop has no idea how to give it. I simply can't do enough to make him happy. I've never been able to. And I'll never be able to. Why do I want to, anyway?

For a minute, I sit down on the bed and place my bag back on the ground. Thoughts continue to ramble.

Growing up, I truly hated him at times. And I feel the impact of what he did to me every day of my life. The self-doubt, social awkwardness, occasional sleepless nights, and episodic memories of the beatings and derisive words still haunt me. *What the hell am I hanging on to here?* I ask myself, as I've done many times before.

I get up from the bed, sling my backpack over my shoulder, grab my pillow with my left hand, and place my right on the doorknob. I take a deep breath. I'm getting the hell out of here, and I'm not coming back. The hell with it. I'm just not coming back this time.

I open the door and step into the foyer.

Helen stops me. She was thrown into the middle of all this shit years ago, and she's still here.

"David, don't go like this. Don't let it end like this."

She senses, correctly, that if I leave now, I won't be back.

Pop sits quietly at the table, looking down, staring at the realigned glass tabletop. He's already straightened it.

I stop for a moment. I look down at Helen and take one final look over at Pop. He doesn't return my glance. I turn coldly and go. I push open the glass front door, step outside, and make my way down the front porch steps. I open the trunk of my car, toss in my backpack and pillow, then close it. I head for the driver's side door, open it, climb in, and push the ignition button.

And then, I don't know why, but I decide to sit for a final minute.

My thoughts travel back once more to my distant, unreachable mother. I think back to that October day so many years ago when she called and tried to take away the money for college. I knew then, without a doubt, that she didn't love me, not even a little. So I cut her loose. At that moment, my heart was cold as frozen snow, and I never looked back for her. Still, a few years ago, I went looking one last time. And I found her—still in Greensboro, living with a family that was paid by the state to take care of her. She had a bedroom, they fed her, and she kept herself clean. That was it. She remembered me. She also told me she worked in secret service protection for Bill Clinton. When I told her about my life, the kids, my work, she said nothing. And, in turn, I felt nothing. When she died, I didn't even know, and when I found out I didn't even care. I'm not sure I'd have even gone to the funeral if I had known it was happening.

I continue sitting in silence and consider that sorry fact.

I think of Danny. I don't think of him as often as I used to, but the truth is, I had more in common with him than with any other member of our family. We genuinely enjoyed being around one another. But so much time has passed. And I didn't think I'd lose him the way I did. He's long gone now, to God knows where. I don't even know if he's alive. And by God, my father had his hand in that.

The thought angers me again.

I think of Billy. He can be as cold as Mama. We talk, but only if I bump into him at Pop's or I call. He's asked for my help financially a few times over the years, and I've given it to him. He's my brother, and I love him. Whether he's truly capable of loving in return, I don't know.

But I have to admit something to myself. The truth is, my decision to drop Mama from my life has stayed with me all these years. I made a moral calculation at the time. I determined that the mental challenges she faced did not excuse her loveless behavior. When she called that day and did what she did, I wrote her off. The inner voice that drives me forward told me to walk away from her, and I did.

But Mama listened to her inner voices too—and they took her down.

Did I do the right thing back then?

I didn't understand her mental illness. The reality of it came on me so quickly. And I was just so young. A bond never formed between us, and because of it, I can't say I feel guilty about the decision I made. But as an adult who has lived through some hard-earned life lessons, I understand better now the fragile balance—the fine line, really—between success and failure, madness and sanity, rising and running, and sometimes even right and wrong. The scale can tip one way or the other very easily, and the world is not always so black and white. In the end, the decisions we make, the things we do, we have to live with. And while I don't miss what I've never had, I have to admit that I do harbor some regret.

But Pop. I've driven myself all these years to prove him wrong. He was wrong about me—by God, they were all wrong about me. Somehow, I knew I was capable of more, and I was hell-bent on proving it. And I suppose by society's definition of success, I have. But so what? What does it all mean? The money, the title, the power, the responsibility—other than improving my family's standard of living, none of that really changes anything. I'm still in the same spot I've been in for the last forty years, carrying my fears, my imagined inadequacies, fighting my demons, including the largest one of all: the man sitting inside that house at the kitchen table. The only thing that has ever really changed anything in my life is my love for Paula and the kids and theirs for me.

So now I've got another decision to make. Am I walking out on my father for good, or not?

I sit quietly, considering my dilemma. And then it finally comes to me—the determinate crucible. It comes down to two questions that I now have to ask myself:

Am I not capable of loving unconditionally? Can I not give what I've been seeking, what I've been looking for my whole life from my father?

I exit the car, take a deep breath, and then climb the steps back up to the front porch. I open the glass door and step back inside the house. I look to my right and see my father, crying soft tears, at the kitchen table.

"I'll call and check on you all in a few weeks," I say. I look briefly at Helen, then quickly head back outside to my car.

In the last years of his life, the two of us hold fast to an uneasy truce, and I keep coming back for more.

There will be no walking away and no regrets for me this time.

Thirty-Six
The Faith Mission

He WAS RENEWED, BUT not recovered, on that road from Omaha to Salt Lake City. There is now dubious hope for an impending change—no longer fatalistic, no longer hopelessly desperate, now more a weary acknowledgment that something has to give, that this nomadic life cannot go on, that some other life can be found. But where and how?

He travels eastward toward familiar territory: Fort Smith, Arkansas, a place he's frequented several times over the years. About six miles southwest of Fort Smith, in nearby Van Buren, is a mission called the Gospel Rescue Mission. It was founded by a former homeless man, Frank Turner. Van Buren is in keeping with Danny's time-informed view that a small city is often better than a big city when it comes to his survival. Also, homeless shelters founded by the homeless usually mean there are decent, clean facilities run by people with a purpose—people who have escaped the road and hope to help others do the same. In this case, Turner is a tough but caring man. He'll put you to work, but he'll also put a meal in your belly.

He allows Danny a short stay, and Danny gratefully enjoys the brief respite.

That first evening, after dinner, he winds up talking to a fellow traveler and shares with him his general interest in getting off the road for a while and finding a new start. The man tells him about a place he's been to in Wichita Falls, Texas: "Faith Mission." They allow long-term stays, up to a year, with an eye toward getting participants to an employable, self-sufficient state. It's a faith-based program that provides job-readiness training with Christian leanings, supplemented by the gospels and teachings of Jesus Christ.

Danny likes the idea of a longer stop in his travels and is open to the possibility of a Bible-based program. His faith—an inheritance bequeathed to him by an erratic father who both helped cause the damage and provided the desperately needed tool—remains present and persistent, a buttress against his various failings and hazardous surroundings.

He leaves the next morning for Wichita Falls and Faith Mission.

Faith Mission's tagline is "Every Story Matters"—or, stated more precisely, "Every person has a story and every story matters to God." Well, my brother has a story to tell. And, as is his custom, he's ready to tell it. But he learns theirs first.

Faith Mission was founded in 1958 in Wichita Falls by Reverend Dick Hogan and his wife, Bee. Dick opened at the corner of 7th and Ohio Street, above a locally owned hardware store, with a sign above the store that told struggling people, "If you are hungry, do not beg or steal. Come eat with us."

Initially, there were few resources and the mission relied, at least partially, on the labor of the Hogan family, along with the generosity of the citizens of Wichita Falls. It was a branch effort of a ministry of the same name in Amarillo, also founded by Reverend Hogan. In the beginning, they only took in transient men with a goal that was clear and direct: to share the gospel of Jesus Christ and to help troubled souls get off the streets. They persisted in the task.

In the spring of 1968, the Mission was able to purchase the Lamar Baptist Church building located at 4th and Lamar with Reverend Jim Cook, who'd come aboard the prior year as superintendent, running the day-to-day operations. This location would house the Mission for the next twenty years. In 1974, a broader ministry to the family, including children, began with the establishment of a community center within the confines of the facility, and in that same year Pete and Sharon Smith came on board. The Smiths took over full operation of the Mission in January of 1975 and it continued to grow, as did community support, and on May 23, 1988, the Mission moved to its current location on Travis Street. With a larger facility and increased donations, that same year the Mission began its "Overcomers Recovery Program," intending to combat homelessness by helping participants overcome their various addictions or deal with their behavioral issues. That program continues today under the name "New Beginnings Drug and Alcohol Addiction Recovery Program." This is the program my brother enters in 2004 when he arrives in Wichita Falls.

He quickly begins a routine of Bible study, anger management, addiction recovery classes (although his only addiction is to the road and his past), work therapy, counseling, and life coaching. Topics covered include specific addictions, methods of recovery, and codependency, and some that are more applicable to him, including taking care of oneself, family issues and patterns, healthy boundaries, accountability, and structure. He lives in a semi-private room and is fed three square meals but is also expected to work; tasks he is assigned include food service, laundry, housekeeping, landscaping, working at the receiving dock or the affiliated resale store, or performing general maintenance on the Travis Street building. He also has to take a breathalyzer test or pee in a cup when requested.

Danny is very good with his hands and that, along with his inability to sit still and desire to keep busy (like his father), quickly wins him the trust and support of the staff at the Mission. The Bible study encourages him, and the counseling feels cleansing; just to talk about Pop, why he ran, and the allure of the road helps him better understand his path to this point in life. It also reinforces the advice he was given in Des Moines a while back—his life now is his responsibility.

Soon, Danny's commitment to the program and good work habits lead him to win a permanent job as an employee there. He lives at the Mission and serves as an acolyte to its homeless constituents. He also serves the administrative team in whatever general helper role is needed. As he becomes increasingly popular with the staff and the clients, he begins to consider the possibility of getting off the road for good, of ending the running, of trying to build some sort of settled-down life in Wichita Falls, Texas.

And then he meets Rhonda. Rhonda is from Azle, Texas, a town located about a hundred miles southwest of Wichita Falls, and she works at a retail store near the Mission. The two of them like each other immediately. And it works. Danny continues his work at the Mission and sees Rhonda on the side, and, in time, they grow closer.

In January 2005, Danny and Rhonda are married in Faith Mission's chapel. The wedding is well attended by a great many of the shelter's residents. They even throw a small wedding reception with a chocolate cake that's greedily devoured—most of this group doesn't get the chance to eat cake very often.

The marriage thrives. My brother has found true love and gotten himself off the road. His running has finally come to an end.

But he continues to be challenged by the trials of his past. He suffers through long bouts of depression and sudden outbursts of uncontrolled anger. His mind races, and sometimes he awakes in the middle of the night crying, remembering events he desperately wants to forget. In particular, he often feels himself being dragged by the foot, grasping at the imagined carpet on a floor that is rumpled sheets in a sleepless bed.

Rhonda and other friends become concerned. Finally, one day in 2009, they confront him. He has to get help. He agrees to try. Through social services, he gets free medical support and learns, for the first time, that he has a form of mental illness. This is critical knowledge that has been a long time coming. He's now given a formal diagnosis for the sickness he's long, if vaguely, suspected he might have inherited from Mama.

My brother has bipolar II disorder. He also suffers from PTSD from the violence and abuse of our youth.

Contrary to popular opinion, PTSD is not just the burden of the battle-tested military warrior; it also impacts others who have been exposed to traumatic events or frightening experiences that create intrusive thoughts, hyperarousal, flashbacks, anger, and sleep disturbances, among other troubling symptoms.

Bipolar disorder, also known as manic depression, is a mental illness that brings severe high and low moods and changes in sleep, energy, thinking, and behavior. The highs and lows can be thought of as two "poles" of mood, which is why it's called "bipolar disorder." Bipolar II is different from bipolar I in the lower severity of the highs or manic episodes. A manic episode is a distinct period of elevated or irritable mood characterized by exceptional energy, restlessness, trouble concentrating, feelings of euphoria, increased sexual desire, reckless behaviors such as spending large amounts of money, and sleeplessness. Bipolar II symptoms include moving from one idea to the next quickly, exaggerated self-confidence, rapid and loud talking, and increased energy, but generally much more time is spent in a depressive mood than in hypomania. In terms of the relative severity of each version, while bipolar II does not include the more severe manic episodes or behavior, it is still believed that it is as disabling as bipolar I, if not even more so, because it can lead to more lifetime days spent depressed and not doing as well overall between episodes. Various medications and means of care for bipolar II include lithium, counseling, psychotherapy, and electroconvulsive therapy. However, there is no cure.

Did our genetic makeup and the abusive environment we suffered as children contribute to my brother's illness? Research suggests there is a genetic linkage with the disease and also suggests, though not as definitively, that certain "trauma factors" (physical, verbal, or sexual assault) endured in youth can cause an earlier onset of the disease. It is quite possible that Danny's bipolar disorder was triggered earlier in life by the emotional and verbal abuse he received in our home, and that the physical abuse he took reduced his ability to cope with the world around him, to operate effectively, to conform to society's norms—it may have led him to become homeless for nearly twenty-five years.

Could the trauma factors in our home have led Mama's already high genetic predisposition to bipolar or schizophrenia to manifest in an earlier and more intense manner? Could my memories, my dreams, my almost PTSD symptoms of those times, those desperately brutal years, and my ongoing battle with self-esteem be partially a result of these factors?

I have no desire to lay all the ills my family members have experienced at the feet of my father, who also provided shelter and assistance at critical times as we grew up and also helped later in life when needed (Billy in particular). I strongly believe that persistence, determination, and choice come into play in the living and the outcome of one's life. I also believe strong faith in a power greater than your own plays a critical role.

But of this I have no doubt: the greater distance we were forced to travel just to achieve normalcy was lengthened by the barbaric hand and callous tongue of my father.

To this day, Danny remains married to Rhonda and lives in Wichita Falls.

I found him there, after so many years, in 2018, and we spent a joyous few days catching up and learning more about our respective lives. We talk on the phone quite often now and are unimaginably grateful for our reconnection. He takes medication for his bipolar and PTSD, and has left his position at Faith Mission for a happier and calmer existence doing maintenance work for several well-to-do families in the area.

But the memories of our merciless childhood linger. To this day, Danny receives ongoing counseling through a caseworker assigned to him by the state. She has helped him reconcile, as much as he can, the abuses of the past, but he says the memories never totally leave his mind.

He says he thinks about that earlier time every day of his life.

Thirty-Seven
Retail Apocalypse

SOME PEOPLE SAY THEY never, for a moment, look back at the story of their lives. Nothing is gained they say; regret is not helpful – after all, what can we change about the past?

But I don't believe those people.

If you've never looked back on the sum of your life, it's only because you're not far enough along in the journey or life hasn't yet brought you to your knees with a challenge so daunting or a moment of accomplishment—or failure—so powerful that it hastens your reflection. Eventually, life requires each of us to confront the merit of how we've lived.

And when we look back—what do we see?

Like a primping eighteen-year-old soon to be crowned home-coming queen at the upcoming high school football game or a hun-gover New Year's Eve partier staring at the morning after red-eyed reflection in a blurry bathroom mirror, we may or may not like the view. But what we see is on us—clear-eyed self-assessment reminds us of an unavoidable truth: *in life, we are the sum of what we do.*

Circumstance and choice lead to actions good and bad that accumulate over time and tell the story of who we are. While a checkered past doesn't mean we can't do better in days to come and stellar accomplishment doesn't ensure an untarnished future, our tale moves closer to completion and we become more assured—and informed—with every page we successfully turn. But sometimes our story takes on an unforeseen twist and satisfactory resolution proves elusive; the expected denouement is suddenly in doubt.

What happens when all that life has taught us is not enough?

Two thousand people. We have over two thousand people in full- and part-time personnel, working and supporting cyclists across the United States. In the day-to-day of running Performance, I'm a heads-down, challenging, committed, driving, analytical, and at times no-nonsense leader, looking for results and accepting nothing less. But those closest to me know how deeply I care about those two thousand people and their families. They're in my thoughts constantly, so much so that Paula gets tired of hearing about them.

In 2013, after the successful momentum in my initial years as CEO, the larger trends of depressed store traffic in retail brick-and-mortar stores and declining demand in the North American cycling market begin to weigh on the business. Performance Bike is experiencing what many have labeled a "Retail Apocalypse"—the closing of a large number of worldwide brick-and-mortar retail stores that began in 2010 (primarily due to the growing consumer preference for the convenience of online shopping). Specific to our industry, millennials don't embrace the avid cycling preferences of their baby boomer predecessors and over time the number of bike shops in North America declines sharply from six thousand to approximately four thousand. We manage to out-perform the cycling market from a sales perspective and effectively meet increased customer demand on our websites (even winning "Multi-Channel Retailer of the Year" at the national bike industry conference in 2016) but the *real* killer for us is that we still have an exorbitant debt load from the sale of the business in 2007. Anxious lenders, seeing brick-and-mortar retailers struggling across the country, simply want their money and are impatient with a downturn in our business. We are suddenly the very definition of a multi-channel retailer caught in the Retail Apocalypse.

The team and I do a hundred different things to respond to our perilous circumstances—some big, some small. A lot of it helps. But with the debt load we carry, none of it materially changes the precarious state of the business. We're in trouble.

I continuously solicit the advice of our board. They concur with my direction and continue to support me throughout this time as CEO—I suspect at least partially because of my earlier successes and the numbers that tell them we're beating the trends in a difficult time in the cycling industry. But despite my aggressive solicitation, they offer no additional insights or particular solutions to the dilemma at hand.

I'd love to say I'm a bastion of strength and fortitude as we fight to save the business. But that's not the truth. Though my staff never sees it—I see it as my burden to carry—I'm afraid. The debt load is overwhelming now—there's no cash and little resources. With more aggressive capital backing, we could play a highly promotional market share game and gradually restore an acceptable level of profitability (see Amazon's first twenty years). But there's no additional capital. There's only business-crushing debt.

My nights are restless; sleep becomes a rare commodity, and my father's voice rings in my ear. "You ain't worth a shit for nothing" becomes louder with each passing day. The one thing I think I'm incredibly good at—running and managing a business—is now being discredited. With each passing day, we move perilously closer to an ignominious fall.

I dream nightly about Performance's two thousand employees and their families—roofs over heads and food in bellies, the team members I'm close to, how they'll be impacted, the hurt, the repercussions, the shame of it all. I can't lie—I think about walking away from it, too.

After all, I didn't decide to put this damn debt on the company. I argued against it. I can easily leave Performance and get another position at a different company. I can wash my hands of it, take the stress out of my life in an instant. But if I leave, the creditors might throw up their hands, and it potentially will be over for those two thousand people and their families. I know that.

I talk with Paula, confide in her my doubts and fears. She says she has faith in me, that I'm the best chance Performance has. I hope that's true, but I'm no longer sure. I pray a lot. I don't know if I can find a way to turn this thing around.

Finally, one bleary-eyed morning, as I lie in bed staring at the ceiling, I decide on two meaningful things: First—financially, however this plays out, my family will be fine. Second—I can't deny the fact that I love Performance and the people I've worked shoulder to shoulder with for years.

And love is not too strong a word. The people I work with, and what we've built together, mean a great deal to me. So, I will continue to work for the two thousand people. And I'll pray nightly for God to help me find a way to reposition the business.

Just as praying helped me get through my abominable adolescence, talking to God now gives me strength and comfort as I face the most difficult professional challenge of my life. God will not let me quit. God—not I—will save those two thousand jobs. And when he does, he will get and deserve the credit.

We meet as a board and decide to attempt to sell the business. If we'd done this three years ago, we might've done well; the chances of selling it now are not great—but we decide to move ahead anyway. My dream goal is to get a large chunk of debt off our balance sheet and gain a business advantage for Performance with a new strategic partner.

And we have one big thing going for us: we're so large in the cycling space that if we fail our vendors are going to feel it. One, in particular, a bike vendor, will feel it in a business-threatening way. Their CEO approaches me about their interest in buying us. They are backed by a bike manufacturer who can sell bikes directly to us at an advantageous price.

Though we dance with several potential suitors, the bike vendor moves quickly to the fore. We agree on ownership split—they will have control—and then work together to secure the financing we'll need to support the new and stronger business model.

There's real interest by multiple banks. They see many of their retail clients struggling and like the vertically-integrated combination we've put together. We eventually secure the needed capital—and a current lender agrees to forgive a large chunk of existing debt in exchange for ownership in the new entity. Finally, the deal closes in August of 2016. With it, the business is given a better, stronger business model, reduces some of its outstanding debt, and now has a chance to make it—a real chance. I'm thrilled and relieved.

But the new owners do not want to go forward with me. They

have their team and this is their show. I'm asked to resign, and I do so quietly.

Once the work to save the business is behind me and I'm let go, I'm emotionally spent.

I've been at Performance for almost twenty-seven years. I started in 1990 as a controller for the smaller retail part of the business, and over time advanced to CEO of the entire business. We grew from barely ten stores to well over one hundred and became the largest cycling specialty retailer in the United States in the process. I led acquisitions totaling over $100 million in sales in my time as CFO, and as CEO led a financial turnaround that netted the second largest earnings year in the company's thirty-six-year history.

But while I had my successes as a CFO and CEO in business, there is also no denying that Performance struggled mightily in the last two years of my watch. Whether it was the changing retail world, the decline in cycling participation, a burdensome inherited debt load, or my own managerial ineptitude, we struggled, staggering, staring at a scary precipice, toward the end of my tenure. My last few working years were not the heroic tale of achievement I hoped to write. In fact, in my black-and-white definition of business success—that is, being a good leader who gets results—I failed at the very tail end of my career, plain and simple. No excuses.

The CEO of the equity team that bought us in 2007 will later tell me that Jack Welch, the role-model CEO of GE back in their headiest, most successful days, could not have produced a better outcome at Performance. I will take solace in that statement, but our lack of results at the very end remains the same and mine to own.

But while I will not ride off in the sunset a resounding success, maybe, with God's help, I was the man to get Performance through that perilous time. I did not quit when it seemed that most all those around me were stepping away, and I found a way, with the help of some key folks at Performance, to shed a meaningful part of our debt load and give the company new life, a fighting chance to move forward. I achieved the only goal I set for myself in what seemed like an impossible situation at the time: to find a way to save those two thousand jobs. That was the sole focus of the last year or so of my professional career, and somehow, we managed to get it done. I take some level of satisfaction in that. I'm also comforted by this Winston Churchill quote, one of my favorites: "Success is not final, failure is not fatal; it is the courage to continue that counts."

God gives me the courage to continue, and Performance continues without me. Because I was asked to leave, I move on. As of August of 2016, their fate is no longer mine to control.

My heart is broken a few years later, in November of 2018, when Performance announced a Chapter 11 bankruptcy. Looking back, it's even more of a disappointment given the positive recovery of the North American cycling market that occurred partially as a result of the Covid pandemic in 2020.

I don't know all that happened after I left. I believe the chance to succeed with the new business model was a good one. But it did not work out. I will leave others to criticize. I understand—I've been the guy in the arena, subject to the uninformed judgment of the masses. Still, those two thousand jobs were not lost on my watch.

I leave the working world at peace with my efforts—at peace with the successes, and the failures, of my career.

And that career, that big part of my life, is now over. I've gone from being responsible for two thousand jobs to being a man who walks his dog alone on a Monday morning.

And I'm okay with that.

Thirty-Eight
Dad

HELEN PASSED AWAY A few years ago. No longer working six-ty-hour weeks, I go to see my eighty-eight-year-old father more fre-quently as he begins to fade. He's talking less often, more abstractly, and sometimes deliriously, as dementia that began to set in a few years ago takes its full and frightful hold. Soon, hospice is in tow, and, almost overnight, he's confined to his bed.

I know this won't stand for long. Pop is an active man, a man who must be doing something all the time.

Some five-odd years ago, when he could still work in his yard, I would take note of the low-cut azaleas and roses, the hedges trimmed knee-high, close and tight, in the freshly mulched ground. He would return to cut them again and again, yet he never quite killed them off. In fact, in the spring the surviving flowers looked beautiful—though the shrubs would never bloom in full. I don't think he meant to overdo it—he simply couldn't stop himself.

But he's dying now—and misses his Helen. She was, without question, the love of his life. He tells me, as he lies in the hospice-pro-vided bed, neck craning up, fingers restlessly tying the bedsheet to the handrails, that he sees her. Says he sees Grandpa and Granny, too. He even tells me he sees Mama—and that she looks well. I don't know what to make of it all, the visages he sees or the innominate place from whence they come.

Death is a mystery and—as it is for most of us—is also vaguely frightening to me. As the years pass and time slips away it only seems more ominous, more imminent. *God give me time, precious time,* I pray—I hope to live to see grandchildren, and my wife's loving face age gracefully. But Pop doesn't seem afraid. No. He's ready. I can tell. A constricted, bed-bound life holds no comfort for this anxious, driven, and sometimes tortured soul.

A month or two ago, as I was typing on my laptop while visiting, I disclosed that I was writing a book. I told him the truth—that it was about my life and what I had learned along the way; that it included stories about our upbringing and he was in it, as were Billy and Danny. I waited. He nodded but proffered no further questions, showed little curiosity. Mentally, he may have been incapable of pressing further—in fact, I'm sure that was the case. Still, I thought long and hard about getting down to it with him that day as I had done, mostly in anger, in the past. I was tempted to bring up some of the bad times between us and what it all meant to me in my life and the lives of my brothers.

But I didn't. Not because I was afraid to, but because it seemed unnecessary. The time to give and receive awaited apologies had long since passed. It would never happen. So I pushed no further, firm in the knowledge that I was telling this story not to hurt my father but to help others. I believe that was the right thing for me to do. I pray that it is so.

Sliding quickly toward finality, no longer struggling, no longer resisting, Pop begins to lose the ability to speak, to respond. One early morning, after getting a text from his live-in nurse updating me on his condition, I decide to rush back to his place from my home at Holden Beach, North Carolina, about an hour and fifteen minutes away.

When I arrive, she needs help cleaning him, so I reach down, put my left hand gently under his neck and my right hand beneath his left shoulder and upper back, then turn and hold him sideways as she slides a clean protective pad between his bottom and the bed, then proceeds to change his diaper. The strongest, most explosive man I've ever known, reduced to an almost infantile state.

Soon, the nurse steps out and we're alone. The sound of my voice can still gain a response, and I speak now.

"Pop, I just came to let you know that, although we had some tough times growing up, I love you. You know that, right?" As I reach down to rub his head and kiss his cheek, I tear up.

He grunts the words, but I can still make them out: "I love you too."

"Helen's waiting for you. It's all right. Whenever you're ready, you go to her."

And I kiss him on the forehead one final time.

I sit quietly for a while in the reclining chair by the bed, in contemplation. Bright sunshine spills through the open blinds over an upright shoulder, reflecting and warming a thinning face as its bearer passes quietly into a restful sleep, no longer fighting the bondage of a certain deathbed; two wet eyes stare vacantly into broken light.

There is no visible outflow of grief or sadness. Not because the son didn't love the father, but rather because he did, and therefore feels secure knowing he did all he could do for that father in this life.

The promise has been fulfilled. I'll harbor no regrets here. I've kept him in his house, made sure he's been cared for until the end and tried to be a good son—just as he tried, I suppose, to be a good father. Neither of us did our jobs perfectly, but we did them, I guess, in the best way we knew how.

There is no more fear, no more anger, just a damaged but resilient family crossing over through the most somber ritual of life passage.

Thirty-Nine
Relative Distance

TODAY IS ONE OF the best days of my life. My youngest, Matthew, is graduating from the Kenan Flagler School of Business at UNC-Chapel Hill, one of the best universities in the country. He's minutes from walking across the stage to receive his undergraduate degree. I'm incredibly proud. I hold Paula's hand tight and look into her eyes, and the gravity of what this moment means is reflected back at me.

I look to my left, down the row of Carolina blue seats in the Dean Smith Center, and appreciate the presence of my extended family. Billy and Danny aren't here and Pop, Mama, and Helen have all passed away. But my father-in-law, my daughter-in-law, my two brothers-in-law, and their families are all present. Seems like they've always been here. I'm grateful for that.

As I continue looking, I spot my elder son, Zack, watching his brother closely. A few years ago, I went to his white coat ceremony at The Brody School of Medicine at East Carolina University. He'd just started medical school there. What a thrill it was! And a few months ago, he took his Step 1 Medical Board exam. With his high score, he finished in the top 4 percent in the entire country! When he called and excitedly shared his wonderful news, that, too, was an unforgettable day in my life.

I understand, quite clearly, the work each of them has put into these exceptional achievements. I understand.

Matthew's name is called to step forward. Paula and I stand and cheer loudly, probably making fools of ourselves in the process. Our shouts of joy find no reverberation, no echo, in the large, flowing arena. Our voices are simply a faint call from a relative distance.

Does he hear us? I wonder. Probably not. It's appropriate, I suppose—both he and his brother will hear less of our voices in the years ahead. We'll be there to help and support as long as we're needed, of course, but they're grown men now. They'll make their own decisions. I pray that we, with God's help, have laid a good foundation that will serve them well.

I watch him amble, as he is wont to do, across the well-lit stage to shake hands with the dean; he pauses for a photo, then exits stage left and returns to his seat. It takes less than two minutes. The distance traveled is minuscule.

And the thought of it overtakes me.

Over time, I've become a great student, observer, believer, and appreciator of the relative distance one must travel to lead a successful and, more importantly, *happy* life. And the relative distance I've traveled—from circling a shotgun shack with pissed-in underwear on my head to disinterested, resentful youth to striving but still damaged young adult to CFO/CEO of a $250 million company and, hopefully, a decent, caring husband and father—is never far from my thoughts.

It is that relative distance—my uniquely personal life journey—that defines me, and because of that I, rightfully or wrongfully, view others through that biased prism. Show me a person who's had to overcome a lot to lead a productive, good life, and my admiration is demonstrably endless. Just as a five-mile run up a lofty mountainside is more arduous than one down an isolated beach road with the ocean wind at your back, our life journeys to personal success and fulfillment are not all the same, and some travel a more difficult path than others. In my heart, I am a disciple of Lincoln, not Roosevelt. Lincoln, who rose from abject poverty, whose greatest early influence was a stepmother who taught him a love of books, who essentially educated himself, who debated one of the great minds of his time with stirring passion, who rose to the presidency in our country's most tumultuous time—he is my idol, my role model. And, in truth, we are members of the same secret society.

Our secret society is one whose members have risen from the ashes of a disadvantaged birth. It is our secret because more often than not we hide our past, cloaking it discreetly in prolonged silence. Yet no amount of time or success can ever wipe it away. It is our lonely burden to carry—for a lifetime. Whether poverty, discrimination, disability, abuse, neglect, violence, or anything else is responsible for handicapping their early existence, anyone who endures these things and finds the path to a fruitful life, contributing to the growth of others, and the betterment of the world is my brother or sister and has earned my greatest respect.

I'm not saying my lofted appreciation for the success of the downtrodden is right or just—perhaps it is narrow-minded. But it's my truth. There are just so many—too many—of us that don't make it. The desperate troubles of the past steal, more often than not, the promise of a successful future.

But not always.

I think of Billy and Danny. The harrowing early journey we took together extracted a high price from each of us. Lives were impacted, some more severely than others, for years to come. Potential was stolen, rest was disturbed, and outcomes were distorted—but in the end, stubborn resiliency won the day. The two of them are in a good place now. That makes me happier than either of them can ever know.

Later that evening at a dinner honoring the graduates, I watch my two sons move easily and converse happily with friends and family, and I hold inside of me a great hope. I hope this will be the first of many happy successes to come in the years ahead.

I will, no doubt, continue to worry and fret over them as they move forward in life. But I've been blessed in my journey to find both gratitude *and* peace in this world—so I know I'm going to sleep well tonight.

Thanks be to God for allowing me to break the cycle of abuse in raising my children. I'll be there for them. I'll always be there for them. But their successes and failures will be their own.

Just like Billy. Just like Danny. And just like me.

Epilogue
My Best Answer

INNUMERABLE CHILDREN ARE LIVING in fear, feeling unloved and unwanted, and will most likely be changed for the rest of their lives by what is happening to them right now—this very second. They're being physically, emotionally, or sexually abused and/or growing up in a home with domestic violence, neglect, mental illness, alcohol or drug abuse, or criminal activity, and these difficult early life circumstances—called Adverse Childhood Experiences (ACEs)—can cause children to have problems in school, with alcohol, and with the police, and later on more likely to have serious health problems in middle age—and even die sooner than they should. The impact of ACEs is overwhelming.

But sadly, we as an American society have become resigned, almost accepting, of the abuse of our children. The numbers are staggering. About six million children are reported to child protection agencies each year. About 400,000 of them are placed in protective custody because of severe neglect or abuse. Children who experience abuse are about nine times more likely to become involved in criminal activity. They are 25 percent more likely to experience teen pregnancy. About 30 percent of abused and neglected children will later abuse their children, continuing the tragic cycle—the sins heaped upon the fathers and mothers brutally passed to the unfortunate sons and daughters. About 80 percent of twenty-one-year-olds who were abused as children meet the criteria for at least one psychological disorder—the iniquitous byproducts of inflicted adolescent pain. The financial cost of child abuse and neglect in the United States is estimated at $585 billion.

But beyond these highly disturbing statistics, there are lives ruined, dreams denied, and potential squandered. Many abused children never take hold of what their lives could be. That seed of inner drive, that kernel of optimism and hope, that ovule of self-belief, can be viciously squashed before a child is even ten years old. It is tragic. It is devastating.

I've seen it. I lived it. Because of it, I wrote this book to help those who, like me and my siblings, are trying to rise above it.

Three divergent paths were started at the foot of the same torturous incline. Three disparate outcomes were derived from a difficult upbringing. Why did our respective lives go in such different directions? Why was one of us a CEO? Why was one of us homeless for almost twenty-five years? Why did one of us flounder for the first twenty-five years of life? These questions have puzzled me all my adult life. Was it predestined by God? Was it genetic? Was it simply individual wants and desires? In the end, I've decided that these questions are, for me at least, unanswerable—and the wrong ones to ask. The right question is, *How did I find the strength to do what I had to do for myself and my family and what does that mean to you as an abused person, a victim of ACE?*

Simply put, there were things that I needed to find to have the chance to succeed in life—things that I could not source from my fractured family, from that volatile, damaging environment at home, things that opened my eyes to what I could be despite what I was told.

Ultimately, I found five things that pushed me forward—that allowed me to survive and thrive in life.

The 5 Finds

There are things an abused child needs to discover in life to have a decent shot at a productive future. Unfortunately, it is much more difficult for an abused child to find these things because the biggest, most important part of a child's life in their formative years is the home in which they live—and an abused child generally will not find these things in their dysfunctional home. But find them you must!

1. Find your role model

A child in a well-adjusted, loving home may find their role model in a parent, a sibling, or another family member. But an abused child in a damaged home isn't as likely to find one within the traditional family structure. To understand there is a better way to behave, a better way to live, you have to see it modeled in others.

My earliest role model was Andy Griffith as the father on *The Andy Griffith Show*.

Yes, it was Hollywood, and yes, it was fiction, and yes, it portrayed the backwoods South—but for an abused child looking for a better father figure, it was as real as it could get. I saw what an even-keeled, caring adult male looked like. I saw how a father could and should approach a relationship with a son. Yes, discipline was part of that relationship, but it was to be meted out in the proper measure and with a purpose, when a behavior needed to change or a lesson had to be taught. There was teaching, there was caring, and there was also, when a mistake was made, an apology from the parent. If you've never watched the show, watch the "Opie the Birdman" or "Opie and the Bully" episodes on YouTube (see Chapter Nine!).

Contrast that with my story growing up. I sat in front of that old black-and-white TV as a child and discovered early on that what was happening to us was wrong. It was a momentous and invaluable find! It made me less accepting of the abusive treatment, less accepting of the idea that I was somehow getting what I deserved—that it was my fault. I told myself and I told my father that if I ever had children, I would never treat them the way he treated me or my brothers. It helped me break the cycle of abuse. I learned a different, better way from a fictional role model.

A second role model for me was my fourth-grade teacher, Mrs. Ross. Demanding but loving, she showed me what a good mother, what a smart and strong woman, what a charismatic leader and committed mentor could look like. I thrived under her prodding to be better, her exacting but caring tutelage. She told me she believed I could be something special and it planted the first seeds of possibility in a battered, immature mind filled with growing resentment and lingering doubt. Later, her early belief and her subtle but persistent calls to action, her repeated efforts to pull the best from me, provided a reminder that maybe I could be better—that maybe if I worked my ass off, I could make something happen. She will never know what she meant to me, but her impact was profound and indelible.

My last two role models, in later life, helped carry my career in the business world to levels I never thought possible.

Terry Smith, a brilliant CPA and capable leader, showed me that the financial guy with the bean-counter label was just a stereotype— that brains, talent, integrity, and partnership could expand influence and ability to make change.

Garry Snook was a tremendous entrepreneur and visionary, always looking ahead, making the toughest decisions when others might waver. He also influenced me personally with the resilient strength of his marriage to his wonderful wife, Sharon. I'm very proud to say he has remained my friend to this day.

When you are abused and the role model can't be found in the home, seek them in other places; they're out there. Internalize the behaviors you see, the lessons to be learned. Make them a part of your understanding of what you're going through now, as well as the human being you aspire to become in the future.

2. Find God (or a person you can trust and confide in)

I will say here, with tremendous gratitude, that I am a Christian. I believe that Jesus died on the cross to save our sins and that I, by His grace, am forgiven for mine. I am by no means perfect—in fact, I sin daily—but I pray nightly to be a better man, husband, father, and son, and I strive to do His will. His grace and mercy provide strength and comfort as I navigate the challenging perils of life. I don't read the Bible as much as I'd like, or go to church as often as I should, but the presence of God in my life has made all the difference. I know it instinctively and carry endless gratitude in my heart because of it.

As a child, in my bed alone at night, I would spill out my hurt and pain to God and ask for both the why and the way—why was this abuse happening to me, and what was the right way to get past it, to persevere, to keep moving forward? In time, doing this became a strengthening and reinforcing exercise for me. The power of prayer buttressed me in the most difficult times of my life—the abuse when I was young, in my responsibilities as a CEO in a challenging professional situation, and even with the death of my father. Given the agonizing but miraculous journey of my life, do not try to convince me there isn't a God! There is, there is only one, and I'm a walking testament to His grace and existence.

But my mission is to explain to you how I got past my abuse as a child to lead a productive life and, even more importantly, how you can do the same. Telling you about a great and wondrous God that pulled me from the ruinous depths of abuse—and He absolutely can do the same for you—is a critical part of my story. But society today is largely secular, and I will acknowledge this by adding the following observation:

You can't shoulder the burden of abuse alone—no one can! Find an outlet through which to share your pain and hurt, to seek solutions, or at least to reconcile yourself to your situation and bring in some healing perspective. Maybe it's a sibling. Maybe it's a teacher. Maybe it's a best friend, a pastor, a counselor, a coach, or a psychiatrist. But find that confidant, that release, because you have to get it out—have to confront your difficult situation head-on—before you can understand how to move forward. You must have support to defeat the tragic impacts of child abuse. It is impossible to do it alone.

My support was and still is, God; in deep, sincere, thoughtful prayer, I found His grace and comfort. But if you don't, or won't—find someone you can talk with about the special challenges of the abused. Find your support, find your outlet.

3. Find a Better World (outside your home)

When you are a child being abused in your home, you are not safe, you are not secure, and you are not free to grow into something better than what you see and experience around you. If you're not careful, you'll start to believe that your abuse and your household is all the world has to offer—that life and people are bad, that you are worthless or damaged, that love is conditional, unattainable, and maybe not even real. But the truth of your damaged and dreaded family home is not the full pallet of available truths in a broader world. Yes, there are bad things and people in the world, but there are also wonderful, kind-hearted souls, charismatic leaders, and loyal and true friends.

Do not let your scope be narrowed to the harrowing halls of your family home. When you leave that desperate, discouraging situation at home for school or work in the morning, open your eyes to the world around you. Look at what good people do for a living, and how they behave. Read books; acquire knowledge about what others have done, where others have been. It's not about wealth. It's about possibility, opportunity, the promise of what one can be. You must understand that the situation you're in is abnormal and dysfunctional, that everyone comes from somewhere, and that many started at a place that was just as bad or worse than yours (impossible as that may seem at this moment in your life) and still somehow found their way to a better place.

The journey from the barbarous abyss begins with one simple realization: there is a better world outside of the abusive one that you were born into or that has been foisted upon you—a place where you belong, a place where you can excel.

Open your eyes to the incredible opportunities in the ever-changing larger world. Be relentless in your search.

4. Find Your Courage

This is perhaps the hardest Find of all for the abused. Perhaps you've been beaten, physically or sexually violated, neglected, demeaned, told you're worthless. In my case, in addition to beating me to a whimpering pulp, Pop told me I wasn't "worth a shit for nothing." On top of his tragic assessment of my self-worth, I was sometimes ridiculed in early life for my appearance by my peers, and I believed all they said about me for almost nine of the most important years of my young life. *Look at how shitty my life is*, I thought. *They must be right.*

I confess that how I found the courage to try, to believe, to go to college, to become a CPA, to try my hand at marriage and parenting, to step forward and lead others on a relatively large corporate stage— it was partially born from anger and resentment. I was angry about the words and the beatings, almost from the very beginning. Still, I floundered mightily for years, until late in that first semester of my freshman year in college when I finally said enough was enough.

Anger, resentment, and a desire to prove your naysayers wrong can play a big role in the rise to a better life, but that alone is not enough. Instead, I believe the Finds that I'm talking about are both critical and cumulative—which means that before you can find the hardest and second-biggest Find of all—the courage to try, the courage to believe—you have to start building toward it.

Once I saw and knew strong and positive role models, prayed and received God's strength, and understood there were reachable possibilities in a larger world, I was able to find the courage to try, to believe that I could reach for something better. Only then did I open those damn textbooks in November of 1980 and study until morning under dim light with drowsy eyes; only then did I begin a different and better journey. What will inspire you to try?

5. Find Your Determination

When you are a child of abuse, you are a child left behind by society. With the hell being unleashed on you in the home, education and social interaction are the least of your concerns. Your chief concern, above all else, is simply survival. You're filled with resentment at your precarious situation and your tormentor's behavior. There is also self-loathing—the mindset bequeathed to you as penance for your helplessness, your inability to stop the abuse.

Because of all this, almost regardless of how long it takes you to cycle through your particular version of the first three Finds and garner the courage to try you will almost certainly be behind the majority of your peers. And since poverty and neglect are typical byproducts of an abusive environment, resources are likely scarce as well. So you're now ready to try, to take control of your life and outcome, but your access to money and knowledge, relative to your peers, is limited or nonexistent.

What's the answer? It is, simply put, this: there is no substitute—none—for finding your determination at this pivotal moment in your life.

I wish the path to rise above poverty, physical abuse, verbal debasement, sexual violation, or parental neglect was an easier road to travel. But it's not. Life is hard for all of us at times, but it's worse for you and me. There are obstacles in front of those of us who have been abused that most others who never faced the hardships of adolescence that were heaped upon us won't ever encounter. And the largest obstacle of all is sustained self-belief in your ability to achieve!

I know you: Your self-esteem was taken at an early age. You were told what you couldn't do, or you were beaten to a pulp, sexually violated, or subjected to some other crippling debasement. The vile acts in your past led you early to the sorry conclusion of predestined failure. As you begin your hard-fought journey to rise, you must remember this: your self-belief will be at its weakest early on—when you first find the courage to stir into action, when the work begins without accomplishment.

People will tell you that you can't, and in truth, you won't know if you can. Worse still, there may be failures in the beginning; if not then, certainly at various points along the way. But while all of that effort may not give you everything you want, you will get something better than anything you've ever had if you just keep working: the satisfaction gained when you achieve a particular goal.

When you begin to achieve and reap the fruits of your determination, your self-belief will finally begin to flower, which will help you down the long, tortuous road to recovery. Completing difficult work and being rewarded for it has a compounding and reinforcing effect on your behavior and outlook, on the endless possibilities of your life and the lives of those you love. I know it's true. I've seen it. I've lived it.

And yes, while talent and intellect matter, nothing matters as much as the willingness to work hard for what you want. So find your determination—the unyielding, immovable, intractable will to work hard and go get it. As the pundits say, there is no substitute for hard work. And you can work as hard as you must only when you have an unshakable will, a relentless drive—only when you are inexhaustibly determined.

So that's it: the five things I found in my life that allowed me to make the long climb up from the underbelly of an abusive home. These five critical elements helped lift me to a better life than I ever imagined possible—a life that, while imperfect and flawed as any other, is also resilient and fulfilled.

Beyond my 5 Finds, I'll share one final statement as a card-carrying member of the fraternal order of abused souls:

Let no one but you, and God, define the outcome of your life. No one.

If you abused your children, or you were abused and are now an abuser—you do not have a built-in or allowable excuse. I have two pieces of advice for you: First, break the cycle, change your ways—it's not too late. Second, if those whom you abused have grown up and left your abode—it's too late to change what you've done, but it's not too late to apologize. So reach out and do so with a sincere heart. I waited for it from my father but it never came. If it had, I'm convinced it would have helped.

If you abused someone in the past, spend the rest of your life behaving better than you did in that earlier time. Maybe you can't fix it, but you might be able to make it better. It could also blow up in your face; you just don't know. But, then again, it's not really about you anymore, is it?

As for my brothers, William Harvey Pruitt and Danny Wayne Pruitt—they have become decent men, leading lives of their own choosing. They don't need my empathy or my empirical questions. What they have is my loyalty, friendship, and sibling love.

They will have that as long as they and I live.

The three of us—wayward sons of abuse no more but forever blood brothers.

Resources

1. google.com – Central Arizona Shelter services – *"Reviews"*

2. Wikipedia.org – *"Edgar Cayce and New Age Movement,""Freight Hopping", Retail Apocalypse"*

3. uncg.edu

4. endhomelessness.org – *"Changes in the HUD Definition of "homeless" - Publication January 18,2012*

5. Faithmissionwf.org – *"About Us; Our history"*

6. webmd.com

7. healthline.com

8. activebeat.com

9. youtube.com

10. invisiblechildren.org

Acknowledgments

ALMOST FORTY YEARS AGO, I shared with family and friends, my desire to write *"The Great American Novel."* I confess I had no particular storyline in mind when I made the statement. I had no expertise, and no qualifying skill set. But for some reason, the vague ambition was there.

Fast forward to 2016, suddenly, at fifty-five, my business career was over. While I didn't particularly like the way it ended, my family's future was reasonably secure. My marriage was strong. My kids were in college and doing well. I felt extremely grateful and a little bit amazed at my good fortune. I also felt I had something more to give.

I can't say I remembered my long-ago ambition when I began writing a fictional story I'd been thinking about. I really can't. But I knew immediately, that I wasn't supposed to write about *that*, at least, not then. The moment I was in, the wonderful gift of time I'd been given, the resulting opportunity—it all felt like it happened for some unknown but more important reason.

I can't say for sure if *"Relative Distance"* was that reason - OR if it was the book in my head waiting to be written forty years later. But somehow, I think it was....

* *

I'd like to acknowledge those who helped me in my publishing journey:

First and foremost, my wife Paula, but also Lauren Keller, Mary Ellen Boelhower, Garry and Sharon Snook, John Davis, John McClenny, Brooke Warner, Lauren Wise, Krissa Lagos, Marika Flatt, and Leslie Barrett.

I'd also like to thank my family, friends, and co-workers that have been part of, what has been for me, a blessed life.

My sincere love, respect, and appreciation to you all.

David Pruitt

July 4, 2022

About the Author

photo credit: Jason Shanahan

DAVID PRUITT is a first-generation college graduate from UNC-Greensboro and previously served on the advisory board for their Bryan School of Business. As a senior leader in the U.S Bicycle industry, he served on the board of "People for Bikes," a national organization with 1.3 million members that works to make riding a bicycle in America safer, easier to access, and more fun. A licensed CPA and a member of the AICPA and NCACPA, David started his business career in an entry-level accounting position before advancing to first CFO, then CEO, of Performance Bike, for a time the largest cycling retailer in the United States. He is an avid reader, a happily married husband for over thirty years, and a proud father of two successful children. He currently resides in Chapel Hill, North Carolina.

SELECTED TITLES FROM SPARKPRESS

SparkPress is an independent boutique publisher delivering high-quality, entertaining, and engaging content that enhances readers' lives, with a special focus on female-driven work. www.gosparkpress.com

Even if Your Heart Would Listen: Losing My Daughter to Heroin, Elise Schiller. $16.95, 978-1-68463-008-0
In January of 2014, Elise Schiller's daughter, Giana Natali, died of a heroin overdose. *Even if Your Heart Would Listen* is a memoir about Giana's illness and death and its impact on her family—especially her mother—as well as a close examination and critique of the treatment she received from health care practitioners while she was struggling to get well.

Roots and Wings: Ten Lessons of Motherhood that Helped Me Create and Run a Company, Margery Kraus with Phyllis Piano. $16.95, 978-1-68463-024-0
Margery Kraus, a trailblazing corporate and public affairs professional who became a mother at twenty-one, shares ten lessons from motherhood and leadership that enabled her to create, run, and grow a global company. Her inspiring story of crashing through barriers as she took on increasingly challenging opportunities will have women of all ages cheering.

Love You Like the Sky: Surviving the Suicide of a Beloved, Sarah Neustadter. $16.95, 978-1-943006-88-5
Part memoir and part self-help in nature, this compilation of emails—written by a young psychologist to her beloved following his suicide—chronicles the process of surviving and grieving the tragic death of a loved one, and of using grief for deeper psycho-spiritual healing and transformation.

The House that Made Me: Writers Reflect on the Places and People That Defined Them, edited by Grant Jarrett. $17, 978-1-940716-31-2
In this candid, evocative collection of essays, a diverse group of acclaimed authors reflect on the diverse homes, neighborhoods, and experiences that helped shape them—using Google Earth software to revisit the location in the process.